Critical Geographies of Resistance

Critical Geographies of Resistance

Edited by

Sarah M. Hughes

Assistant Professor, Department of Geography and Environmental Sciences, Northumbria University, UK

Cheltenham, UK • Northampton, MA, USA

© Sarah M. Hughes 2023

All rights reserved. No part of this publication may be reproduced, stored in a retrieval system or transmitted in any form or by any means, electronic, mechanical or photocopying, recording, or otherwise without the prior permission of the publisher.

Published by
Edward Elgar Publishing Limited
The Lypiatts
15 Lansdown Road
Cheltenham
Glos GL50 2JA
UK

Edward Elgar Publishing, Inc.
William Pratt House
9 Dewey Court
Northampton
Massachusetts 01060
USA

A catalogue record for this book
is available from the British Library

Library of Congress Control Number: 2023939807

This book is available electronically in the Elgaronline
Geography, Planning and Tourism subject collection
http://dx.doi.org/10.4337/9781800882881

Printed on elemental chlorine free (ECF)
recycled paper containing 30% Post-Consumer Waste

ISBN 978 1 80088 287 4 (cased)
ISBN 978 1 80088 288 1 (eBook)

Printed and bound in the USA

Contents

List of figures		vii
List of contributors		viii
Acknowledgements		xii
Foreword		xiv
1	Introduction to *Critical Geographies of Resistance* Sarah M. Hughes	1

PART I   RETHINKING RESISTANCE, REFRAMING DEBATES

2	Feminism, resistance and the archive Maria Fannin and Julie MacLeavy	26
3	Resisting beyond the human: animals and their advocates Catherine Oliver	41
4	Resistance without subjects: friction and the non-representational geography of everyday resistance Sage Brice	59
5	Towards a more-than-human theory of resistance: reflections on intentionality, political collectives and opposition Carlotta Molfese	76
6	Activism and resistance: activist dispositions and the hidden hierarchies of action Charlotte Lee	92
7	Making space: relational ethnography and emergent resistance Sarah Zell and Amelia Curran	107

PART II   EMERGENT RESISTANCE: REFLECTIONS FROM THE FIELD

8	'My existence is resistance': an analysis of disabled people's everyday lives as an enduring form of resistance Angharad Butler-Rees	124

9	'Bollocks to Brexit': the geographies of Brexit protest stickers, 2015–21 *Hannah Awcock*	138
10	Struggles around housing: La Plaza De La Hoja in Colombia *Karen Schouw Iversen*	153
11	'What size is the room?': using the law to resist the UK's bedroom tax *Mel Nowicki*	168
12	Bearing witness at a Home Office reporting centre *Amanda Schmid-Scott*	182
13	'Unleashing the beast': emergent resistance in White charity *Kahina Meziant*	199
14	Around, despite, and without reference to domination: crafting oppositional human geographies in migrant detention *Leah Montange*	217

Index 235

Figures

3.1	'Collie Steak' being served at Veggies and Animal Aid's 2010 'Friend or Food' campaign	47
3.2	'Puppy on a Plate'	50
3.3	A group of ex-commercial hens awaiting being collected to go to their new domestic homes	52
9.1	Stickers referring to the EU referendum	141
9.2	A selection of Brexit stickers	143
9.3	Stickers that have been interacted with	150
10.1	Plaza de la Hoja (left) and the mural (right), February 2018	153
13.1	Song written on the night, 13 January 2020	209
14.1	Vase of flowers made by Patricia at the Northwest Detention Center, USA	227

Contributors

Hannah Awcock is a University Teacher in Human Geography at the University of Edinburgh, UK. She received a PhD in Geography from Royal Holloway, University of London, UK in 2018. Hannah is interested in the historical, cultural, social and political geographies of urban resistance, including: conflict over control of, and access to, public space; the commemoration and memorialisation of protest; and protest stickers. She blogs at TurbulentIsles.com.

Sage Brice (she/her) combines research in cultural geography with a lively contemporary art practice. She is a British Academy postdoctoral fellow and assistant professor at the Department of Geography, Durham University, UK. Her research interrogates the ontologies and politics of nature, particularly in relation to queer and trans ecologies of identity. Her current project, in collaboration with trans and non-binary participants, examines the conditions of vulnerability through which Covid-19 elicits a new and different concept of subjectivity. She has an affinity for watery and fluid landscapes, and other recent work explored problems of identity and ecology in the Huleh wetlands, in northern Israel–Palestine.

Angharad Butler-Rees is a Research Fellow in the Department of Sociology at the University of Warwick, UK. Her current research explores the life trajectories of disabled young people. Prior to this, she undertook her doctorate in the School of Geography and Environmental Science at the University of Southampton, UK, where she explored disability activism in response to austerity. Angharad has a longstanding interest in disability rights, activism and social justice.

Amelia Curran, PhD, University of Winnipeg, Canada. Amelia is an Instructor in the Criminal Justice Department at the University of Winnipeg. Her work studies geographies of crime and criminal justice, currently with an interest in the intersection between housing and criminal justice. Her most recent project studied gang territories as urban spaces made and maintained through embodied and other material practices. Her work has been published in *Canadian Journal of Law and Society*, *Critical Sociology* and *Critical Social Policy*.

Maria Fannin is Professor of Human Geography at the University of Bristol, UK. Her research focuses on the geographies of reproduction and the social and economic dimensions of human tissue donation.

Sarah M. Hughes is an Assistant Professor in Human Geography in the Department of Geography and Environmental Sciences at Northumbria University, UK. She is a political geographer working on asylum politics, resistance, citizenship and the politics of epistemology within the academy.

Charlotte Lee is an Associate Lecturer in Geography and Sustainable Development at the University of St Andrews, UK; prior to this she held a Teaching Fellowship at Newcastle University, UK and carried out her PhD at Durham University, UK. Her research interests sit largely within cultural geography, in particular around the agency of activism, political and cultural geographies of climate change, and affective and non-representational geographies.

Julie MacLeavy is a Professor of Economic Geography at the University of Bristol, UK. Her research concerns both economic production and social reproduction. In particular, she attends to the gender relations that operate across these two spheres, which have been a key focus of feminist political struggles.

Kahina Meziant trained and worked as a journalist before moving to the UK and starting a PhD in the Department of Geography and Environmental Science at Northumbria University, UK. Her research is situated at the crossroads between alternative spaces of citizenships, activisms, sound and social justice. She has a particular interest in using creative, participatory approaches as a way to navigate complex, multiple identities in the context of forced migration.

Carlotta Molfese is a PhD student in Human Geography at the University of Plymouth, UK, and a passionate small-scale farmer, off-gridder and DIY-er resisting the state–corporate takeover of peasant agriculture and alternative lifestyles. She has received a 1+3 Economic and Social Research Council (ESRC) scholarship to investigate the radical ecologies and more-than-human geographies of 'back-to-the-land' (BTTL) farms from an auto-ethnographic and activist perspective. She was trained as a biologist but eventually found human geography to be more welcoming towards her passions and radical spirit, which she cultivates both in the academy and in the field. Her broader research interests include social movements and counter-cultures, environmental politics and science, and the geographies of agriculture and conservation, which she approaches through engaged, creative and participatory practices.

Leah Montange is a human geographer. Her work addresses the relations between human life and state power in contexts of bordering, detention and labour; contexts where freedom, unfreedom and mobility are at stake. Her work is published in *Citizenship Studies*, *Environment and Planning D: Society and Space*, *Globalizations*, the *Annals of the Association of American Geographers*, *ACME: An International Journal of Critical Geographies*, and *Population, Space and Place*. She is the Bissell-Heyd Lecturer and Assistant Professor, Teaching Stream in American Studies at the University of Toronto, Canada. Leah received a PhD from the University of Toronto, where she was a recipient of the Vanier Canada Graduate Scholarship and was a Pruitt Dissertation Fellow of the Society of Women Geographers.

Mel Nowicki is a Reader in Urban Geography at Oxford Brookes University, UK. Her research focuses on urban housing exclusion and geographies of home. Her research projects have included exploring the global rise of shrinking domestic space, and documenting homeless families' experiences of life in emergency accommodation in the UK and Ireland. Mel has published widely in academic journals (for example, the *Geographical Journal*, *Geoforum*, *Social and Cultural Geography*), for policy audiences, and in the media (for example, *The Guardian*). Her first book, *Bringing Home the Housing Crisis: Politics, Precarity and Domicide in Austerity London*, explores the impact of three UK government housing policies (the bedroom tax, the rise of temporary accommodation, and criminalisation of squatting) on low-income Londoners.

Catherine Oliver is a geographer and lecturer in the sociology of climate change based at Lancaster University, UK. Her research interests span animals (specifically birds), more-than-human theory, and urban studies. Between 2020 and 2022, Catherine was researching backyard hens and their keepers in gardens and allotments in London. Previously, she researched veganism in the UK, and her book *Veganism, Archives and Animals* was published with Routledge in 2021.

Amanda Schmid-Scott is an Economic and Social Research Council (ESRC) postdoctoral fellow in the School of Geography, Politics and Sociology at the University of Newcastle, UK. Her research, which engages with feminist theories of violence and resistance, explores the intersections between bureaucracy and violence within the UK's asylum system. She has previously worked as a research consultant in East Africa, as well as in the migrant charity sector in London.

Karen Schouw Iversen is a Fellow at the London School of Economics and Political Science (LSE), UK. Her research focuses on resistance by internally displaced persons in Colombia, where the state has rolled out a set of humanitarian policies targeting this group for assistance. Specifically, she explores the opportunities for resistance provided by humanitarian policies and discourses in this context. Karen holds a PhD from the School of Oriental and African Studies (SOAS), University of London, UK, and an MSc from the LSE.

Sarah Zell, PhD, University of Winnipeg, Canada. Sarah is an Assistant Professor in Urban and Inner-City Studies at the University of Winnipeg. She is a political and urban geographer whose research primarily focuses on international human migration, with specific interests in migration and border policy and governance, citizenship and belonging, and labour mobility. She is also interested in questions related to housing and urban change. Sarah's most recent project, 'Outsourcing the Border', examines spatialisations of borders and sovereign power in the recruitment and migration of temporary migrant workers to Western Canada. She has published in both academic and policy circles, with recent work appearing in *Studies in Social Justice* and the *International Journal of Migration and Integration*.

Acknowledgements

I owe a huge thank you to all the authors contributing to *Critical Geographies of Resistance*. This book was written during various and varying Covid-19 lockdowns across multiple continents and countries, and this placed additional stresses on all the contributors. I really appreciate you staying with the book, and for being so generous, flexible and accommodating to each other's work schedules during this challenging period. Thank you for being so supportive when I took a leave of absence from work. Thank you also to the peer reviewers for your careful and considerate feedback. The book really is much improved by your input. I am indebted to Professor Cindi Katz for agreeing to write the Foreword to this book and for providing such a powerful, interesting and insightful commentary on the book.

To the team at *Edward Elgar Publishing*, in particular to Stephanie Hartley, Katy Crossan, Marina Bowgen, Cathrin Vaughan and Wendy Graham, thank you for your support in bringing this manuscript to publication. Thank you also to the Economic and Social Research Council (ESRC 1332625 and ESRC ES/S010262/1), and the British Academy (SRG2021\210498) for grants which have helped me to develop my research on the geographies of resistance.

This book would not have been possible without invaluable debates and discussions on all things 'resistance' with a wider group of academics. Thank you for challenging my thinking, encouraging me to keep writing, and helping me to navigate a wealth of interdisciplinary literature. Special thanks are due to: Louise Amoore, Johanne Bruun, Kathryn Cassidy, John Clayton, Kate Coddington, Rachel Colls, Anish Chhibber, Angharad Closs Stephens, Alice Cree, Jonny Darling, Phil Emmerson, Mara Ferreri, Dan Fisher, Peter Forman, Wenying Fu, Phil Garnett, Nick Gill, Paul Griffin, Jason Luger, Kate Maclean, Gaja Maestri, Hannah Martin, Lauren Martin, Olivia Mason, Francis Massé, Ingrid Medby, Isabel Meier, Kahina Meziant, Jacob Miller, Leah Montange, Alison Mountz, Amber Murrey, Katie Oven, Harry Pettit, Vanessa Schofield, Olivia Sheringham, Vicki Squire, Joe Williams and Diana Zacca Thomaz.

Thank you to Northumbria University's Geography Department, in particular to the Social and Cultural Geography Research Group; the wonderful PhD students I have (had) the absolute pleasure of supervising: Kahina Meziant, Anish

Chhibber and Bina Limbu, and our undergraduate geographers who genuinely continue to inspire and challenge my thinking.

Finally, this would not have been possible without Pete. Thank you for your encouragement, feedback, love and support.

Foreword

Critical Geographies of Resistance is a provocation that builds on a provocation: Sarah Hughes's (2020) incitement to think otherwise about resistance. Her writings here and elsewhere discourage any predetermined construction of resistance so that its everyday possibilities and emergent forms are recognized and appreciated. The chapters gathered here are alive with finding and thinking new formations of resistance that do not require intentionality, that may skirt linearity, and that locate agency in the animacies and even inanimacies that exceed the human. They understand that power is always entangled with resistance, rather than some sort of fixed object or totalizing force of domination that calls forth emancipatory acts of resistance and opposition. Those entanglements of power create infinite possibilities for spurring resistance in emergence across time, space, and scale.

The collection makes good on Hughes's and others' desire to reinvigorate debates on resistance, and in so doing to attend to the 'ambiguous, unremarkable, less coherent' practices that may conjure something like resistance, or not (Hughes 2020: 1145; cf. Hughes et al. 2022). In resisting the idea that resistance calls for or requires conscious intent, the authors find hope and promise in the material social practices and spaces through which worlds and next moves are created, new horizons are glimpsed, and everyday acts of care and restoration stretch the ambit of the possible. Not insisting on or waiting for any sort of resistance "big bang"—a protest, a social movement, an uprising, a public act of opposition—can inspire hope and keep alive the making, moving, seeing, saying, and going, through which resistance emerges, and may arouse more intentional moves toward something else; something more just.

The idea of emergence around resistance is compelling because of all the flowering possibilities and prospects for change it makes visible. In focusing on emergence these chapters refuse a predetermined understanding of resistance, one that usually encumbers it with conscious intent around doing something against domination, exploitation, unfreedom. I have been an encumberer of resistance as such, insisting on intentionality in conscious opposition to something unjust, exploitative, or threatening domination (Katz 2001, 2004). For me it was a way to tame what seemed to be an unruly florescence of every and any autonomous gesture as resistance, and a way to think hard about the sorts of responses I was witnessing to the political economic, political ecological, social, and cultural changes taking place in the Sudanese village where I worked. In the process I created the "3Rs"—resilience, reworking, and resistance (with an imagined fourth R, revolution, flickering on the horizon)—to think about the material social practices through which people withstood, coped with, and confronted oppressive situations and unanticipated futures.

While this collection has encouraged me to rethink the presumed linearity of this triad of material social practices as building up to conscious intent to confront oppressive situations, I imagined fluid relationships and lively overlaps among the three that is not so different from the lively frameworks offered by the authors herein. Perhaps it was my commitment to conscious oppositional intent as definitional of resistance that obscured the ways I saw and might understand practices of resilience or reworking as part of, and even necessary to, a resistant flow; something akin to resistance in emergence. Even if I am not sure that I can give up the ghost of conscious intent in the last instance, the chapters in this book have got me thinking about the vibrancy of imagining resistance otherwise, and made me realize that determining anyone's intent, let alone consciousness, is difficult if not impossible, and certainly presumptuous to attempt. Sometimes the intention behind our own actions is opaque to us. Recognizing these limits opens broad terrains for rethinking resistance, and the chapters in this book travel that terrain beautifully and compellingly.

Each chapter shimmers with evidence of possibilities of and for resistance everywhere—interstices, (in)visibilities, stickers, configurations of space, everyday acts of care, quiet refusals—that do not hew to predetermined categories of what counts as resistance, but which alter the conditions that confine people and limit their prospects for wellbeing in the broadest sense. In Chapter 12 on migration and asylum, for instance, Schmid-Scott argues that the critical work of bearing witness in Home Office reporting centers by volunteers accompanying asylum seekers through the often long and alienating bureaucratic entanglements of the application process provides a "counter-gaze" that is at once "quietly disruptive" of the surveillant spaces of immigration, and oppositional in intent. Likewise, Chapter 13 by Meziant documents how members of a cultural center frequented by asylum seekers and others for music lessons and other activities staged a music session at a pub not generally visited by migrants, which turned out to create new mutual recognitions across the altered soundscape of the pub, and with them the outlines of new modes of resistance in emergence. In a similar vein, Montange (Chapter 14) found that residents of an immigration detention center engaged in making crafts in ways that reshaped the spaces of their confinement, offering a chance for conviviality that was life-enhancing. Each of these examples reveals embodied modes of presence-making that at once enable people to endure difficult circumstances—practices I think of as "resilience"—while cultivating emergent practices of resistance. As with any mode of resistance, whether quietly emergent or clangingly palpable, the outcomes are indeterminant. Yet, as this collection beautifully makes clear, everyday acts of feeling, seeing, hearing, making, singing, create possibilities for new social relations and new realms of becoming; for making more survivable futures, for recognizing shared concerns, for creating more just conditions of everyday life, and for sustaining the activities that make these possible.

Moving away from any predetermined sense of what constitutes resistance opens the terrain not just to all those acts that make the world every day, but also to the ways it could be—and often is—made different at every turn. These practices of social reproduction not only create the conditions of everyday life and social relations of production, but through them and their shortcomings and failures we can also see and start to make worlds—big and small—in which there is room for imagination, thriving, and the sustenance of all life. It happens all the time, and one of the powerful effects of the geographies of resistance collected here is the ways in which these unspectacular acts are recognized, theorized, and valorized. For example, Maria Fannin and Julie MacLeavy (Chapter 2) focus on the sorts of resistant politics that are "immanent to everyday practices and relationships" in their study of the making and maintenance of the Feminist Archive South held at the University of Bristol. They consider the archive to be alive with possibilities for reconfiguring relationships among the past, present, and future; understanding the feminist activists who created and added to the collection as both documenting and enacting resistance to the fluid conditions of domination in which they lived and worked. Far from static boxes of dusty documents, the archive is a space of active engagement through which new modes of resistance might emerge. The Lesbian Herstory Archive in New York City works in similar ways: its unconventional cataloguing may spur people drawing on the archive to bump into the unexpected. These feminist and queer archives are built and rebuilt in the course of their use, wherein conditions past and present may collide in ways that inspire new directions of thinking and doing, even remaking the archive itself as new frames of reference spark new connections across space, time, and practice.

In Chapter 6, Charlotte Lee steps away from what she terms a hierarchy of activism to think through resistance as a "disposition," such that everyday acts—hardly noticed, perhaps not directed specifically at any sort of target—at once create and are forms of activism. Lee champions "quiet," "slow," and "implicit" activism as key to how oppressive conditions might be confronted and changed, deflecting some of the attention given to the most visible acts understood as activist, and pointing to the everyday practices of social reproduction that may or may not be specifically directed at reworking or resisting something, but condition the possibilities for change. But beyond what is liberated in letting go of fixed ideas about what constitutes resistance, it is strategically astute because predetermining an act or set of actions as resistance may expose them to co-optation or subversion.

As its title suggests, *Critical Geographies of Resistance* offers nuanced attention to space and place in theorizing resistance, examining not just sites of resistance but the ways in which space itself is part of the practice of resistance. The entanglements of domination and resistance are manifest, for instance, in chapters on borders, stickering, housing, and the United Kingdom's "bedroom tax." Zell and Curran (Chapter 7) reflect on how borders are encountered and negotiated in places far from formally demarcated boundaries. Examining the encounters of would-be labor migrants to Canada in offices in Mexico City, and the experiences of walking through what are gang territories in Winnipeg, but realizing how they may be insensible to non-participants, they argue these spaces come "alive in practice." Recognizing the embodied creation of these spaces as distinct from what they might seem on the surface, Zell and Curran suggest that they can be seen as "emergent forms of resistance," which awakens them to thinking about how non-human actors and actions may themselves be resistance. In Awcock's Chapter 9 on stickering against Brexit, the space of the city itself is activated in hailing people's attention, along with possible responses, whether contacting an organization provided in a hashtag or defacing and removing stickers in disagreement, or maybe just idle boredom. Whatever the response, urban space is activated as a site of and for resistance. In a more intimate register, Caitlin Cahill and the Fed Up Honeys mounted a sticker campaign in New York City, plastering stickers depicting stereotypes of young women of color all over their Lower East Side neighborhood and elsewhere in the city intended to mock the sexual sell of advertisements and "make people think" (Cahill 2006). Finally, Karen Schouw Iversen (Chapter 10) addresses the entanglements of power and resistance in the plaza of a public housing project in Bogotá Colombia built to house internally displaced people. The plaza, like many quasi-public spaces in state-sponsored housing, is a site of surveillance and policing, and what Iversen frames as a "technology of invisibility" in seeming to serve, yet hiding from political scrutiny, marginalized groups of displaced people. Residents, however, insisted on their presence in the space: meeting and organizing with neighbors against problems encountered in the project, and staging large-scale demonstrations that draw people from elsewhere in Bogotá to block major traffic arteries nearby. They keep this policed space open to contestation and remaking in their everyday practices.

While all of the authors in this book are alive to the spatiality of resistance, and I can see the agentic capacity of space and place in creating realms of practice enlivened by people's attention, attunement, and possible action, the arguments recognizing non-anthropocentric ideas of resistance—the agency of the more-than-human—may be more than I can accede to, though several of the chapters here have stretched my imagination. I can see where animals "resist" to avoid pain or discomfort, to circumvent doing things they do not want to do, to seek particular kinds of companionship—I live with two cats after all—but how do we thread these actions with our own practices of resistance and the aspirations they encompass? While I recognize that the worlds we inhabit are co-produced by and with animals, plants, objects, technologies, and elemental forces, as Catherine Oliver (Chapter 3) argues, I am not sure how our modes of resistance coalesce, though Oliver offers some provocative ideas about interspecies "friendship" that "[unsettle] the subject of resistance between and beyond the human and the animal." I am moved by this idea, but I am going to draw a line (perhaps a wobbly one) in naming what the object of resistance is, which can be indistinct even to us. Chickens in factory farms clearly suffer, and may find ways to limit or even resist the hideous conditions in which they are kept; but to say that they are resisting capitalist violence is to exceed their frame of reference and dilute what it means to resist capitalist violence. Resistance to capitalism—whatever its tenor or scale—is shaped by people. Working in conditions not of our own choosing, we make room for action— quiet or loud, intentionally or even unconsciously—that might make the world differently for us and for our co-producers. Our actions, in "friendship" and otherwise, are "perpetually becoming" as Meziant (Chapter 13) drawing on Deleuze and Guattari suggests, and I am grateful to have been encouraged by these chapters to see things differently.

The current moment—of war, of sprawling acts of state violence, global and intimate, of the immediate and looming effects of climate change, of the viscosity of white supremacy—calls for resistance in every register, and for seeing its abundant material social practices outside of conventional frames. This collection is a gift, offering nuanced and original perspectives on the contours and possible subjects, spaces, and times of resistance in emergence and otherwise, encompassing everyday activities, quiet and loud dissent, the daily work of care, witnessing, and refusals to look away from troubling circumstances. The ambiguities, intensities, contradictions, entanglements, and hazy horizons of these material social practices create possibilities and paths to social and environmental justice, and building solidarities across difference here, now, there, then.

Cindi Katz
City University of New York, Graduate Center

REFERENCES

Cahill, C. (2006). "'Risk'? The Fed Up Honeys Re-Present the Gentrification of the Lower East Side." *WSQ: Women's Studies Quarterly* 34(1–2): 334–363.

Hughes, S.M. (2020). "On Resistance in Human Geography." *Progress in Human Geography* 44(6): 1141–1160.

Hughes, S.M., A. Murrey, S. Krishnan, K. van Teijlingen, P.O. Daley, M. Nowicki, M. Fannin, J. MacLeavy (2022). "Interventions in the Political Geographies of Resistance: The Contributions of Cindi Katz, 15 Years On." *Political Geography* 97. https://doi.org/10.1016/j.polgeo.2022.102666.

Katz, C. (2001). "On the Grounds of Globalization: A Topography for Feminist Political Engagement." *Signs: Journal of Women in Culture and Society* 26(4): 1213–1234.

Katz, C. (2004). *Growing up Global: Economic Restructuring and Children's Everyday Lives*. Minneapolis, MN: University of Minnesota Press.

1. Introduction to *Critical Geographies of Resistance*
Sarah M. Hughes

Critical Geographies of Resistance emerges from a recognition that the contemporary geopolitical moment is characterised by an increase in actions that are recognised as, or claim to be, 'resistant'. The rise of the far right, the decimation of the natural environment and the responses to the so-called refugee 'crisis' are illustrative of these disturbing times. This book contends that revisiting debates on what we mean by 'resistance' may go some way to question how geographers can, or should, respond to the contemporary moment.

The chapters comprising this edited book therefore critically interrogate the political work of resistance in the contemporary moment. The authors carefully explore the multiple and everyday spaces, subjects and temporalities of resistance, and in doing so provide a novel approach to the study of resistance within geography. Together we aim to push forward debates on resistance in geography that perhaps have been stagnant over the last decade. That is not to say that there has not been scholarship on resisting and on resistance, but that a critical discussion on terminology of resistance remains missing. Whilst resistance has a long and rich history within geography, the book emerges from a recognition that tracing the concept of resistance within geography reveals a paradox: resistance is everywhere, and yet, surprisingly, elusive. Furthermore, whilst the conceptual vocabulary for resistance is increasingly diverse and splintered, and work on practices of resistance has proliferated, a critical engagement with resistance 'itself' has rarely been systematically engaged with, despite its apparent centrality to many geographical debates (for previous work, see Staeheli 1994; Pile 1997; Cresswell 1996; Sharp et al. 2000a; Routledge 1996, 1997; Rose 2002; Amoore 2005; Sparke 2008).

The conceptualisation of resistance is of importance for geography as the discipline has focused upon theorising power. Over the last decade, a wealth of scholarship interrogating the various and emergent multiplicities, intensities, modes, forms and genres of power has developed (Anderson 2017; see also Crampton and Elden 2007; Allen 2011). Tracing the trajectory of resistance cannot be separated from power, and yet, crucially, the shape of such resistant forms remains delineated a priori (with the exception of Horton and Kraftl

2009). That is, the (in)actions that come to be framed as resistance are not traced in their emergent becoming; geographers remain wedded to particular coordinates – of intention, linearity and opposition – that serve to determine in advance what comes to be termed as resistance. Further, these developments in how power is conceived are now ontologically dissonant with prevailing understandings of resistance. It is now recognised in several areas of the discipline, (particularly within social and cultural geography), that the non-human is lively and agentic (Braun and Whatmore 2010; Clark et al. 2008; Anderson and Wylie 2009; Gregson and Crang 2010). Yet, this focus upon the vitality of the non-human can serve to displace intention, which is a pivotal component of how resistance is determined in many dominant geographical accounts (Pile 1997; Routledge 1997; Martin and Pierce 2013). How, then, does a focus upon the non-human unsettle the assumption of an intentional, resistant subject?

Critical Geographies of Resistance aims to rekindle debates on resistance within the discipline. It rejects grand narratives or predetermined accounts of the form of resistance, and instead focuses on what a critical approach to resistance in its emergence might mean in the contemporary moment. Refuting a singular conceptualisation of resistance, the chapters are nonetheless united by an attempt to unpack how, where and for whom resistance does political work within geography. Moving beyond binary accounts of power versus resistance, the authors of this edited book think critically about the work that the concept of resistance does in their scholarship. What forms of politics does a focus on resistance open up, and what does it risk foreclosing? How might geography engage with resistance in the context of the 'material turn'? How does a focus upon the non-human unsettle the assumption of an intentional, resistant subject? Can geographers recognise and research resistance without recourse to such a predetermined form? In this way, *Critical Geographies of Resistance* takes stock of, and advances, geographical understandings of resistance.

In sharing these ontological, epistemological and political premises, the authors of *Critical Geographies of Resistance* demonstrate the potential of rethinking the work that resistance does within geography in productive ways, engaging in positive critical thinking and aimed at the identification of new voices, possibilities and agencies, and also at deframing established knowledges.

The idea for this book emerged gradually over five years. It began during my doctoral research, which explored resistance within the United Kingdom's (UK) asylum system. Taking stock of the literature on resistance in geography, I began to note that debates on the conceptualisation of resistance had perhaps reached an impasse. Since the debates on resistance in the late 1990s and early 2000s – including the edited books *Geographies of Resistance* (Pile and Keith 1997), and *Entanglements of Power: Geographies of Domination/*

Resistance (Sharpe et al. 2000b) – debates on what geographers mean by resistance became stagnated. There has not been an edited or single-author book specifically exploring the role of resistance within geography for two decades. Accordingly, the chapters that comprise *Critical Geographies of Resistance* address this important lacuna in geographical scholarship. The authors advance debates on resistance in geography by interrogating what a critical geography of resistance might look like in the contemporary moment.

This chapter traces a history of resistance in geography, reflecting on the trajectories of the term 'resistance'. This includes a discussion of the possible impasse in scholarship in the late 1990s, and also Marxist, anarchist and post-political accounts of resistance, recognising the feminist and post-colonial contributions pushing the criticality of accounts of resistance. This Introduction specifically addresses what is 'critical' in this book's engagement with resistance, before outlining the rest of the book so that the reader can navigate the arguments put forward.

I begin by outlining engagement with resistance in geography, exploring approaches that conceive resistance as oppositional to power, and then addressing scholarship whereby resistance is always-already entangled with power, including attending to the diversity of the many terms that have arisen to ground the specificities of particular resistant relations. I then move to identify two interrelated logics which have come to undergird much scholarly attention in this area: first, that resistance as distributed or 'everywhere' reduces the conceptual purchase of the term; and second, that resistance requires (a recognition of) intention. The chapter then takes up these pervasive conceptual threads and frays them to critically destabilise these seemingly fixed coordinates of resistance, arguing that a non-reductive attention to the always-already entangled forces, claimed as power and resistance, necessitates acknowledging the potentiality of forces. Such an approach to resistance prevents a foreclosure of these forces into predetermined forms (for example, of activist, intentional subject, protest, tactic or dispute), and thereby keeps open the category of resistance to other subjects, materials, spaces and temporalities which do not always cohere to an expected, coherent, resistant form.

As I will demonstrate throughout this Introduction, a rethinking of resistance within geography is important both within and beyond the academy, for a foreclosure of debate into 'what counts' as resistance risks denying recognition to those involved, and shutting down the multiple possible futures that may, or may not, emerge. This chapter, therefore, does not settle on a specific definition of resistance, for this risks excluding and ignoring the 'pluralities of resistance' (Foucault 1978: 95) which I will continue to detail. I follow Caygill's (2013, 7) comments that '[*a*] philosophy of resistance has itself to resist the pressure of concept-formation, of reducing the practices of resistance to a single concept', and therefore avoid the 'conceptual unification of "a Resistance"'. However, attention to the potentiality of resistant relations, I argue, does necessitate a discursive shift; new dis-organising grammars (of ambiguity, inconsistency and non-linearity) and vocabularies (of genre, intensity and mode), are needed for geographers to meaningfully engage with resistance in its emergence. This chapter thereby details areas where scholarly debate on resistance could be productively reanimated.

RESISTANCE AS OPPOSITIONAL

Resistance has traditionally been viewed as an oppositional binary to power: a 'central dialectic of opposing forces' (Sharp et al. 2000a: 9). Such structural accounts, whereby society is understood in relation to an overarching system or framework, posit power as possessed and deployed by those who control the institutions comprising the sovereign state. This, often (neo-)Marxist, scholarship focuses upon the hegemony of state and society, linking power with domination, control and coercion. When resistance is articulated thus, it is primarily recognised as mass mobilisations against a top-down, hierarchical manifestation of (sovereign) power; resistance is framed as power's antonym. Indeed, 'traditional' notions of resistance, as Cresswell (2000: 261) notes, pivot on this idea that power, 'through force or persuasion, diverts people from pursuing their "real interests"'.

Power and resistance are thus conceptualised as a dualism: resistance is considered emancipatory and acts against the seemingly totalising force of hegemonic state power (Hoy 2005). Across the wider social sciences, scholarship on resistance has its origins in this structural shared sense of counter-movement from below, double movement, or an identity-orientated approach to resistance, looking at how 'collective actors strive to create the identities and solidarities that they defend' (Sharp et al. 2000a 9; see Laclau and Mouffe 1985; de Certeau 1988; Polanyi 2001; Gramsci 2007).

More specifically, as Rose (2002) notes, geography has also focused upon theorising organised opposition (see Brown 2007; Peters 1998; Routledge 1996, 1997; Martin and Pierce 2013). This focus upon the geography of collective action cuts across many sub-sections of the discipline: Cloke et al. (2016) look at religion and contemporary activism in the Occupy movement, Flusty (2011) examines play as resistance to new developments in Los Angeles; Naseemullah (2018) analyses riots in India, and Murrey (2016) focuses upon community-led activity to fight against the Chad–Cameroon oil pipeline. Common across these empirically disparate accounts is an understanding of resistance in response to a particular configuration of power relations: resistance is placed in a dialectical relationship to power.

This dialectic is further developed in the influential work of feminist geographer Katz (2004, 2009), whose alternative categorisations of agency as reworking, resilience or resistance has had significant traction across the discipline. As Sparke (2008: 424) explains, Katz 'contrasts *resistance* that involves oppositional consciousness and achieves emancipatory change, with forms of *reworking* that alter the organization but not the polarization of power relations'. Katz's (2004) requirement for resistance to be oppositional has dominated much geographic scholarship, including: class and agency in post-industrial Glasgow (Cumbers et al. 2010), feminist accounts of intimate warfare in South Sudan (Faria 2017), migrant workers in Can Tho, Vietnam (Hauge and Fold 2016), and hip-hop cultures in Cape Town (Hammett 2012). Importantly for this chapter's argument for geographers to expand their engagement with resistance, Katz's delineation of resistance determines a priori what form resistance can take, which risks denying recognition to those actions and actors that do not fit within a preassigned 'oppositional' narrative.

Moreover, following calls in the 1990s for geographers to 'challenge social oppression ... putting ourselves "on the line" as academics, and engage with activism as academics' (Chouinard 1994: 5), the discipline has seen a rise in work on activism as a particular form of oppositional resistance directed at influencing change. Here, '[r]adical and critical geographers seek not only to interpret the world, but also to change it through the melding of theory and political action' (Blomley 2008: 285). Activism can be broadly understood to be a 'practice of political action by individuals or collectives in the form of social movements, non-government organizations' (Routledge 2009: 5), and is commonly understood as actions directed as opposition to particular configurations of power relations. Feminist scholars have further 'begun to expand the category of activism to include modest, quotidian acts of kindness and creativity' (Pottinger 2017: 215). Through this lens, activism does not need to be revolutionary, and is conceptualised beyond a revolutionary overthrowing of power. This attention to activism 'beyond the militant subject' (Chatterton and Pickerill 2010: 478; see Larner and Craig 2005; Horton and Kraftl 2009; Pottinger 2017) has arisen 'partly in response to the machismo that besets notions of wholesale revolution, giving rise to a need to understand post-heroic forms of activism more clearly' (Gill 2016: 168). These 'quiet' actions at the level of the everyday remain purposeful and oppositional; they are action on behalf of a cause, deliberate tactics with political orientations (Pottinger 2017).

Indeed, geographers have paid close attention to quotidian tactics of oppressed groups, often utilising the work of de Certeau, who proposes that many everyday practices of resistance are tactical, deployed by those who lack the backing of institutions of power, who seize the 'possibilities offered by circumstances' to oppose and eventually overthrow the forces oppressing them (de Certeau 1988: 37). Geographers have utilised the work of de Certeau to understand resistance in a wide range of contexts, including migration (Gill et al. 2013), citizenship (Secor 2004), online mapping technologies (Elwood and

Mitchell 2013), and through the 'dumpster diving' tactics of 'contemporary anarchist collective, CrimethInc' (Crane 2012). This approach to everyday, individual resistance is also characterised by opposition, coherence and intention.

These oppositional accounts are disparate in their ontologies, empirical focus and articulation of 'resistance', and yet they all broadly resonate within a framework of resistance as oppositional to power, resistance as 'challenging oppressive power relations' (Routledge 2009: 6). Within (neo-)Marxist accounts of (organised) opposition, resistance remains antonymic to power. Yet outside of an explicitly Marxist framework, dialectics haunt resistance: the residues of autonomous Marxism, sidelined by the post-structural and material turn within geography, continue to surface in how resistance is defined, researched and recognised as oppositional. Recognising this undergirding dialectic is important for geographic scholarship engaging with practices of resistance, for in predetermining what form resistance must take before its emergence, concerns over co-option emerge.

Concerns about Co-option

This narrative, of resistance as oppositional to power, results in concerns around co-option, and consequently with what form 'real' resistance can take. Pierce and Williams (2016: 171) argue that scholarship from the 1990s has tended to 'use the term resistance to link a myriad of oppositional responses to existing, unjust, power relations', and voice their concerns about a resultant co-option of resistance into existing power relations. They note that (neo-)Marxist oppositional accounts of resistance are often concerned with those for whom resistance is seeking inclusion within a particular system. Furthermore, post-political scholarship, with its varying emphases on antagonism (Mouffe 2005), dissensus (Rancière 2010) and foreclosure (Žižek 2004), emphasises – and critiques – the need for emancipatory change (Wilson and Swyngedouw 2014). These scholars variously call for radical transformative, revolutionary resistance; although Žižek (2004) argues that even when power is seized through a revolution, prior structures remain. The post-political view that those resisting power will 'inevitably reproduce a variation of the unjust institutions they have displaced' (Pierce and Williams 2016: 175) has had much traction within geography; such scholarship is concerned with co-option as reproducing the hegemonic order and resulting in structures and subjects becoming enveloped back into powerful systems (Wilson and Swyngedouw 2014).

These concerns with co-option extend beyond a post-political approach and are found throughout broader narratives of resistance as oppositional to particular forms of power relations. For example, Johnston (2017: 653), exploring the relationship between queer lives and normative institutions, suggests in relation to the 2010 UK Equalities Act that '[t]raditional forms of activism – that oppose the state – are no longer necessary, yet these leave some questioning the incorporation of queer lives into normative institutions'. Furthermore, Naylor (2017: 26) looking at reframing autonomy within political geography, argues for 'a feminist geopolitics of autonomous resistance', moving beyond simply framing this as a 'form of political resistance driven by social movement action against the state and/or neoliberal capitalist systems' and instead reinserting agency into geopolitics. Gill, writing in the context of the UK asylum system, is also sceptical about 'the potential of compassion to be truly emancipatory' (Gill 2016: 158) and consequently argues against particular forms of activism that try and bring asylum seekers into contact with state actors.

These empirically diverse accounts, underpinned by autonomy, emancipation and a concern with what 'counts' as resistance, reflect broader anxieties around co-option when resistance is framed as oppositional to power. Whilst these authors do engage with the complexity of power, an at times paradoxical and essentially binary view of resistance can be traced throughout much of this literature. This chapter now turns to examine scholarship that attempts to refute this separation, framing resistance as intimately entangled with power relations (Sharp et al. 2000a), discussing post-structuralist conceptualisations of the term, before moving to unpack the logics that underpin these dual framings of resistance.

RESISTANCE AS ALWAYS-ALREADY ENTANGLED WITH POWER

> [D]omination and resistance cannot exist independently of each other, but neither can they be reducible to one another: they are thoroughly hybrid phenomena, the one always contains the seeds of the other, the one always bearing at least a trace of the other that contaminates or subverts it. (Sharp et al. 2000a: 20)

Sharp et al.'s (2000a: 27) influential account of the geographies of domination/resistance draws upon Foucault to put forward an argument for an 'ambiguous, entangled view of power' deploying the term 'entanglements' to refute a binary separation of power and resistance. For Sharp et al. (2000a: xv), resistance and domination are both inherently linked; neither can 'escape from the endless circulation of power'. Indeed, Foucault's conceptualisation of power and resistance as multiple and relational, produced by certain forms of social relationship and therefore unable to be possessed, contained or localised (Foucault 1978; Allen and Cochrane 2010), has become close to orthodoxy within (and beyond) geography. Within this framework, 'where there is power, there is resistance, and yet, or rather consequently, this resistance is never in a position of exteriority in relation to power' (Foucault 1978:

95). Consequently, resistance does not entail escaping power relations, as the 'strictly relational character of power relationships [whose] existence depends on a multiplicity of powers of resistance ... present everywhere in the power network' (Foucault 1978: 95).

For geographers, conceptualising this relationship as 'entangled', Sharp et al. argue, brings forward a new spatial metaphor of 'knotted thoughts' (Sharp et al. 2000a: 1), or as Massey (2000: 283) frames it, 'a ball of wool after the cat has been at it'. An entanglement framework necessitates alternative ways of thinking about resistance beyond the metaphorical, looking practically at how 'knots' of forces become grounded in the multiple materialities of space (Sharp et al. 2000a). Therefore, recognising these entangled resistant power relations may not mobilise individuals or groups in any definitive way; but, crucially, this does not disqualify these (in)actions as resistance, rather it changes the way in which resistance is recognised as a multiplicity of potential relations. This is because, for Foucault, unlike the aforementioned accounts of resistance as oppositional, 'no matter how terrible a given situation may be, there always remain the possibilities of resistance, disobedience, and oppositional groupings' (Foucault 2002: 354). Yet this apparent optimism is in contrast with claims made by Thrift that Foucault, in his reliance upon discourse, does not leave space for lively, agentic subjects, resulting in 'a certain rather gloomy outlook' (Thrift 2007: 53). Such claims of futility are important to address when thinking about the possible limitations of this approach to resistance within geography, as Thrift (despite an acknowledgement that Foucault does leave some space for resistance) argues that 'the overwhelming impression is, too often, of a world that has given up the ghost' (Thrift 2000: 269), implicitly reinforcing resistance as intentional, linear and directed at a particular configuration of power relations.

What becomes apparent here is that debates over the nuances of Foucauldian framings of agentic subjects serve to highlight how particular forms of resistance and power continue to be held apart, or in opposition, for analysis. Returning to the quotation that opens this section: 'the one always contains the seeds of the other' (Sharp et al. 2000a: 20). Indeed, Sharp et al. remain with the domination/resistance couplet; for them, power is 'operative in moments of both domination and resistance', a focus upon entanglements of power, uses the terminology of 'dominating power' and 'resisting power' (ibid.: 3, 20) to name the forms that these various relations take. Such a focus has resulted in resistance placed as proxy for power relations, a 'form of power' (Bale 2000: 148), an attunement to a different force. Grounding these forces in writing becomes difficult as the terms 'power' and 'resistance' imply a dualism, and entanglements of domination/resistance require the naming of a particular force; a discursive dialectic (re)emerges within this framework. Indeed, this separation of entangled forces can be traced throughout many

Foucauldian-inspired accounts that have emerged within geographic literature, as this section will now continue to outline.

For example, Sparke (2008: 424) draws upon this entangled framework to comment that 'writing on the geography of resistance is especially indicative of the widened field of political geography'. Political geography emphasises power: there is a large and widely acknowledged body of work which conceives power to be dispersed through multiple actors; a 'tangled array of forces' (Allen and Cochrane 2010: 1073; see, e.g., Agnew 1999; Allen 2004, 2006; Hyndman 2004; Allen and Cochrane 2007; Crampton and Elden 2007; Sharp 2009). Furthermore, there is significant attention to discussions over sovereign power as multiple and diffuse (see Connolly 2007; Painter 2006; Gill 2010; McConnell 2009; Mountz 2013; Amoore 2013). As a consequence of the development and intersection of these bodies of literature, sovereignty is now widely considered to have migrated 'from states to a loosely assembled global system' (Connolly 2007: 36). This attention to the multiplicity of power relations has resulted in, as Chatterton and Pickerill (2010: 482) argue, 'resistance ... not usually articulated against a clear figure of oppression, be it the state, capital or the global corporation'. Yet whilst the 'target' of resistance has been interrogated and splintered, far less attention has been given to the multiplicity of forces of resistance within political geography (Sparke 2008).

Furthermore, post-colonial scholarship has also been concerned with a multiplicity of intertwined forces. In Bhabha's critique of Edwards Said's 'binary' account of 'the other' (Said 1978), Bhabha (1990) articulates how fluid, mixed, ambivalent and uncertain identities of emerge through colonialism: a mutual construction of subjectivities. Here the coloniser attempts to make those who have been colonised act or behave like the coloniser, reforming a more-familiar, but always-different 'other' (Sambajee 2015). Yet, this mimicry 'continually produces its slippage, its excess, its difference' (Bhabha 1984: 126), opening up an unstable and ambivalent 'third space' whereby different identities come together; a space 'holding its opposite within it' (Mitchell 1997: 536). An attention to such hybridity for post-colonial geography means that separation of domination and resistance is considered 'analytically unsatisfactory' (Radcliffe 2000: 170). The hybridity of third space is important for understanding resistance as entangled, argues Radcliffe, writing on the politics surrounding indigenous clothing in Ecuador, for unpacking binaries illuminates the 'complexities of power engaged in cultural contact and social change, highlighting the deeply entangled an impure, non-essential nature of societies and identities' (ibid.: 169).

An acknowledgement of the complex entanglements of forces, is further evident within actor network theory (e.g., Pickering 1993; Latour 1996; Law 1999). Here 'modern societies cannot be described without recognizing them as having fibrous, thread-like, wiry, stringy, ropy, capillary character' (Latour

1996: 370). Comparably, geographers drawing upon the rhizomatic assemblage thinking of Deleuze and Guattari (1987) and DeLanda (2016) also acknowledge that 'assemblage connotes not a central governing power, nor a power distributed equally, but power as plurality in transformation' (Anderson and McFarlane 2011: 125). This flat ontology, which refutes a privileging of the human, means that resistance here also includes acknowledging the 'vibrant materiality' that Bennett (2010) argues runs alongside humans: seeing things as having the capacity to act as quasi agents and as forces of their own. Whilst these accounts focus upon the multiplicity of non-hierarchical power relations that assemblage thinking obligates, the (albeit implicit) assumption here in this literature is that resistance is also splintered, multiple and non-hierarchical (see also McFarlane 2006, 2009; Allen and Cochrane 2007, 2010). An important exception here is Legg (2011: 128), who discusses 'Deleuze's commentary on Foucault's work, in which he [Deleuze] stressed that "the final word on power is that resistance comes first" (Deleuze 1988, 89)'.

Such a relational approach has had considerable traction within urban geography (e.g., McFarlane 2009, 2011; Shaw 2014; Jacobs 2012; Storper and Scott 2016), with McGuirk et al. (2016: 129) arguing that understanding the city as an assemblage means conceiving it to be 'performed, emergent and diversely constituted ... enacted in socio-material "frictions" and negations of the everyday'. This non-hierarchical multiplicity also emerges within Wideman and Masuda's (2018: 387) account of resistance to planning interventions in Downtown Eastside in Vancouver, where they argue that an assemblage approach which engages the material is a 'powerful analytic tool for uncovering the contested production of place'. Such accounts of the liveliness of materials, that form new relations beyond (although not excluding) any human intention, destabilises intention as a criterion for determining resistance a priori, for – as this chapter will continue to interrogate – Bennett's concept of distributed agency 'does not posit a subject as the root cause of an effect' (Bennett 2010: 31). This multiplies the potential for resistance into material and other non-human actors, which aligns with the concern that a multiplicity of resistant relations is a dilution of the purchase of the term, resulting in particular predetermined coordinates (of intention, coherence, opposition) that delineate the form of resistance.

LOGIC 1: THAT RESISTANCE 'EVERYWHERE' DILUTES THE PURCHASE OF THE TERM

A focus upon entanglement can be traced throughout much geographic scholarship on resistance since the cultural turn. Yet, literature premised upon this understanding of power and resistance continues to separate them for analysis: to entwine, to entangle, requires a separation; the possibility to disentangle, unravel or untwine is inevitable within such a discursive capture. Even for Foucault, resistances are 'the odd term in relations of power; they are inscribed in the latter as an irreducible opposite' (Foucault 1990: 88). This enduring dialectic has resulted in a wide variety of productive terms emerging to detail particular manifestations, nuances and specificities of entanglements. For example, geographers have explored 'counter conduct' (Cadman 2010; Conlon 2013; Rosol 2014), resilience (Munt 2012; Pugh 2014; Weichselgartner and Kelman 2015) and the complexities of social movements (Creasap 2012; Fairhurst et al. 2004) to conceptualise the nuances of these entanglements within the broader bracket of resistance. These reclassifications of the term have emerged to (re)define, delineate and capture particular manifestations of the complex relationship between power and resistance.

For example, Jones (2012: 686–687), researching contested spaces at the India–Bangladesh border, distances himself from Sharp et al.'s (2000a) 'capacious definition of resistance', arguing that:

> if everything is understood as part of the interplay of dominance and resistance in power relation, the analysis becomes increasingly meaningless because it fails to consider whether the resistance actually produces any changes to the power relationship or whether it was even intentional, a decision often left to the researcher, not the individual (Pile and Keith 1997; Rose 2002; Sparke 2008).

In contrast, Jones (2012: 687) develops the framework of refusal to 'conceptualize everyday actions ... that disregard the rules of the state in these not completely administered spaces but are not politically motivated resistance to sovereignty'. Here Jones rejects the conceptual purchase of a multiplicity of resistances, and his articulation of spaces of refusal can be considered to delineate what form the interplay of power and resistance must take for it to be considered resistance, or refusal.

Jones's (2012) concerns are illustrative of an impasse in accounts of resistance within geography. That is, with the splintering of potential sites and subjects of power and resistance, further curtailment around what 'counts' as resistance is required to prevent a romanticisation of resistance. Cultural geographer Rose (2002: 383) succinctly explains this impasse:

> [T]he challenge for geographers has been to develop theories that recognize and categorize 'resistant' practice. Despite the interest that this new subfield has garnered, the challenge has created a theoretical crossroad. If we choose criteria narrowly, we risk ignoring certain forms of contradictory practice, yet, if we accept every moment of contradictory practice as an example of resistance, our concepts of resistance become devoid of any practical use.

In limiting our understanding of resistance, geographers constrain opportunities for the recognition of subjects, materials, spaces (in)actions that do not cohere with a preset form to be woven into narratives of resistance. This 'theoretical crossroad' (Rose 2002: 383) is therefore important; for, as Amoore (2005: 7) notes, 'we tend to recognise resistances to take a particular form, and that in doing this we increase the visibility of these modes of politics whilst simultaneously rendering other modes invisible'.

Therefore, whilst the move away from binary accounts of resistance towards a pluralised and relational understanding has (somewhat) displaced accounts of acts of opposition, it has also led to concerns that resistance is becoming romanticised in its multiplicity:

> Just as Foucault's lesson is that power is everywhere and inescapable, this new concern with resistance sees it in the most mundane activities. The discourse on resistance moved from strikes, protests, riots and the production of alternative cultures through the resistance of carnival, having fun and telling jokes to a whole plethora of unremarkable activities such as walking, eating, shopping and taking shortcuts. I do not wish to offer any definitive statement on resistance here but I will suggest a difficulty with defining certain kinds of activities, which seem to lack a crucial element of choice, as resistance. (Cresswell 1996: 422)

In short, the argument is made here that if resistance is everywhere, it becomes 'increasingly meaningless' (Jones 2012: 687; Cresswell 1996, 2000; Ferguson and Golding 1997). As Cresswell later expands: 'It is fair to say that human geography, and cultural studies even more so, have been guilty of romanticising resistance' (Cresswell 2000, 258). Whilst for Pile, resistance as ubiquitous does not mean that that 'resistance becomes "anything" or "everywhere"', but precisely that resistance is understood where it takes place' (Pile 1997: 3), Cresswell raises particular concerns that 'there is a danger that no area of social life will not be described as resistance', and any act that is not definitively linked to dominant structures is held up as an example of 'resistance' (Cresswell 2000: 259). Massey echoes some of these concerns, noting that a recognition of resistance as everywhere should not mean that structural inequalities of power become lost and 'dissipated in a plethora of multiplicities' (Massey 2000: 280). It is important, she cautions, not to 'trivialise resistance, nor to underestimate what real resistance costs' (ibid.: 281). These narratives continue to hold traction within geography; the logic that Foucauldian-inspired entanglements of power and resistance risks overextending and romanticising the term persists.

A notable exception to this viewpoint can be found, however, in the work of Chatterton and Pickerill (2010: 479) who, writing about the activist subject in relation to post-capitalist worlds, highlight that what 'our findings point to is an altogether more complex and often contradictory process of activist-becoming-activist through trends that include the rejection of binaries between activists and their other, an embracing of a plurality of values, a pragmatic goal orientation and a growing professionalism'. In splintering the 'assumed unified activist subject' to reveal 'messy impurities' Chatterton and Pickerill's work contributes to critiques of what, for Nealon (2008: 105), is the predominant 'old-fashioned, gold-standard thinking of resistance'. This is the view that 'if it's not scarce and it doesn't refer to some grounding version of a "real thing", then it's not valuable. It's not actual resistance, it's just a programmed product of power' (Nealon 2008: 105).

Further, understanding resistance as potentially percolating everywhere has led to concerns that 'true' resistance is futile, for resistance cannot be necessarily linked to observable change (Hoy 2005; Jones 2012: 687). Should every disruption be theorised as resistance? This is by no means to suggest that challenging inequalities should not be a driving force behind scholarly attention to resistance, but instead to note that the assumption of linearity towards a telos – an end goal – is bound up in predetermined forms of resistance. Yet, as this chapter will continue to explore, is an explicit causal link to change required for an (in)action to be considered resistance? Can the critique that 'resistance goes nowhere in particular, has no inherent attachments, and hails no particular vision' (Brown 1995: 49) be turned on its head? Hoy's (2005: 229) reading of Derrida is useful here, as it critiques 'the sense of direction suggested by any line of criticism proffered with the tacit implication that it knows the true picture and the best solution, even if it never fully articulates this knowledge'. A growing body of work on resistance as opening other possible futures has been examined in diverse spaces: for example, Joronen (2017) discusses play, potentiality and form-of-life in Palestine; Bagelman and Wiebe look to political acts of resistance where 'other possibilities may be glimpsed' in their work on the intimacies of global toxins in the Aamjiwnaang First Nation's reserve (Anderson 2014, cited in Bagelman and Wiebe 2017: 83); and even Jones (2012: 698), who articulates concern over the multiplicities of resistance, explains that '[b]y emphasizing nuance, fragmentation, and process, the possible remains'.

Resistance has thus been framed within geography as entangled with power, present within everyday actions, and not restricted to oppositional movements against (primarily) state power. This opening up of the term has resulted in scholars narrowing the scope of resistance, predetermining what forms actions must take before being identified as resistance; classifications emerging a priori; a privileging of form. The most significant and pervasive logic of this is that resistance requires (a recognition of) intention.

LOGIC 2: THAT RESISTANCE REQUIRES INTENTION

> I use the term 'resistance' to refer to any action imbued with intent that attempts to challenge, change or retain particular circumstances relating to societal relations, processes and/or institutions. (Routledge 1997: 360)

The word 'intent' is derived from the Latin *intendere* (verb), or *intentus* (adjective). It means 'to stretch out, to strain' (*tendere*) 'towards' (*in*), to direct action towards a purpose (Ainsworth et al. 1823). Importantly therefore, the aforementioned notion of telos, an end goal, is bound up with the idea of a subject acting with intent. This understanding of intent as being associated with the idea of an end goal is therefore crucial when thinking about how resistance has been conceptualised as intentional and linear, as future-orientated actions are directed by a subject to resolve, at least in part, some problem of the present moment. This is not to say, however, that intention is itself a binary: whilst the confines of language frame intentional as oppositional to unintentional, subject (in)coherence is far more complex than this simple delineation of terms suggests. A destabilisation of intent, however, is bound up within the dangers of romanticising resistance: the concern that multiplying the possible points of resistance results in a dilution of the political utility and potential of the term.

Conceptualisations of resistance within and beyond geography have been framed by the view that 'acts of resistance' require the intention of subjects and/or a recognition of intent by a target or observer (see Cresswell 1996, 2000; Routledge 1996, 1997; Pile 1997; Jones 2012; Martin and Pierce 2013; Crane 2015; Nicholls 2016). Resistance is thus seen as a conscious practice, whereby a subject overcomes or, crucially, intends to overcome, a particular configuration of power relations: 'the person engaging in resistant acts must do so consciously and be able to relate that consciousness and intent' (Leblanc 1999: 18); in doing so, a resistant subject is invoked. For example, in their work on radical democracy Martin and Pierce (2013: 77) argue that '[r]esistance ... needs to intentionally and deliberately employ the state to sow greater lines of contradiction within the state's neoliberal project'. The concern that resistance necessitates conscious intent, Hollander and Einwohner (2004) argue, is central to debates over whether an act constitutes resistance throughout the social sciences.

Furthermore, a recognition of intention within (in)action is frequently linked to scalar analysis of resistance. Scott's work on local-scale, intentional actions, the 'hidden transcripts of subordinate groups', has influenced much work on resistance within geography (Scott 1990, 15). Scott (1990) privileges intent as a better indicator of resistance than the outcome of actions, because acts of resistance do not always achieve the desired effect. However, Scott's argument that it is reasonable to read intent in actions has been criticised by those who note that assessing intent is difficult, if not impossible (Hollander and Einwohner 2004). Pile also critiques accounts of resistance, such as Scott's (1990), that prioritise intentional actions, arguing that determining intent is not straightforward (Pile 1997). Pile suggests that resistance may be unintentional but not accidental; rather than acting against perceived oppression, other motives may inspire resistant subjects (ibid.). This continues to resonate with intention as a binary, that can be located within a coherent subject (ibid.), and supports the work of Cresswell (1996) who also points to the need to decouple intention from action, Yet Rose reads in Pile's argument an underlying assumption that resistance is still reacting: how reacting takes form shapes the debate, but 'that resistance is a responsive act, however, is an assumed part of the equation' (Rose 2002: 387). This problematic of recognising resistance aligns with concerns within animal geography on the use of the term resistance, which Wilbert (2000: 238) argues 'raises political and ethical questions about who, or what, can or cannot act purposefully to bring about change'. Wilbert's account again aligns with a purposeful action directed at a particular end goal (Wilbert 2000), a focus upon a recognition of an inscription of agency. These views are further premised upon the idea that there is a binary between intentional and unintentional actions, which relies upon the assumption of a coherent actor able to determine when, how or why they or 'others' are acting with intent.

Importantly for tracing the multiple trajectories of resistance within geography, what becomes visible when attention is paid to this logic of intention is that such a priori delineations of resistance decouple from recent theorisations of power as emergent and 'lived as part of the composition of experience' (Anderson 2017: 501). In short, the work that resistance does within geography is not ontologically compatible with new directions in power. The contributors to this book work – in different, and deliberately incoherent ways – to variously decentre these logics, arguing that accepting the potentiality of resistant relations allows for different questions to be asked of the conceptual purchase of this term within geography.

ORGANISATION OF *CRITICAL GEOGRAPHIES OF RESISTANCE*

Critical Geographies of Resistance is a book in two parts. The chapters comprising Part I of the book, 'Rethinking Resistance, Reframing Debates', focus upon reconceptualising approaches to the *concept* of resistance. The authors do not prescribe a singular or overarching framework of resistance. Instead, they explore multiple positions on the work that resistance does within human geography. Part II, 'Emergent Resistance: Reflections from the Field', then takes up these conceptual threads and grounds them empirically, through a series of rich case studies that unpack the nuances of what a critical geography of resistance might look like in practice. Throughout, the authors make suggestions for future areas of research and reflection in this area.

The authors in this book are united in their focus on the critical geographies of resistance. It is important to state from the start that this is not to claim that previous work on resistance has not been critical. Instead, we are interested in pushing, playing and pulling apart the expected conceptual boundaries of resistance in geographical scholarship. With this in mind, Part I, 'Rethinking Resistance, Reframing Debates', aims to reflect upon and advance understandings of resistance within geography. Contributors revisit the concept of resistance in the context of ontological developments in the discipline. Part I opens with a reflection on the role of feminist geographies of resistance. Maria Fannin and Julie MacLeavy (Chapter 2) describe such resistance 'not as a constant, shared or even necessarily antagonistic activity, but as something achieved through inconsistent behaviours and actions'. They explore this framing of resistance by tracing the spatial-political practices of the UK-based Feminist Archive South, looking at the 'political dimensions of collecting, cataloguing and preserving materials as a form of resistance'.

Catherine Oliver's Chapter 3 continues to unsettle the expected form of resistance in her focus on resistance beyond the human subject. Oliver argues that animal resistance is too often understood within 'an anthropocentric framework which is obscured by dominant epistemological assumptions about animals'. Moving to disrupt this narrative, Oliver's careful account of role of interspecies friendship provides a rethinking of the subject/object binary of many predetermined categorisations of resistance. Sage Brice (Chapter 4) furthers this discussion of subjectivity in the context of current geographical approaches – informed by a range of posthumanist and non-representational theories – that aim to decentre the pre-individuated subject as a unit of social and political analysis. Her work examines frames resistance both as a 'practice oriented towards opening up space to thrive in the face of oppressive systems, and a force of opposition or obstruction to that practice: an opposition experienced in the everyday as a kind of "friction"'. In doing so, Brice explores how geographers engage gender variance and transition, to ask what kinds of politics of resistance might be facilitated by emerging non-representational theories of subjectivity.

A conceptual engagement with intentionality and resistance beyond a coherent human subject is also threaded through Carlotta Molfese's Chapter 5, which considers how more-than-human perspectives can assist in 'developing a non-anthropocentric framework of resistance in critical geography'. Building upon a post-phenomenological understanding of intentionality, Molfese argues that a rethinking of resistance beyond the traditional (human) subject of resistance, requires 'an expansion of what a political collective is, how it comes into being and the political work it does'. Charlotte Lee (Chapter 6) unpacks the relationship between activism and resistance within geography and argues for greater attention to the nuances of this terminology. Lee identifies a hierarchical understanding in some accounts of activism and argues against this, claiming that that resistance 'should be considered a disposition present in some activism'. Finally, Sarah Zell and Amelia Curran (Chapter 7) reflect upon how an emergent understanding of resistance emerged in and through their ethnographic fieldwork. Drawing across their different research projects – on gang territories in Winnipeg, Canada, and the recruitment process and the Canadian border for Mexican migrant workers – they argue that their methodological approaches helped them shift from thinking about 'resistance in space, to space as resistance'. Focusing on the ethnographic methods used to research resistance Zell and Curran discuss how a 'materialist orientation focused on practices helped [them to] encounter elusive spatial forms, and concomitantly, emergent and seemingly unremarkable instances of resistance'.

Part II of the book, 'Emergent Resistance: Reflections from the Field', develops from Part I by critically interrogating how we account for resistances as the develop in practice. Building upon the conceptual groundwork of Part I, these contributions use case studies to push forward critical geographical understandings of resistance. Each chapter in Part II represents one of these possible ways of tracing, reading and researching resistance, thus carrying a value that is related both to its specific content and to its wider applicability and contribution to the approach proposed by the book. First, Angharad Butler-Rees (Chapter 8) challenges conventional notions of resistance by drawing upon disabled people's direct narratives of how their everyday lives and bodies may constitute material forms of resistance. Through her detailed research on disability activism in response to austerity in the UK, Angharad Butler-Rees argues that resistance may not constitute solely that of predetermined forms, but also be 'lived out' through 'disabled people's everyday existence (and practices of self-care and mutual aid) along with their tenacity to keep accessing public space in uncompromising ways'.

In the next contribution, Chapter 9, Hannah Awcock analyses the material politics of protests stickers in the context of urban spaces. Grounding her discussion in her photographic archive of 'Bollocks to Brexit' stickers that have emerged in the UK in the wake of the 2016 European Union Referendum, Awcock explores the forms for resistance that these stickers enable. Focusing on the material politics of these common forms of protest, she argues that stickers 'blur the boundaries of what constitutes resistance' as they are 'frequently unclear in their authorship and/or intention'. Karen Schouw Iverson (Chapter 10) also focuses on urban spaces of resistance, examining the struggles in and around a housing project (Plaza de la Hoja) built for displaced victims of the armed conflict in Bogota, Colombia. Schouw Iverson's argument that this project represents 'a spatial technology of control that renders the continued socio-economic marginalisation of the internally displaced politically invisible' emerges from her rich empirical reflections, which serve to nuance binary approaches to 'power' or 'resistance', and calls instead for attention to the mobility of the category of resistance itself. Continuing with housing, in Chapter 11 Mel Nowicki explores the multiple ways by which small-scale grassroots activism utilises the law as a method of resistance to housing inequality in the context of the UK's 'Bedroom Tax' (implemented as part of the 2012 Welfare Reform Act). Nowicki's research with social tenants, housing associations and welfare charities has identified how people navigate legal spaces to 'to resist its imposition in largely mundane settings not usually equated with resistance movements: online social media groups and housing association offices'.

Following this, the book turns to the role of resistance within migration geographies. First, Amanda Schmid-Scott (Chapter 12) explores the significance of volunteers bearing witness to asylum seekers reporting to the Home Office. This purposefully oppositional response to the violence of border control and management practices may not typically constitute a discrete 'act of resistance', but Schmid-Scott argues that – by making usually discrete practices visible – the act of witnessing constitutes 'a mode of resistance which holds potency, both through its ability to disrupt the hegemonic gaze of the Home Office officers over signers'. Next, Kahina Meziant (Chapter 13) explores 'how quiet transgressions and sonic practices (and properties) can rework power structures in organisations'. Meziant draws upon a situated ethnographic study of community music practices in an organisation in the UK voluntary and community sector to show how subtle transgressive acts contribute to the emergence of resistance. Finally, in Chapter 14, Leah Montange engages with frameworks from two Black feminist thinkers, Saidiya Hartman and Katherine McKittrick, to explore crafting and resistance in United States immigration detention centres. Montange offers a reading of crafting within detention and argues that it is 'agentic practice that does not demonstrate political subjectivization, or acquiescence with spatio-temporal domination' instead those within immigration detention 'use and make space and place around, despite, or without reference to the logics of spatio-temporal domination'.

ACKNOWLEDGEMENT

Sections of this chapter have already been published in Hughes, Sarah M. (2020). 'On Resistance in Human Geography', *Progress in Human Geography* 44(6): 1141–1160. Copyright © 2019, © SAGE Publications.

REFERENCES

Agnew, J. (1999). 'Mapping Political Power beyond State Boundaries: Territory, Identity, and Movement in World Politics.' *Millennium* 28(3): 499–521.

Ainsworth, R., Morell, T., and Carey, J. (1823). 'Intendus.' In *Ainsworth's Latin Dictionary*. Edited by Ainsworth, R., Morell, T., and Carey, J. London: C. & J. Rivington.

Allen, J. (2004). 'The Whereabouts of Power: Politics, Government and Space.' *Geografiska Annaler: Series B, Human Geography* 86(1): 19–32.

Allen, J. (2006). 'Ambient Power: Berlin's Potsdamer Platz and the Seductive Logic of Public Spaces.' *Urban Studies* 43(2): 441–455.

Allen, J. (2011). 'Topological Twists: Power's Shifting Geographies.' *Dialogues in Human Geography* 1(3): 283–298.

Allen, J., and Cochrane, A. (2007). 'Beyond the Territorial Fix: Regional Assemblages, Politics and Power.' *Regional Studies* 41(9): 1161–1175.

Allen, J., and Cochrane, A. (2010). 'Assemblages of State Power: Topological Shifts in the Organization of Government and Politics.' *Antipode* 42(5): 1071–1089.

Amoore, L. (2005). 'Introduction: Global Resistance – Global Politics.' In *The Global Resistance Reader*, edited by Amoore, L. Abingdon: Routledge.

Amoore, L. (2013). *The Politics of Possibility: Risk and Security beyond Probability*. Durham, NC: Duke University Press.

Anderson, B. (2017). 'Cultural Geography 1: Intensities and Forms of Power.' *Progress in Human Geography* 41(4): 501–511.

Anderson, B., and McFarlane, C. (2011). 'Assemblage and Geography.' *Area* 43(2): 124–127.

Anderson, B., and Wylie, J. (2009). 'On Geography and Materiality.' *Environment and Planning A* 41(2): 318–335.

Bagelman, J., and Wiebe, S.M. (2017). 'Intimacies of Global Toxins: Exposure and Resistance in "Chemical Valley".' *Political Geography* 60: 76–85.

Bale, J. (2000). 'Sport as Power: Running as Resistance?' In *Entanglements of Power: Geographies of Domination/Resistance*, edited by Sharp, J.P., Routledge, P., Philo, P., and Paddison, R. London: Routledge.

Bennett, J. (2010). *Vibrant Matter: A Political Ecology of Things*. Durham, NC: Duke University Press.

Bhabha, H. (1984). 'Of Mimicry and Man: The Ambivalence of Colonial Discourse.' *October Discipleship: A Special Issue on Psychoanalysis* 28: 125–133.

Bhabha, H.K. (1990). *Nation and Narration*. London: Routledge.

Blomley, N. (2008). 'The Spaces of Critical Geography.' *Progress in Human Geography* 32(2): 285–393.

Braun, B., and Whatmore, S. (2010). 'The Stuff of Politics: An Introduction.' In *Political Matter: Technoscience, Democracy, and Public Life*, edited by Braun, B., and Whatmore, S. Minneapolis, MN: University of Minnesota Press.

Brown, W. (1995). *States of Injury: Power and Freedom in Late Modernity*. Princeton, NJ: Princeton University Press.

Brown, G. (2007). 'Mutinous Eruptions: Autonomous Spaces of Radical Queer Activism.' *Environment and Planning A* 39(11): 2685–2698.

Cadman, L. (2010). 'How (Not) to be Governed: Foucault, Critique, and the Political.' *Environment and Planning D: Society and Space* 28(3), 539–556.

Caygill, H. (2013). *On Resistance: A Philosophy of Defiance.* London: Bloomsbury Academic.
Chatterton, P., and Pickerill, J. (2010). 'Everyday Activism and Transitions towards Post-Capitalist Worlds: Everyday Activism and Transitions towards Post-Capitalist Worlds.' *Transactions of the Institute of British Geographers* 35(4): 475–490.
Chouinard, V. (1994). 'Reinventing Radical Geography: Is All That's Left Right?' *Environment and Planning D: Society and Space* 12(1): 2–6.
Clark, N., Massey, D., and Sarre, P. (eds) (2008). *Material Geographies: A World in the Making.* London: SAGE Publications.
Cloke, P., Sutherland, C., and Williams, A. (2016). 'Postsecularity, Political Resistance, and Protest in the Occupy Movement: Postsecularity in the Occupy Movement.' *Antipode* 48(3): 497–523.
Conlon, D. (2013). 'Hungering for Freedom: Asylum Seekers' Hunger Strikes – Rethinking Resistance as Counter-Conduct.' In *Carceral Spaces: Mobility and Agency in Imprisonment and Migrant Detention*, edited by Moran, D., Gill, N., and Conlon, D. Aldershot: Ashgate.
Connolly, W.E. (2007). 'The Complexities of Sovereignty.' In *Sovereign Lives: Power in Global Politics*, edited by Edkins, J., Pin-Fat, V., and Shapiro, M.J. New York: Routledge.
Crampton, J W., and Elden, S. (eds) (2007). *Space, Knowledge and Power: Foucault and Geography.* Aldershot: Ashgate.
Crane, N. (2012). 'Are "Other Spaces" Necessary? Associative Power at the Dumpster.' *ACME: An International Journal for Critical Geographies* 11(3): 352–372.
Crane, N.J. (2015). 'Politics Squeezed through a Police State: Policing and Vinculación in Post-1968 Mexico City.' *Political Geography* 47: 1–10.
Creasap, K. (2012). 'Social Movement Scenes: Place-Based Politics and Everyday Resistance.' *Sociology Compass* 6: 182–191.
Cresswell, T. (1996). 'Writing, Reading and the Problem of Resistance: A Reply to McDowell.' *Transactions of the Institute of British Geographers* 21(2): 420–424.
Cresswell, T. (2000). 'Falling Down. Resistance as Diagnostic.' In *Entanglements of Power: Geographies of Domination/Resistance*, edited by Sharp, J.P., Routledge, P., Philo, P., and Paddison, R. London: Routledge.
Cumbers, A., Helms, G., and Swanson, K. (2010). 'Class, Agency and Resistance in the Old Industrial City.' *Antipode* 42(1): 46–73.
De Certeau, M. (1988). *The Practice of Everyday Life.* London: University of California Press.
DeLanda, M. (2016). *Assemblage Theory.* Edinburgh: Edinburgh University Press.
Deleuze, G., and Guattari, F. (1987). *A Thousand Plateaus. Capitalism and Schizophrenia.* Minneapolis, MN: University of Minnesota Press.
Elwood, S., and Mitchell, K. (2013). 'Another Politics Is Possible: Neogeographies, Visual Spatial Tactics, and Political Formation.' *Cartographica: The International Journal for Geographic Information and Geovisualization* 48(4): 275–292.
Fairhurst, F., Ramutsindela, M., and Bob, U. (2004). 'Social Movements, Protest, and Resistance.' In *Mapping Women, Making Politics*, edited by Staeheli, L., Kofman, E., and Peake, L. London: Routledge.
Faria, C. (2017). 'Towards a Countertopography of Intimate War: Contouring Violence and Resistance in a South Sudanese Diaspora.' *Gender, Place and Culture* 24(4): 575–593.

Ferguson, M., and Golding, P. (1997) 'Cultural Studies in Question. An Introduction.' In *Cultural Studies in Question*, edited by Ferguson, M., and Golding, P. London: SAGE Publications.

Flusty, S. (2011). 'Thrashing Downtown: Play as Resistance to the Spatial and Representational Regulation of Los Angeles.' *Cities* 17(2): 149–158.

Foucault, M. (1978). *The History of Sexuality*. New York: Vintage.

Foucault, M. (1990). *The Will to Knowledge. The History of Sexuality, Volume 1.* London: Penguin Books.

Foucault, M. (2002). 'Space, Knowledge, and Power.' In *Power*, edited by Faubion, J.D. London: Penguin.

Gill, N. (2010). 'New State-Theoretic Approaches to Asylum and Refugee Geographies.' *Progress in Human Geography* 34(5): 626–645.

Gill, N. (2016). *Nothing Personal? Geographies of Governing and Activism in the British Asylum System.* Chichester: John Wiley & Sons.

Gill, N., Conlon, D., and Moran, D. (2013). 'Dialogues across Carceral Space: Migration, Mobility, Space and Agency.' In *Carceral Spaces: Mobility and Agency in Imprisonment and Migrant Detention*, edited by Gill, N., Conlon, D., and Moran, D. Farnham: Ashgate Publishing.

Gramsci, A. (2007). *Selections from the Prison Notebooks of Antonio Gramsci.* Edited by Hoare, Q., and Nowell-Smith, G. London: Lawrence & Wishart.

Gregson, N., and Crang, M. (2010). 'Materiality and Waste: Inorganic Vitality in a Networked World.' *Environment and Planning A* 42(5): 1026–1032.

Hammett, D. (2012). 'Reworking and Resisting Globalising Influences: Cape Town Hip-Hop.' *GeoJournal* 77(3): 417–428.

Hauge, M., and Fold, N. (2016). 'Resilience and Reworking Practices: Becoming the First-Generation of Industrial Workers in Can Tho, Vietnam.' *Geoforum* 77: 124–133.

Hollander, J.A., and Einwohner, R.L. (2004). 'Conceptualizing Resistance.' *Sociological Forum* 19(4): 533–554.

Horton, J., and Kraftl, P. (2009). 'Small Acts, Kind Words and "Not Too Much Fuss": Implicit Activisms.' *Activism and Emotional Sustainability* 2(1): 14–23.

Hoy, D.C. (2005) *Critical Resistance From Poststructuralism to Post-Critique.* Cambridge, MA: MIT Press.

Hyndman, J. (2004). 'Mind the Gap: Bridging Feminist and Political Geography through Geopolitics.' *Political Geography* 23(3): 307–322.

Jacobs, J.M. (2012). 'Urban Geographies I: Still Thinking Cities Relationally.' *Progress in Human Geography* 36(3): 412–422.

Johnston, L. (2017). 'Gender and sexuality II: Activism.' *Progress in Human Geography* 41(5): 648–656.

Jones, R. (2012). 'Spaces of Refusal: Rethinking Sovereign Power and Resistance at the Border.' *Annals of the Association of American Geographers* 102(3): 685–699.

Joronen, M. (2017). '"Refusing to Be a Victim, Refusing to Be an Enemy". Form-of-Life as Resistance in the Palestinian Struggle against Settler Colonialism.' *Political Geography* 56: 91–100.

Katz, C. (2004). *Growing up Global: Economic Restructuring and Children's Everyday Lives*. Minneapolis, MN: University of Minnesota Press.

Katz, C. (2009). 'Social systems: Thinking about society, identity, power and resistance.' In *Key Concepts in Geography*, edited by Clifford, N., Holloway, S.L., Rice, S.P., and Valentine, G. London: SAGE Publications.

Laclau, E., and Mouffe, C. (1985). *Hegemony and Socialist Strategy: Towards a Radical Democratic Politics*. London: Verso.

Larner, W., and Craig, D. (2005). 'After Neoliberalism? Community Activism and Local Partnerships in Aotearoa New Zealand.' *Antipode* 37(3): 402–424.

Latour, B. (1996). 'On Actor-Network Theory: A Few Clarifications.' *Soziale Welt* 47(4): 369–381.

Law, J. (1999). 'After ANT: Complexity, Naming and Topology.' *Sociological Review* 47(1): 1–14.

Leblanc, L. (1999). *Pretty in Punk: Girls' Gender Resistance in a Boys' Subculture*. New Brunswick, NJ: Rutgers University Press.

Legg, S. (2011). 'Assemblage/Apparatus: Using Deleuze and Foucault.' *Area* 43(2): 128–133.

Martin, D.G., and Pierce, J. (2013). 'Reconceptualizing Resistance: Residuals of the State and Democratic Radical Pluralism.' *Antipode* 45(1): 61–79.

Massey, D. (2000). 'Entanglements of Power. Reflections.' In *Entanglements of Power: Geographies of Domination/Resistance*, edited by Sharp, J.P., Routledge, P., Philo, P., and Paddison, R. London: Routledge.

McConnell, F. (2009). 'Governments-in-Exile: Statehood, Statelessness and the Reconfiguration of Territory and Sovereignty.' *Geography Compass* 3(5): 1902–1919.

McFarlane, C. (2006). 'Transnational development networks: bringing development and postcolonial approaches into dialogue.' *Geographical Journal* 172(1): 35–49.

McFarlane, C. (2009). 'Translocal Assemblages: Space, Power and Social Movements.' *Geoforum* 40(4): 561–567.

McFarlane, C. (2011). *Learning the City: Knowledge and Translocal Assemblage*. Oxford: Wiley Blackwell.

McGuirk, P.M., Mee, K.J., and Ruming, K.J. (2016). 'Assembling Urban Regeneration? Resourcing Critical Generative Accounts of Urban Regeneration through Assemblage.' *Geography Compass* 10(3): 128–141.

Mitchell, K. (1997). 'Different Diasporas and the Hype of Hybridity.' *Environment and Planning D: Society and Space* 15(5): 533–553.

Mouffe, C. (2005). *On the Political*. Routledge: London.

Mountz, A. (2013). 'Political Geography I: Reconfiguring Geographies of Sovereignty.' *Progress in Human Geography* 37(6): 829–841.

Munt, S.R. (2012). 'Journeys of Resilience: The Emotional Geographies of Refugee Women.' *Gender, Place and Culture* 19(5): 555–577.

Murrey, A. (2016). 'Slow Dissent and the Emotional Geographies of Resistance.' *Singapore Journal for Tropical Geography* 37(2): 224–248.

Naseemullah, A. (2018). 'Riots and Rebellion: State, Society and the Geography of Conflict in India.' *Political Geography* 63: 104–115.

Naylor, L. (2017). 'Reframing Autonomy in Political Geography: A Feminist Geopolitics of Autonomous Resistance.' *Political Geography* 58: 24–35.

Nealon, J.T. (2008). *Foucault beyond Foucault: Power and Its Intensifications since 1984*. Stanford, CA: Stanford University Press.

Nicholls, W.J. (2016). 'Producing-Resisting National Borders in the United States, France and the Netherlands.' *Political Geography* 51: 43–52.

Painter, J. (2006). 'Prosaic Geographies of Stateness.' *Political Geography* 25(7): 752–774.

Peters, E.J. (1998). 'Subversive Spaces: First Nations Women and the City.' *Environment and Planning D: Society and Space* 16(6): 665–685.

Pickering, A. (1993). 'The Mangle of Practice: Agency and Emergence in the Sociology of Science.' *American Journal of Sociology* 99(3): 559–589.

Pierce, J. and Williams, O.R. (2016). 'Against Power? Distinguishing Between Acquisitive Resistance and Subversion.' *Geografiska Annaler: Series B, Human Geography* 98: 171–188.

Pile, S. (1997). 'Introduction: Opposition, Political Identities and Spaces of Resistance.' In *Geographies of Resistance*, edited by Pile, S., and Keith, M. London: Routledge.

Pile, S. and Keith, M. (eds) (1997). *Geographies of Resistance*. London: Routledge.

Polanyi, K. (2001). *The Great Transformation: The Political and Economic Origins of Our Time*. Boston, MA: Beacon Press.

Pottinger, L. (2017). 'Planting the Seeds of a Quiet Activism.' *Area* 49(2): 215–222.

Pugh, J. (2014). 'Resilience, Complexity and Post-Liberalism: Resilience, Complexity and Post-Liberalism.' *Area* 46(3): 313–219.

Radcliffe, S. (2000). 'Entangling Resistance, Ethnicity, Gender and Nation in Ecuador.' In *Entanglements of Power: Geographies of Domination/Resistance*, edited by Sharp, J.P., Routledge, P., Philo, P., and Paddison, R. London: Routledge.

Rancière, J. (2010). *Dissensus: On Politics and Aesthetics*. London: Continuum.

Rose, M. (2002). 'The Seductions of Resistance: Power, Politics, and a Performative Style of Systems.' *Environment and Planning D: Society and Space* 20(4): 383–400.

Rosol, M. (2014). 'On Resistance in the Post-Political City: Conduct and Counter-Conduct in Vancouver.' *Space and Polity* 18(1): 70–84.

Routledge, P. (1996). 'Critical Geopolitics and Terrains of Resistance.' *Political Geography* 15(6–7): 509–531.

Routledge, P. (1997). 'The Imagineering of Resistance: Pollok Free State and the Practice of Postmodern Politics.' *Transactions of the Institute of British Geographers* 22(3): 359–376.

Routledge, P. (2009). 'Activism.' In *The Dictionary of Human Geography*, edited by Gregory, D. Malden, MA: Blackwell.

Said, E. (1978). *Orientalism*. Pantheon Books: New York.

Sambajee, P. (2015). 'Rethinking Non-traditional Resistance at Work: The Case of the Indian Diaspora in Mauritius.' *Culture and Organisation* 21(5): 386–408.

Scott, J.C. (1990). *Domination and the Arts of Resistance: Hidden Transcripts*. New Haven, CT: Yale University Press.

Secor, A. (2004). '"There Is an Istanbul That Belongs to Me": Citizenship, Space, and Identity in the City.' *Annals of the Association of American Geographers* 94(2): 352–368.

Sharp, J. (2009). 'Geography and Gender: What Belongs to Feminist Geography? Emotion, Power and Change.' *Progress in Human Geography* 33(1): 74–80.

Sharp, J.P., Routledge, P., Philo, P., and Paddison, R. (2000a). 'Entanglements of Power: Geographies of Domination/Resistance.' In *Entanglements of Power: Geographies of Domination/Resistance*, edited by Sharp, J.P., Routledge, P., Philo, P., and Paddison, R. London: Routledge.

Sharp, J.P., Routledge, P., Philo, P., and Paddison, R. (eds) (2000b). *Entanglements of Power: Geographies of Domination/Resistance*. London: Routledge.

Shaw R. (2014). 'Beyond Night-Time Economy: Affective Atmospheres of the Urban Night.' *Geoforum* 51(1), 87–95.

Sparke, M. (2008). 'Political Geography – Political Geographies of Globalization III: Resistance.' *Progress in Human Geography* 32(3): 423–440.

Staeheli, L.A. (1994). 'Empowering Political Struggle: Spaces and Scales of Resistance.' *Political Geography* 13(5): 387–391.

Storper, M., and Scott, A.J. (2016). 'Current Debates in Urban Theory: A Critical Assessment.' *Urban Studies* 53(6): 1114–1136.

Thrift, N. (2000). 'Entanglements of Power. Shadows?' In *Entanglements of Power: Geographies of Domination/Resistance*, edited by Sharp, J.P., Routledge, P., Philo, P., and Paddison, R. London: Routledge.

Thrift, N. (2007). 'Overcome by Space: Reworking Foucault.' In *Space, Knowledge and Power: Foucault and Geography*, edited by Crampton, J., and Eldon, S. London: Ashgate Publishing.

Weichselgartner, J., and Kelman, I. (2015). 'Geographies of Resilience: Challenges and Opportunities of a Descriptive Concept.' *Progress in Human Geography* 39(3): 249–267.

Wideman, T.J., and Masuda, J.R. (2018). 'Toponymic Assemblages, Resistance, and the Politics of Planning in Vancouver, Canada.' *Environment and Planning C: Politics and Space* 36(3): 383–402.

Wilbert, C. (2000). 'Anti-This–Against-That: Resistances Along a Human–Non-Human Axis.' In *Entanglements of Power: Geographies of Domination/Resistance*, edited by Sharp, J.P., Routledge, P., Philo, P., and Paddison, R. London: Routledge.

Wilson, J., and Swyngedouw, E. (2014). *The Post-political and Its Discontents: Spaces of Depoliticisation, Spectres of Radical Politics*. Edinburgh: Edinburgh University Press.

Žižek, S. (2004). 'The Parallax View'. *New Left Review* 25: 121–134.

PART I

RETHINKING RESISTANCE, REFRAMING DEBATES

2. Feminism, resistance and the archive
Maria Fannin and Julie MacLeavy

INTRODUCTION

If resistance is perhaps the most familiar understanding of what feminist political engagement has made possible, one might expect to find much of contemporary feminist scholarship characterised by accounts of resistance: of subjects working against the state and capital, against dominant constructions of masculinity and femininity, and other elaborations of an oppositional consciousness characteristic of the women's movement. But very few scholars now position themselves as working on explicitly feminist or indeed gendered projects of resistance. This may be a legacy effect of the powerful notion of resistance as an exterior force – in Matt Sparke's (2008: 423) language, 'the basic idea of resistance [as] people "pushing back"' that obscures the complex entanglements of people with the forces to which they are subject and made subjects by – and of the historically limited recognition of forms of resistant politics as immanent to everyday practices and relationships.

In this chapter, we consider resistance not as a constant, shared or even necessarily antagonistic activity, but as something achieved through inconsistent behaviours and actions: both collective and personal, inventive and also sustained by care, 'outside' mainstream institutions and yet also deeply invested in the creation of new ones. In doing so, we seek to build on recent scholarship on feminist activism which points towards the tensions, but also the collective projects, that emerge as actors with progressive social or political commitments seek to achieve individual goals and targets (Jupp, 2017; Newman, 2012). We draw a line between resistance in the pure and 'romantic' sense, and activism which is generally understood to be 'experimental, messy and heavily context-dependent' (Chatterton and Pickerill, 2010: 476). While resistance (often) implies a reaction – that is, an expression of dissent or objection based on firmly held values or ideals – feminist activism tends to be conceived as emerging in and through everyday practice. Hence, we use the term 'activism' – alongside resistance – in what follows as a means of placing emphasis upon strategies of 'everyday making': the small-scale, gradual changes that are made possible through localised actions (Davies, 2013).

Our empirical focus is on the United Kingdom (UK)-based Feminist Archive South, which began as a personal collection, the Feminist Archive, and was 'devoted to identifying, collecting, preserving and producing women's work and documenting the development of the Women's Liberation Movement' ('Constitution "draft"' folder, DM2123/1/Archive Boxes 68). Founded in 1978, the creators of the Feminist Archive, and the many volunteers who supported them, brought together personal papers and materials from the homes and organisations of those active in the Women's Liberation Movement, primarily but not exclusively in the UK. The Feminist Archive also sought to collect and preserve materials related to the many issues that affected women's lives and interested them, from trade unions, motherhood and peace movements, to lesbian and gay rights, masculinity and under-recognised women artists. The materials in the Feminist Archive date primarily from the period 1958–2000. Acquisitions, though not actively sought, continue to be made where the materials relate to that period of feminist activism. Today, the materials collected are housed in two regional archives: Feminist Archive North at the University of Leeds, and Feminist Archive South (henceforth, 'the Archive'), upon which much of our discussion will focus, at the University of Bristol. Increasing in size over the years, the Feminist Archive South now comprises over 160 metres of material documenting feminist politics from the latter half of the 20th century, and contains 'periodicals, books, pamphlets, diaries, calendars, conference papers, personal letters, photographs, stickers, postcards, drawings, posters, banners, badges, vinyl records, mini-disks, audio cassettes, video cassettes, a 16mm film, clothing, digitized audio and film and various other ephemera' (http://feministarchivesouth.org.uk/). In tracing the origins of this collection, we consider how the Archive's founders and supporters articulated its purpose and aims as a form of resistant practice both within and outside of formal institutional initiatives.

We consider how those activists involved in the Archive's creation expressed the political dimensions of collecting, cataloguing and preserving materials as a form of resistance. The notion of 'activist' archives both troubles and reaffirms our argument about the importance of feminist archives as spaces of resistance. Cindi Katz's (2004) work provides a framework with which we consider the complicated and strategic manoeuvring through which feminist actors positioned themselves in relation to prevailing matrices of power and dominance when establishing the Archive as a space of resistance. For Katz, the concept of resistance affords 'a peculiar and wonderful vantage point on the nexus of creative and recuperative impulses' (2004: xi) that enable 'people to get by, reconfigure themselves, and reimagine if not reconstruct their worlds' (ibid.: 239). We argue that it is through cultural forms and practices of archiving that the possibility – at least – of reconfiguration, reimagination and reconstruction of the relationship of the past to the present and the future come to the fore. We view the Archive not as a repository of the past, but as a space replete with possibility for both creation and recuperation, where new orientations to other feminisms (at other historical times and in other spaces) might emerge out of archival encounters.

In what follows, we explore how we might theorise the Feminist Archive South as a space of a reconfigured resistance, especially in light of the attention given to archives by historical and, increasingly, political geographers. We describe how the founders of the Archive sought to collect and catalogue the many different forms of creativity emerging from feminist movements, notably by collecting the visual and ephemeral records of the struggle for women's liberation (badges, posters, pamphlets, and so on). Drawing on records in the Archive of its own history as an archive, we trace how its changing fortunes reflect the complexities of everyday spaces of resistance. These everyday resistant spaces are imperfect and experimental endeavours that see social relations developed, worlds constituted and politics enacted. Recuperating the Archive as a space of feminist knowledge production and preservation, once separate from the patriarchal spaces of established institutions (such as universities), the accounts of the Archive's inception and the ongoing labour to ensure its survival push us to consider the more everyday tools for advancing the cause of gender justice, equality and difference. These seemingly mundane responses to oppression may intersect with and alter processes of domination and subordination, making '[t]he process of transformation ... uneven, slippery and shot through with as many derailments as possibilities' (Katz, 2008: 15). Given its age and acquired institutional status, the Archive can no longer be considered a fringe development. Through a series of moves to different locations, the changing composition of volunteers, librarians and supporters, as well as the shifting social, technological and political terrains of feminist activism, the Archive has been resituated within an academic context (the University of Bristol), granting it an institutional legitimacy that both strengthens and strains its potential to remake the present through the 'fragments' of history it embodies (Lorimer, 2009). We reflect upon the implications of its (re)positioning.

THE FEMINIST ARCHIVE SOUTH

In this section, we draw on documents housed within the Feminist Archive South that narrate and tell a (partial) story of its origins. We focus on these texts to demonstrate how the Archive as a space of resistance is shaped by practices of invention and care. In so doing, we position archiving as a form of everyday making which is not only in or of the past, but also crosses temporal boundaries: although 'different politics have calcified around different eras [there is] potential for archives to foster productive political alliances across seemingly distinct generations and eras' (Eichhorn, 2013: 56). In this respect, attention to the spatial-temporal dynamics of archiving offers a generative way to interpret the many feminist forms of resistance, from the enacted through to the (to be) imagined.

Approaching the Archive in this way requires confronting the different possibilities for reading historical sources. Through a process of continuous interaction between past, present and future temporalities, the researcher must attend to 'the remnants of the past that continue to exist in the present' (McBean, 2014: 50). As Kate Boyer (2004: 170) writes:

> it may appear as though archival material is '"there for the taking" in a relatively unproblematic way' as the collection of texts, objects and other media within archives appear to act as objective windows to historical truths. However, their gaps and silences as well as their contradictions and complexities elude such easy interpretation. What we see within archives is 'not "what really happened" ... but what lives on from that happening' (Brown 2001: 150).

What we must contend with is 'what is conjured from it, how past generations and events occupy the force fields of the present, how they claim us, and how they haunt, plague, and inspire our imaginations and visions of the future' (Brown 2001: 150).

Documents in the Archive recount its 'origins' and development over time, albeit in different registers. This excerpt from its founding Constitution in an application for charity (non-profit) status sets out the Archive's aims in formal and legal terms, in many ways belying or even obscuring its radical, visionary and political roots:

> the objects of the Charity shall be to advance public education by maintaining a reference library and museum to identify preserve and produce material which inter alia tells the story of women and to make it available for reference, [and to] ...
> (i) Assist the research and study into all aspects of women in society and to publish material relevant to such work
> (ii) Train women in the work of archive maintenance
> (iii) Publish important works not otherwise available
> (iv) Serve the South West region principally as a comprehensive reference centre and as a prototype for regional centres
> (v) Raise funds and invite and receive contributions from any person or persons whatsoever
> (Folder 'Trust Deed', DM2123/1/Archive Boxes 68)

The Archive sought charitable status to benefit from state funding in the form of government grants offered to non-profit organisations, and to enable the Archive to apply for support from other larger charitable and cultural organisations. To that end, the formal legal text establishing the Archive clearly explains its aims and purpose in language that speaks to these other institutions and imagines the Archive as its own institution: to become a 'reference library and museum' in the service of 'public education'.

Yet the Archive's founding ethos and the milieu from which it emerged was also much more radical. The materials related to the Archive's own history also include letters and notes from its founder, Jean Freer, about the Archive's inception. Freer writes that the 'Feminist Archive is an ambitious project, hopefully to one day form the core library of a Feminist University, where we can research, study and learn on our OWN terms' (Freer, undated letter, DM2123/1/Archive Boxes 68). Freer wrote insistently of the need for the Archive to differentiate itself from other institutions, such as universities, that many people involved in the women's liberation movement found alienating, and to embed alternative forms of knowledge within the Archive's day-to-day practice, even down to the very architecture of how the materials collected were assembled and classified.

The Archive was not to conform to the standard conventions of libraries, but was to organise itself along different principles. To that end, the classification system used by the Archive was one designed by Freer herself, and grouped materials within its own distinctive hierarchy in which the categories of Cosmology, Communication and Healing/Divination were foremost, followed by 'Humun Society' (which would include reproduction and family as well as work, production and economics), the study of 'Hystory and Politics', and finally Ecology and Technology. On the final category, Freer notes that its subcategories were only suggestions, 'as neither of us [Jean and another person unnamed] feel competent to classify this in detail' ('Feminist Archive Classification Scheme', DM2123/1/Archive Boxes 75).

In a detailed explanation of the Archive's particular and idiosyncratic classification system attributed to Freer, she explains its alternative logic as well as the spiritual sensibility that she sought to infuse into the practice of archiving:

> The commitment of the Feminist Archive is to help womyn restructure knowledge to strengthen our wymn's culture and to further undermine the patriarchy. Therefore the classification scheme has seven sections rather than ten and spelling is changed. Reintegration of spirituality into our everyday lives is seen as part of the task of the feminist revolution by many or even most of the women who have sustained the Archive over the years. It is my deepest wish for the Feminist Archive that wherever she is housed and whomever looks after her, the focus of separatist spirituality expressed primarily as feminist witchcraft will infuse her spirit and provide motivating energy. ('FEMINIST ARCHIVE: Explanatory Notes by the Founder', July 1986, DM2123/1/Archive Boxes 68)

These sensibilities, however, did not prevent Freer and others from being pragmatically attuned to the material and embodied labour required to ensure the Archive's growth and survival, and to the mundane problems of day-to-day organising. In personal correspondence dated 7 April 1979, 'Lee' (as Freer was then known) writes to 'Barbie':

> The Archive is growing steadily, and beset with the usual problems of no money, too few helpers, makeshift premises and equipment, and so on A jumble sale in Shepton today netted the grand total of £2.00. For all that bloody work. The morning was miserable, of course, and I wouldn't have come out if I hadn't had to. But on top of it one of our helpers alienated most of the women on the estate, so <u>none</u> of them came. There are times when I wish I could pack it all in ... (DM2123/1/Archive Boxes 75)

Without a steady income, and relying on donated labour and materials, the Archive's appeals for support speak directly to the temporal dimensions of its presence and ongoing survival as 'living memory', and indirectly to the marginal place occupied by the work of women in mainstream cultural institutions. The Archive sought materials related to the women's liberation movement from anyone willing to donate, redefining the many forms of cultural production emerging from feminist social movements (whether spiritualist or not) as worthy of preservation and study:

> The growth of the Feminist Archive is entirely dependent upon the support of the people for whom it exists, as we are not able to buy material. The Archive is the living memory of our history, our development and change. We must be sure that, as such, it reflects and embraces all aspects of women's creativity: her energy, her concerns, her interpretation of the world. The content and form of the Archive depends on the material you send. It is by this process of re-cognition of our hystories that we will be able to adequately document our background and shape our future. The Archive is a place where this material will be maintained, developed and displayed ... Posters, badges, records, clothing, photographs, postcards and other ephemera are also important to a representative collection: especially as much women's work uses different forms than are traditionally preserved in libraries and museums, employing many different forms of resistance. (Undated statement, DM2123/1/Archive Boxes 75)

The Archive's recognition of resistance as a neglected or overlooked part of 'women's work' and of the importance of collecting 'grassroots, ephemeral and personal material', emphasising these materials as the most likely to be discarded or lost over time – as opposed to published books and magazines – reflects how practices of seeking out and caring for such materials occupied much of the efforts of volunteers over the early years of the Archive's existence. In the first instance, this led Freer to admonish volunteers of the importance of retaining multiple copies of work, not loaning them out, stating that she is 'pleased that women find the contents of the collection exciting ... the purpose of the Feminist Archive is to <u>PRESERVE</u> the material'. She also explains why the Archive would seek to retain at least three copies of materials, asking pointedly, 'Have you never stolen from a library? I have, and many feminists I know stole from the Fawcett library in their enthusiasm in finding feminism in the early seventies. Can we please not be too short sighted?' (p. 1, 'FEMINIST ARCHIVE: Explanatory Notes by the Founder', July 1986, DM2123/1/Archive Boxes 68).

By 1998, the collection had grown too large for its existing location and was split into two archives: the Feminist Archive North, which was relocated to Leeds (currently Leeds University), and the Feminist Archive South, which remained in Bristol. In these later years, the Archive's practices of care were shaped in part by the vulnerability of collected materials to degradation over time. Volunteer and librarian Jane Hargreaves wrote many years after Freer of the need for resources to preserve materials adequately:

> the Archive is at present we do not have the resources to safeguard films and tapes properly for the future. We also need more room. (I have had to pack the fiction into boxes in order to achieve adequate shelf space for the other items which are more needed by researchers). Much of our newsprint is yellowing with age and as many of you will know from your personal collections, the life of a paperback is limited. Glue gets brittle and pages crack. We have done the primary job of collecting and looking after all the items. Now we need to look to the future ... (FAS Newsletter, April 2005, FA/Arch/74)

This highlights that such archiving projects, which are often limited by their funding constraints, and in turn the space and (volunteer) expertise available, need to remain resourceful to sustain their presence and role. A politics of 'resourcefulness' (MacKinnon and Derickson, 2013) which saw volunteers cultivate links with academic institutions meant that ten years after the split, in 2008, the Feminist Archive South moved to the Special Collections of the University of Bristol, where it is now housed. The Archive's future was still uncertain, Hargreaves suggests in her final letter to supporters as it prepared to move (and she prepared to move on from her role as librarian), as she asks of supporters:

> This is not the first time the archive has had to reassess its position. We have always come through bigger and better. However I have done my stint (twelve years is a long time!) and feel it is time for a new direction. I know there are loyal friends out there and I really would like some response from you as to what we might do in the future. Would anyone like to take over or even help?

Hargreaves continues:

> I am happy that the archive has a permanent home at the university. I am happy that feminism is alive and well. There are young people out these promoting their ideas by internet. This archive website has already been archived in its own right! The

next generation of archives will not be on paper. But the second wave of feminism has been recorded at least in part.

While the act of archiving brings with it the possibility of empowerment and transformation, the multiplicity of potential relations it enables is entangled with forces of domination and oppression: 'co-option', as Hughes (2020: 1146) remarks, 'is always-already present'. The Archive's fate, then, seems mixed. Today, materials in the Archive are no longer classified using Freer's inventive (but ultimately unworkable) system, but rather with the classification system of the European Women's Thesaurus, a system developed as an alternative to the dominant classification systems whose generic terms tend to refer to men. The Archive is organised through labels searchable on a database and remains in large part under-catalogued; that is to say, many items are not catalogued individually (at what archivists would call 'item level') but are grouped into boxes by topic or by date, reproducing and preserving the original groupings by which materials were organised when the Archive arrived at the University. Materials are no longer directly accessible by the public, but housed in off-site storage and must be requested by contacting a librarian at Special Collections. This is a barrier for those who would find making a special request to a university archivist daunting, or who expect that their request must 'prove' that it relates to scholarly research.

At the same time, the collection is no longer managed by volunteers, but is staffed by professionals who are institutionally tasked with ensuring its sustainability and the care of vulnerable materials over time. The Archive's charitable status requires it to retain an independent Board of Trustees who are tasked with promoting the Archive's original aims but also retain the rights to decide the fate of the Archive in the future. And, although accessing the Archive requires effort on the part of researchers, it is now the most used and requested archival resource held by the University of Bristol (personal communication, 2021). Furthermore, the Archive itself has been the subject in recent years of efforts to both disrupt and critically interrogate the structures of knowledge and assumptions about feminism's history that shape feminisms today, including the conventions of metadata and classification (Withers, 2018; Withers and Fannin, 2019), and with respect to the Archive's pedagogical role in the contemporary university (Perrier and Withers, 2016).

These efforts support Dydia DeLyser's (2014) argument that work with archival materials is irrefutably transformative. Through the process of participation with enthusiast communities, the public and interested institutions, as well as through the outputs of research, scholars can make contributions to liberatory agendas. It is through these engagements that scholars confront not only the precarious nature of the collected materials they work with, but also the multiple and changing temporal and spatial contexts surrounding archives which alter their understanding and use (Geoghegan, 2014). In many respects, the Archive's fate mirrors that of feminists and feminism: once marginalised and excluded from institutions of higher education, feminist theories of gender and gender difference, and feminists themselves, are now part of these institutions (MacLeavy et al., 2016). It is through the provision of 'useable pasts' (Griffin, 2018) that archives enable 'a new stage of self-consciousness, of self-reflexivity' (Hall, 2001: 89): at the point of becoming more ordered and considered, their contents are transformed into objects of reflection and debate.

ARCHIVES AND RESISTANT PRACTICE

Archives are generative sites to think through how history is 'invented, reworked, and also destroyed' by forms of resistant practice (Brown, 2001: 158). Archives – in the sense of material places where artefacts and accounts of the past are housed – are fluid spaces that embody and produce forms of everyday resistance. They are not fixed, asocial or timeless, but dynamic spaces that connect the times of past, present and future. Indeed, recent efforts to reread and revisit archival sources situate archives as generative sites for remaking and rethinking feminist action in the present. Briony McDonagh's (2018: 1564) review of the work of feminist historical geography emphasises the importance of enquiries into the lives of women and other marginalised groups, and their role in relation to colonial, imperial and modernist projects of geographical knowledge and power. Other histories challenge the heroic masculinist story of the discipline's origins and development, while also informing critical feminist geographical work seeking to tell the less dominant stories of women involved in the mundane making of domestic, labouring and commercial spaces within the city, the countryside and the home. Work by Chatterton and Pickerill (2010: 476), for instance, notes how participants in their research on everyday activism 'express identities that attempt to go beyond exclusionary labels such as "militant" or "activist", which are set apart from the everyday and simply oppose the present condition'. Critiques which they cite of the militant and revolutionary 'god-man' evince how such labels carry with them gendered notions of the revolutionary subject of political change.

Reclaiming 'activism' in its many feminist guises might be one way to undermine these presumptions. Yet the label of 'militant' has also been used to marginalise and stereotype some feminists, and to preclude closer attention to the specific issues that animate their struggles over time. The role of naming and labelling feminists and feminisms, and historians' and others' reflections on these names, are detailed in the work of Cott (1989) and Rupp and Taylor (1999), amongst many others, and in a recent special issue of 'Country and Region Reports' of the journal *Gender, Place and Culture* (see Blidon and Zaragocin, 2019 for an introduction). In this chapter we use the term 'feminist' to refer to those who founded and maintained the Archive, under the presumption that at a minimum, and borne out by our reading of materials from the Archive's history, it is a term that many of the individuals involved would have used to describe themselves.

By attending to 'the routine, banality and rhythm ... [of] the everyday as a feminist project', geographers have been able to 'connect small scale actions with larger scale inequalities' (Hall, 2020: 813) and so subvert the symbolic institutionalised heritage upon which individual and group projects might build. Such a task is not easy. Rather, those striving to tell stories about 'unspectacular ordinary things and happenings' (Phillips, 2018: 181, quoted in Hall, 2020) recognise the difficulty of tracing the lives of those marginalised from official historical accounts, and of learning from the lives, experiences and stories of the marginalised that are less often the subject of formal archival practice. Scholars have also read the silences embedded within historical archives as an imaginative and potentially subversive act (Domosh and Morin, 2003). But what is most striking from McDonagh's (2018) review are the relatively rare instances in which archives created by and for feminists or activists have been the subject of geographical study. In particular, geographers have only begun to attend to how feminists made spaces of knowledge in the past, especially spaces of knowledge devoted to their own political movements, and how those acts of resistance were riven with power relations that lie at the heart of the process of constructing an archive.

Geographical research on community or activist archives and the imperfect and experimental nature of such endeavours offers a means of exploring how archives activate a political process that 'carries threads of past lives into our present' (DeSilvey, 2007: 405). We see the selection and categorisation of materials for and within an archive as a profoundly geographical practice, but one that within the Feminist Archive South (and other archives tracing the histories of the non-dominant) also speaks to efforts to circumvent official or hegemonic forms of knowledge production and to actively create spaces of knowledge relevant to one's own experience. As scholars of the histories, geographies and pedagogies of radical social justice movements note, 'the widening of access to knowledge production ... is the goal of the enterprise' of political movements, enabling people 'to realize their relative position in society, which may in turn lead to more active agitation for change' (Stephenson 1974: 101, quoted in Heyman 2007: 105). How feminists produced their own knowledge to inform everyday actions, outside of the spaces of formal institutional privilege, and with a view to providing resources for present and future feminists, is therefore of interest, not least because of the historical ontologies and claims to truth that this work generates, as gender difference and movements seeking liberation from domination may be expressed in different ways and at different points in time (see also Duncan, 1999).

As archives attend to the past with a view to protecting or preserving memories for the future, they are marked by fundamental uncertainties, which mean that rather than be 'wedded to particular coordinates – of intention, linearity, and opposition – that serve to determine in advance what comes to be termed as resistance' (Hughes, 2020: 1142), they operate as sites through which to activate politically in potentially unforeseen ways. The Feminist Archive South, for instance, entails the assertion of alternative ways of knowing and being that, while never nostalgic, build on and affirm solidarity among women, even as they question and strain the boundaries of that identity and the historical (and ongoing) struggles over who is included, and how, within that category. The many different feminisms that make up the Archive's history, and its constituencies and readers in the present and in the future, are brought into being through the (anticipated) creation of new liveable cultures and relations in the face of gender injustice.

Thus, while we are not alone in theorising from the location of archives and in seeking to mobilise an understanding of time as 'something deeply nonteleological and antiprescriptive – something that, like space, might just as easily be occupied as passively received' (Eichhorn, 2013: 55), our work has a particular emphasis. In thinking through archival practices in feminist and other activist movements, we wish to delineate how the act of collecting is not only driven by the will to overturn, upend or heroically emancipate, but is necessarily sustained through more ongoing work to attend to the ephemeral and to care for the future. Care for knowledge – what we are calling the archival labour of feminists committed to documenting, collecting, preserving and sharing the material presence of feminist and women's liberation movements, as well as many other aspects of women's lives – has been positioned as a 'craft' of everyday making (Awcock, 2020; Heyman, 2007). The foundation and maintenance of the Archive, in this vein, might be considered not just an end but also – and importantly – a beginning of or opening to emancipatory change, both for those whose political struggles and alternative forms of knowledge are currently included in the Archive and for those who encounter it from beyond or 'outside'. The Archive provides a way to understand how feminism's past, and the work of feminists in the past, can shape the possible futures for feminist activism and forms of resistance; a means of harnessing the potential generated by the serious commitment to record women's dissenting practices in a manner that 'breaches or displaces temporal, spatial boundaries or social conventions' (Vijay et al., 2021: 490).

CONCLUSION

In this chapter we have sought to consider how a feminist archive – and, by extension, other archives of the lives and histories of the non-dominant – constitutes resistance as a spatial-political practice, not because it corresponds to heroic notions of a group's organised political mobilisation, but because it houses and records the complex, mundane and everyday work of transformation that is less often viewed as self-evidently political (for example, the work of classification). We also point to how an encounter with a feminist archive can become a resource for thinking past, present and future feminisms, and the relationships between and across the 'times' of feminism. The archive which we describe in this chapter reminds us that those involved in struggles for liberation knew then, as we argue here, that feminism involves 'many different forms of resistance' (Undated statement, DM2123/1/Archive Boxes 75). Moreover, attention to the 'unromantic' everyday practices of 'doing feminism' within the Archive provides a generative way of thinking about political subjectivity, where politics is understood as necessarily messy and complex.

Archiving is, then, best characterised as 'resistance in its becoming' (Hughes, 2020: 1143), given that it creates the space for – rather than certainty of – transformation. This rests on the idea that '[t]he future is a potentiality in the present that is aimed or worked toward, even if it may never be reached or achieved' (Coleman, 2018: 38). Although the aspiration to 'found an archive' is a bold act which presumes that the materials within will be worth saving for the future, the labour required to maintain a collection of materials and ensure its survival is a daily and ongoing act of care. Gleaning the ephemerae of the subaltern that would be 'excluded, forgotten, discarded or otherwise destroyed' (Mills, 2013: 706) demonstrates a commitment to create and claim a space for different forms of knowledge, but also relies upon quiet, non-spectacular and mundane forms of care that are less often viewed as self-evidently political. The burden of this care for an archive can also, however, strain the capacities for making that enable a new beginning through 'the founding of a new body politic for public participation and collective action' (Ranson, 2012: 252).

We see archives as active sites for producing – rather than simply recording or preserving – a consciousness and political agency through the awareness that history is socially made and (can be) remade. The impossibility of mastering the past through archives, and the persistence of our insecure knowledge of their bearing on the present, offers a means of galvanising grassroots organising, activism and solidarity work. In this sense, archival research is 'an activist practice, frequently associated with a political agenda aiming at social transformation and challenging discrimination' (Flinn, 2011: 1). It pushes those striving for gender and social justice to confront the absence of an objective or comprehensive route from the past through to the future, and to work with (rather than against) the paradoxes and contradictions of the political present. For feminism, this presents an opportunity for reinvention. Anxieties about the progress, loss or return of feminist campaigns may be absolved through the recognition of the temporal and situational complexities of individual and group struggles. In short, the realisation that narratives of feminism through time are born from efforts to give coherence, authority and legitimacy to feminist subjectivity, which is disintegrated and yet held together by the array of entanglements through which political actors and subjects are contingently formed, obliges an affirmative and prefigurative politics (see also MacLeavy et al., 2021).

In placing emphasis upon forms of everyday resistance, our aim is not to expand the category of resistance such that it becomes all-encompassing (cf. Katz, 2004: 241–243), but to expose how discursive or cultural forms of resistance, which we see as emergent from feminist efforts to develop alternative spaces and networks of knowledge-making, can co-exist with dominant narratives, and in some instance overcome and ultimately come to inhabit critical spaces; as seen with the movement of the Feminist Archive into the institutions of higher education. Kate Eichorn (2013: 4) explores the creation of three feminist archives by, in Eichorn's words, 'activist archivists and librarians' in United States universities since the year 2000. She situates these archives as examples of how 'feminist scholars, cultural workers, librarians, and archivists born during and after the rise of the second wave feminist movement are seizing the archive as an apparatus to legitimize new forms of knowledge and cultural production in an economically and politically precarious present'. Eichorn's work prompts us to reflect on how the objects and subjects of feminist analysis are (increasingly) framed, regulated and disciplined by institutional interests. In the UK context, this includes the Research Excellence Framework (REF), a national evaluation of academic research that determines each higher education institution's public funding and, in turn, feeds into its national and international league table ranking. The use of metrics such as the REF and the accompanying increased marketisation of higher education raises an important question. Would projects of alternative knowledge-making like the Feminist Archive South be possible to invent today within these institutions, given the pressures facing academics working and studying within them? Despite our uncertainty about the answer to this question, we acknowledge the success of feminist scholars in creating space within the academy for gendered political analysis, and in creating internal pressure to take up women's experiences and understandings, thereby challenging the predominance of masculinist approaches and ways of knowing and doing. In its new institutional space, the Feminist Archive South supports and enables questions that return us to the potential radical dimensions of scholarship and practice; questions that collectively signal how such archives might in turn nurture future forms of resistance.

REFERENCES

Awcock, Hannah (2020) New protest history: exploring the historical geographies and geographical histories of resistance through gender, practice, and materiality, *Geography Compass*, 14(6): 124–191.

Blidon, Marianne and Zaragocin, Sofia (2019) Mapping gender and feminist geographies in the global context, *Gender, Place and Culture* 26(7–9): 915–925.

Boyer, Kate (2004) Feminist geography in the archive: practice and method, pp. 169–174 in Women and Geography Study Group of the RGS-IBG (ed.), *Geography and Gender Reconsidered*, London: WGSG. Available at: https://gfgrg.co.uk/wp-content/uploads/2010/08/Boyer.pdf (last accessed 13 July 2021).

Brown, Wendy (2001) *Politics out of History*, Princeton, NJ: Princeton University Press.

Chatterton, Paul and Pickerill, Jenny (2010) Everyday activism and transitions towards post-capitalist worlds, *Transactions of the Institute of British Geographers*, 35(4): 475–490.

Coleman, Rebecca (2018) Affective futurity, pp. 37–52 in Sellberg, Karin (ed.), *Gender: Time*. Farmington Hills: Macmillan Reference.

Cott, Nancy F. (1989) What's in a name? The limits of 'social feminism'; or, expanding the vocabulary of women's history. *Journal of American History*, 76(3): 809–829.

Davies, Jonathan S. (2013) Just do it differently? Everyday making, Marxism and the struggle against neoliberalism, *Policy and Politics*, 41(4): 497–513.

DeLyser, Dydia (2014) Towards a participatory historical geography: archival interventions, volunteer service, and public outreach in research on early women pilots, *Journal of Historical Geography*, 46: 93–98.

DeSilvey, Caitlin (2007) Salvage memory: constellating material histories on a hardscrabble homestead, *Cultural Geographies*, 14: 401–424.

Domosh, Mona and Morin, Karen M. (2003) Travels with feminist historical geography, *Gender, Place and Culture: A Journal of Feminist Geography*, 10(3): 257–264.

Duncan, James S. (1999) Complicity and resistance in the colonial archive: some issues of method and theory in historical geography, *Historical Geography*, 27: 119–128.

Eichhorn, Kate (2013) *The Archival Turn in Feminism: Outrage in Order*, Philadelphia, PA: Temple University Press.

Flinn, Andrew (2011) Archival activism: independent and community-led archives, radical public history and the heritage professions, *InterActions: UCLA Journal of Education and Information Studies*, 7(2). http://dx.doi.org/10.5070/D472000699. Retrieved from https://escholarship.org/uc/item/9pt2490x.

Geoghegan, Hilary (2014) A new pattern for historical geography: working with enthusiast communities and public history, *Journal of Historical Geography*, 46: 105–107.

Griffin, Paul (2018) Making usable pasts: collaboration, labour and activism in the archive, *Area*, 50(4): 501–508.

Hall, Sarah Marie (2020) Revisiting geographies of social reproduction: everyday life, the endotic, and the infra-ordinary, *Area*, 52: 812–819.

Hall, Stuart (2001) Constituting an archive, *Third Text*, 15(54): 89–92.

Heyman, Rich (2007) 'Who's going to man the factories and be the sexual slaves if we all get PhDs?' Democratizing knowledge production, pedagogy, and the Detroit Geographical Expedition and Institute, *Antipode*, 39(1): 99–120.

Hughes, S.M. (2020) On resistance within human geography, *Progress in Human Geography*, 44(6): 1141–1160

Jupp, Eleanor (2017) Home space, gender and activism: the visible and the invisible in austere times, *Critical Social Policy*, 37(3): 348–366.

Katz, Cindi (2004) *Growing up Global: Economic Restructuring and Children's Everyday Lives*, Minneapolis, MN: University of Minnesota Press.

Katz, Cindi (2008) Childhood as spectacle: relays of anxiety and the reconfiguration of the child, *Cultural Geographies*, 15(1): 5–17.

Lorimer, Hayden (2009) Caught in the nick of time: archives and fieldwork, pp. 248–273 in DeLyser, Dydia, Aitken, Stuart, Crang, Mike A., Herbert, Steve and McDowell, Linda (eds), *The SAGE Handbook of Qualitative Research in Human Geography*, London: SAGE.

MacKinnon, Danny and Derickson, Kate Driscoll (2013) From resilience to resourcefulness: a critique of resilience policy and activism, *Progress in Human Geography*, 37(2): 253–270.

MacLeavy, Julie, Fannin, Maria and Larner, Wendy (2021) Feminism and futurity: geographies of resistance, resilience and reworking, *Progress in Human Geography*, 45(6): 1558–1579.

MacLeavy, J., Roberts, Susan and Strauss, Kendra (2016) Feminist inclusions in economic geography: what difference does difference make? *Environment and Planning A*, 48(10): 2067–2071.

McBean, Sam (2014) Feminism and futurity: revisiting Marge Piercy's 'Woman on the edge of time', *Feminist Review*, 107: 37–56.

McDonagh, Briony (2018) Feminist historical geographies: doing and being, *Gender, Place and Culture*, 25(11): 1563–1578.

Mills, Sarah (2013) Cultural-historical geographies of the archive: fragments, objects and ghosts, *Geography Compass*, 7(10): 701–713.

Newman, Janet (2012). *Working the Spaces of Power: Activism, Neoliberalism and Gendered Labour*, London: A&C Black

Perrier, Maud and Withers, Deborah (2016) An archival feminist pedagogy: unlearning and objects as affective knowledge companions, *Continuum*, 30(3): 355–366.

Ranson, Stewart (2012) Remaking public spaces for civil society, *Critical Studies in Education*, 53(3): 245–261.

Rupp, Leila J. and Taylor, Verta (1999) Forging feminist identity in an international movement: a collective identity approach to twentieth-century feminism. *Signs: Journal of Women in Culture and Society*, 24(2): 363–386.

Sparke, Matthew (2008) Political geographies of globalization (3): Resistance, *Progress in Human Geography*, 32(1): 423–440.

Vijay, Devi, Gupta, Shalini and Kaushiva, Pavni (2021) With the margins: writing subaltern resistance and social transformation, *Gender, Work and Organization*, 28: 481–496.

Withers, D.-M. (2018) Meta-data diaries 1: The feminist archive, in Johansson, Karl-Magnus (ed.), *Inscription*, Göteborg, Sweden: Regional State Archives in Gothenburg.

Withers, D.-M. and Fannin, Maria (2019) Digital literacy in the age of the screen? Re-imagining the social pedagogy of the archive, pp. 127–139 in Vansieleghem, N., Vlieghe, J. and Zahn, M. (eds), *Education in the Age of the Screen: Possibilities and Transformations in Technology*, Routledge.

3. Resisting beyond the human: animals and their advocates

Catherine Oliver

INTRODUCTION

In January 1998, two pigs escaped from a lorry at an abattoir in England. The 'Tamworth Two', later named Butch and Sundance, used 'wily tricks' to escape their fate and in doing so, captured the empathy of the British public. The resourceful pigs slipped under a fence and swam across a river in their dash for freedom, hiding in a thicket for six days before capture. The pair were rescued from slaughter by a journalist, Barbara Davies, and rehomed at the Rare Breeds Centre in Kent. Fourteen years later, the deaths of first Butch and then Sundance were announced. They could not resist death forever. This story received widespread attention as a story of animals' escape, adventure, and struggle for freedom.

Following Butch's death (at a slaughterhouse after a short illness) in 2012, the journalist who led the call to save them in 1998 said:

> I'm devastated to hear of her death but it's comforting to know that she lived a long and full life. She and Sundance might so easily have ended up in the abattoir, but they shared a spirit of survival which struck a chord, particularly with the British, but also with animal lovers all over the world.

The Tamworth Two 'struck a chord' with a public who kill almost 11 million pigs annually for food (Animal Clock, 2021). The pigs' 'spirit of survival' made them exemplary animals through an empathetic resistance. Ultimately, they did end up in the abattoir, albeit 14 years later. Farmed animals' resistance has been the target of physical and technological manipulations, enclosing animals, and breeding docility. However, as for Butch and Sundance, animal resistance can sometimes breach these enclosures. In this chapter, I argue that animals and human–animal relationships offer vital contributions to the critical geographies of resistance. I do so by bringing more-than-human geographical theory into conversation with the practice of friendship, contending that resistance can be rethought through the productive tensions between the two from popular culture, to eating, to animals themselves.

As I have written elsewhere (Oliver, 2021), friendship has been a vital force in animal activism for at least the last century, defining human networks of power and care. Friendship is a force that works on multiple registers: as a protective force of the powerful, and as a mode of resistance for those on the margins, 'both an inclusionary and exclusionary bounding' (ibid., 39). As bell hooks (2000) has written, friendship in its truest form acts as a kind of enduring love, freed from historically contingent violence, with bonds and responsibilities. However, friendship is not utilitarian in form; Stroud (2006) eschews such a 'properties' view of friendship, and Sokolowski (2002, 462) argues that friendship is found in the 'contingencies and vicissitudes of life'. Ideas of non-human animals as 'family' are common in popular culture and in academic accounts (Flynn, 2000; Sutton, 2018), but these ideals are difficult to extend beyond close, familiar relationships. This chapter thus turns to friendship-as-resistance by looking in turn at animal activist slogans, eating, and animals themselves, weaving together case studies to argue that friendship has a close connection with non-human resistance (Wilbert, 2000).

I begin by critically introducing 'more-than-human' geographies' literatures and their relationship with geographies of resistance. There are then four empirical sections, drawing on analysis of activist campaigns and ethnographic work. The first, on 'friends not food', explores how friendship is used in animal slogans as a kind of activist resistance. The next section, on 'the stomach', takes up the idea that liberation – and thus resistance – begins in the stomach. In the section on 'Resistance in rescue', I draw on ethnographies to think about friendship in relation to the resistance of farmed chickens as they face 'freedom'. In the conclusion, I bring together these distinct sites and examples to contend that friendship as resistance can be found in myriad ways with, by and for animals, and that it is an important site for thinking about resistance beyond the human. Ultimately, I argue that these are not distinct sites, but intimately connected in understanding the extension of friendship across species as resistance.

RESISTING MORE-THAN-HUMAN GEOGRAPHIES

Over the last 30 years, animals have been 'brought back in' to geography (Wolch and Emel, 1995), most recently being captured and theorised from 'more-than-human' perspectives. More-than-human geographies weave together animals, plants, technologies and affects to understand the space as never human alone. As Whatmore (2002, 2) contends, more-than-human geographies developed in response to the life being 'sucked out of' geography. A significant portion of geography is *de facto* concerned with the more-than-human; so 'cultural geographers have found their way (back) to the material in very different ways that variously resonate with what I take to be amongst the most enduring of geographical concerns – the vital connections between the geo (earth) and the bio (life)' (Whatmore, 2006, 601).

The very foundations of the geographical (human) subject rely on the interconnection between people and place, humans and land, society and space. More-than-human thought is attending to the interconnectivities at the heart of the geographical discipline (Panelli, 2010). Hughes (2020, 1152) argues that a focus on predetermined resistant forms fails to engage with resistance in emergence and fails to cohere the 'subject as shot through with multiple, incoherent forces', reanimating debates on who or what constitutes a resistant subject. There is thus rich potential to expand understandings of non-human resistance through engaging critically with these more-than-human geographies.

Whatmore (2006) situates this geographical turn within a broader engagement by cultural geographers towards politically 'molten' modalities of life. Isaacs (2020) contends that more-than-human geographies 'revisit the category of the human by better attending to the capacity of matter – both living and nonliving – to affect and be affected', raising new problematics for social, cultural, political and economic geographies, as well as the physical sciences. However, the ever-expansive more-than-human geographical subject risks homogenising non-human matter and experience.

More-than-human geographies' overemphasis on entanglement has reinstated anthropocentric worldviews that homogenise individuals and species, and undermine political action (Giraud, 2019). This tendency to flatten ontologies has been critiqued by critical scholars; for example, Haraway's work with companion animals has been critiqued as trailblazing depoliticised animal scholarship (Weisberg, 2009). Critical animal geographies offer politicised alternatives to this, where animals are understood as 'subjects of and in spatially uneven practices' (Hobson, 2007, 253). Critical animal geographies contest this human–animal border, and the exclusions and inclusions of always-already 'multispecies' spaces (Wolch and Emel, 1995; Philo and Wilbert, 2004), critiquing the relationships between animals and space where the 'fundamental interconnectedness of humans and animals ... [which] authorizes oppressions based on gender is the same ideology which sanctions the oppression of animals' (Hovorka, 2015, 5).

Thus, when animals are considered political subjects (Hobson, 2007), their resistance challenges anthropocentric orderings of space, but more-than-humanism often falls short of theorising power and resistance as constitutive of capitalist relations (Mumby et al., 2017). Thinking resistance beyond the human requires pushing back against the depoliticisation of more-than-human geographies. Here, wider animal studies thinking is relevant, where resistance has become a topic of increasing interest for animal scholars across disciplines. Colling (2020) pushes back against 'saviour narratives' of animal activists, instead seeking out animals' own practices and languages of resistance, conceptualising these active refusals of capitalist exploitation as political acts.

Meijer (2019) similarly understands animals' voices and actions as engaging in kinds of politics, and worthy of inclusion in an 'interspecies democracy', realised in part through their vocal rejection of painful circumstances. In a history of animals 'from below', Hribal (2007) argues that animals have engaged in similar 'weapons of the weak' as working-class human populations that are not organised but are effective. Humans exploiting animals are cognisant of these forms of resistance and have spent centuries trying to 'break' them (see Wadiwel, 2016). It is clear from these accounts that not only do animals have agency (as recognised from multiple viewpoints; McFarland and Hediger, 2009), but also that animals resist, with purpose (Hribal, 2010; Wadiwel, 2016).

While these emerging bodies of literature in more-than-human geographies look to non-human animals, and longer lineages of activist and social movement studies analyse human resistance on behalf of animals, the two are typically treated as distinct. This chapter addresses brings the two, specifically to think about resistance in more-than-human geographies. By considering these sometimes complementary, sometimes contradictory resistances in this chapter, I offer a reading of this landscape of resistance through different assemblages of 'friendship'.

FRIENDS, NOT FOOD

In the 2003 Disney film *Finding Nemo*, Marlin, a cartoon clownfish, and his new friend Dory, a royal blue tang fish, are looking for Marlin's son, the eponymous Nemo, when they find themselves in a cave with three sharks. In the cave, a group of sharks are having a Fish-Friendly Sharks support group meeting, beginning with their pledge: 'I am a nice shark, not a mindless eating machine. If I am to change this image, I must first change myself. Fish are friends, not food.'

This meeting is part of a shark rehabilitation programme to stop eating fish, to which the sharks must bring a fish friend. When Marlin is called up to the podium to introduce himself, he is interrupted by the sound of Nemo calling to him. Marlin tells the sharks his son has been captured by divers, and the sharks empathise, growling that 'humans think they own everything'.

Finding Nemo 'represents an opportunity to teach environmentally friendly attitudes' (Tidwell, 2009) but is also 'laced with dangerous environmental ideas'. Tidwell takes issue with the representation of the sharks as 'a perfect example of our inability to deal with the reality of nature' (ibid.). She argues that 'vegetarian'[1] sharks reveal the anthropocentric tendency to smooth nature out. This Disneyfied learning moment creates dramatic conflict, tapping into what Herzog (2010) would describe as complicated and 'inconsistent' relations with animals, even though these relations often make logical geographical, if violent, sense. Far from being surface-level, these popular iterations of this phrase show how friendship is not beyond the realm of imagination between different species.

'Friends, not food' has long been a slogan in animal activist campaigns, usually accompanied by cartoon pigs, cows and chickens on t-shirts, tote bags and sweatshirts. 'Friends, not food' signals a shifted relationship with animals. In 2018, Vancouver Humane Society (VHS) ran a 'Go Veg' bus ad campaign, featuring a 'young girl petting a pig, [aiming] to remind us that when we were children, we instinctively saw animals as friends and not food' (Pickett, 2018). Their full slogan, 'Friends, Not Food. When we were children, we knew', works as a spatial intervention, asking people to choose kindness when they sit down to eat (VHS, in Pointing, 2018). Invoked in their campaign is a temporal pull to remember the supposed simpler, kinder time of childhood (Cole and Stewart, 2014). By bringing in friendship, it asks people to reconsider putting animals on their plate.

The United Kingdom (UK)-based GoVegan also unveiled a 'Friends Not Food' campaign in 50 cities in 2019. Its billboards read 'Fight Climate Change with Diet Change', along with a link to a website hosting a counter of the numbers of land and water animals killed since you loaded the page. The counter reaches tens of thousands of land animals and over 1 million fish in 30 seconds. The same year, GoVeganWorld launched a large Christmas and New Year campaign across the UK, based on the premise that: 'there is everything right about connecting with family and friends. But our celebration shouldn't carry the high price that it does to the animals who are killed for us; to the people who are overworked and exploited to cope with our demand for consumerism; and to the environment' (GoVeganWorld, 2019). These vegan campaigns reframing animals as 'friends, not food' attempt to shift veganism away from a fringe or extremist belief, and into the social and cultural mainstream (Oliver, 2021).

In 1985, The Smiths released *Meat is Murder*, the title track of which was inspired by anarcho-punk band Conflict, whose *Meat Means Murder* is about factory farming and animal suffering. Anarchists and punks have long had an affinity with veganism (Haenfler, 2006); as Cherry (2006, 159) explains, 'punk describes a state of mind and a willingness to change society more than a sartorial display'. Through a do-it-yourself (DIY) ethic and a politically progressive lifestyle, punks and anarchists have long foregrounded the centrality of a vegan ethic to resisting societal hierarchies. The Smiths, through their frontman Morrissey (more recently known for his far-right political views), were pioneers of bringing animals as 'friends, not food' to a wider public, as a resistant challenge to normative human–animal relations.

This slogan – 'friends, not food' – does little to think about what friendship or resistance might actually look like for animals. For Slicer (2014, 59): 'We don't eat those with whom we play, joke, laugh. This isn't an empirical claim. In fact, some people do eat those with whom they play, joke and laugh. But many of us find it odd, even incomprehensible, a kind of category mistake, or worse.'

The idea that animals can move from 'food' to 'friend' through human campaigns is one that has captured the imaginations of animal activists and the cultural mainstream. However, it largely omits animals themselves as resistant subjects. In the next section, I turn to campaigns of resistance that use animal representations to evoke more visceral senses.

LIBERATION BEGINS IN THE STOMACH

Where 'friends, not food' campaigns promote an image of animals as cuddly friends, many forms of resistance to eating animals tend towards shock tactics, seeking out affects of anger or disgust to start a conversation. Veggies is a Nottingham-based catering campaign group which had an active role in the 1980s 'What's Wrong with McDonald's?' campaign. The campaign gathered stories of McDonald's from worker exploitation to deforestation to animal welfare. Whilst the leaflet still circulates today (Giraud, 2019), there is also a factsheet which has fallen out of popular knowledge. In thinking about what (and who) is not eaten as a kind of resistance, this factsheet contends that: 'Liberation begins in the stomach' (London Greenpeace Group, 1986).

Veggies makes food playful in its catering campaigns; in 1984, it presented the president of McDonald's with a giant veggie burger (Giraud, 2019). For Veggies, vegan food becomes a creative site of resistance that uses category-shifting tactics of shock to represent human relations with different animals. Following Hughes (2016), this resistant creativity is a process, not a singular moment of resistance, where food, eating and cooking are collective socio-cultural doings. Hocknell's (2019, 3) playful experiments create a space for navigating self-performance, finding that participants 'were prompted to examine why things are the way they are and what food framings deflected them from thinking about'. Playing with our food challenges eating as ordinary, shifting it into the space of the political.

When Veggies plays with food, it conceptualises the stomach as a space where resistance begins: as a site for intervention. It was no surprise, then, that in 2010 Veggies lent its campaign and catering van to Animal Aid's 'Friend or Food' tour (Figure 3.1). The Veggies van was 'decorated as a spoof organic and free-range dog meat catering trailer' (Veggies, 2010) on a tour: 'featuring pictures of happy healthy dogs running through fields, chasing balls and swimming in streams, and the words "organic" and "free-range", the trailer will be offering dog meat to the public, with the assurance that all the animals were loved and well cared for before being butchered' (Animal Aid, 2010).

Source: Copyright Veggies Nottingham, veggies.org.uk/2010/10/friend-or-food/.

Figure 3.1 *'Collie Steak' being served at Veggies and Animal Aid's 2010 'Friend or Food' campaign*

Its 'dog meat' stall was set up at farmers' markets. People were invited to 'try a free sample of Dog Meat' and told that it was 'as tasty as pig meat'. Met with disgust, Veggies challenged Nottingham council's distaste for their tour when the same council invited 'exotic meat' farms to serve ostrich, kangaroo, crocodile and wild boar: 'then why not dog!' (Veggies, 2010).

Through these spatial interventions, playful resistance was brought to the streets. The van blended into the farmers' market but, as passers-by draw closer, dogs being sold as food evoked disgust, horror and anger. This was not just a clever comparative tactic, but deliberately evoked reactions from the audience through the stomach as a source of embodied knowledge, particularly powerful in disgust: 'everyone knows what it is like to feel disgust. The stomach heaves, the nose wrinkles, the mouth opens a little and one's tongue comes out, and one shudders with displeasure' (Schroeder, 2012, 430).

These campaigns of disgust are affective, playing with a 'gut sympathy' (Markley, 2021, 1) where the 'body's physiological and affective processes of ingestion and expulsion mirror ongoing, often contradictory, processes of assimilation and exclusion that determine how political subjects are made'. The stomach is ripe for resistance beyond the human: by replacing a 'food' animal with a 'friend' animal, the goal is to produce behaviour change through this disgust. In a 2008 essay, Annemarie Mol considers who she becomes when she eats, locating her subjectivity in her stomach. When 'we play with our food ... [we] explore the possibilities of models to do with growing, cooking, tasting and digesting' (Mol, 2008, 34). Some foods become distasteful through their political entanglements, such as eating animals for vegans, in turn having visceral effects. Mol (2021, 71) thus takes eating as an exemplary situation for philosophy:

> Eating changes the conditions of possibility on which getting to know a dish depends. Eating may warm a subject to the taste of her foods or impede any further tasting. Getting to know a dish may lead to valuing it ever more positively or, alternatively, make appreciating another bite altogether impossible.

Mol argues that digestive processes are beyond rational control, but this essential activity – eating – transforms us, and the world around us. In the stomach, human and more-than-human entities coalesce, challenging a human politics: 'Only *thinking* elevated "the human" over "nature," his *eating* did not' (Mol, 2021, 126). In the stomach as a site of resistance, eating is brought back under control.

'Friends, not food' campaigns attempt to make the human stomach's relations with animals an externality. It is not the mind that these campaigns target, but the stomach: the gut feeling. Our stomachs can be trained as sites for liberation, challenging socio-cultural positions of animals by removing them (Taylor and Signal, 2009). Ultimately, however, producing resistance in and from the stomach relies on reaching the stomach through category-shifting campaigns. If liberation begins in the stomach, it implicates the spaces of production and consumption preceding the stomach. The stomach is no longer just a site for digestion and nourishment, but one that is actively related to the world outside of it; it is a site not only for political action, but for political relations.

Animal campaigns commonly focus on the similarities between different categories of animals, often through imagery that places cows, pigs and chickens next to cats, dogs and horses, and accompanied by a slogan such as 'why love one but eat the other?' (AnimalAid). Kimberley Caroll organised a campaign that placed a kitten and a puppy alongside a chick and piglet for Toronto Vegetarian Association. She explains that: 'we hope that in connecting with these animals and the grievous suffering that is behind every burger, omelette, and hot dog, people will be motivated to make more compassionate food choices' (Caroll, in Alter, 2018). The stomach is a connected entity, and while digestion is beyond our control, the matter of digestion is ripe for resistance.

Another iteration of this category-shifting tactic is to put 'pet' animals 'in the place of' food animals. For example, an image produced by the Vegetarian Society (Figure 3.2), sees a small dog sitting on a plate with a knife and fork on either side.[2]

The slogan reads: 'Why not, you eat other animals don't you?' The puppy is 'out of place', creating a jarring image in the British context, where dogs are usually valued as friends (which of course is geographically and culturally variant; see Avieli, 2012). This category-challenging work is the 'bread and sunflower spread' of animal activists seeking to challenge 'speciesism', a label coined by Richard D. Ryder (2010, 1) in the 1970s.

However, the feeling of resistance in the gut – of disgust – often continues to centre the intentional human subject, asking them to reconsider who their animal 'friends' are. In the next section, I move to look directly at animals' own resistance, specifically in the case of chickens, and consider whether this has any connection with these human campaigns.

RESISTANCE IN RESCUE

> Lou is dead and we don't know where his body might be. I believe that Lou is dead in part because we forgot about other bodies while we were so busy trying to protect his
> (Jones, 2014, 192)

In 2014, cofounder of VINE Sanctuary Pattrice Jones told the story of how two of VINE's community members, Bill and Lou, had been condemned to death in the small town of Poultney, Vermont. After a long campaign, Bill escaped death, but Lou was killed, and his body never found. Jones had fought to bring both community members into their sanctuary but, despite a bitter battle, Lou was killed and buried alone in a dark spring night in 2012.

> Where did we go wrong? I bear some responsibility for what allies of Bill and Lou did or didn't do in a campaign we tried to coordinate. Even before the college killed Lou, I began to suspect that we, the oxen's allies, had erred badly in allowing so much of the discourse about the oxen to be so disembodied (Jones, 2014, 13)

Jones had launched a campaign to prevent Bill and Lou from being killed, made into hamburgers, and eaten. For years prior to this, Bill and Lou had been

Source: Published in *The Vegetarian* (a publication of the Vegetarian Society), September 1992.

Figure 3.2   *'Puppy on a Plate'*

enlisted to walk in circles, generating electricity every day at the agricultural college which 'owned' them. On special occasions, they were co-opted into 'parading' through the town centre, with crowds gathering to watch this spectacle. When looking for Lou's buried body, Jones finds herself frustrated with her own misplacing of the body in the campaign for Bill and Lou's life. The disembodiment of this campaign has stuck with Jones; VINE Sanctuary today foregrounds the material circumstances of its community members in their spaces, whilst emphasising 'multispecies' living (see Blattner et al., 2020).

In 2020, I began working with a hen rehoming charity in London and eastern England. The work involves collecting hundreds of chickens at the end of their 'productive lives' from egg-laying farms, loading them into vans, and transporting them to rehoming centres across the country (Figure 3.3). These centres are temporarily set up at sanctuaries, with people coming to collect the birds to rehome in gardens and allotments on the same day (for more detail on this process, see Oliver, 2021). In the middle of a large animal sanctuary in Cambridgeshire, about once a month, a group of people convene to coordinate the unloading, comforting and rehoming of these hens. The first time I arrived, apprehensive, I was hit simultaneously by the stench of sweat and ammonia emanating from the chickens, and the warmth of a well-oiled team there to welcome them.

Chicken-keeping has seen a huge surge in interest in the UK and the United States, leading to a burgeoning non-profit sector that moves chickens from the industrial farm to backyard keepers. In the Uk, rehoming organisations procure laying hens from farms at the end of their industrially productive lives, at around 18 months old. These organisations will usually buy the entirety of the farmer's stock of birds, and then deliver these birds around the country to backyard keepers. On this journey, some chickens will die. The volunteers say that it is usually the weakest, or those who were already ill, who had escaped the attention of farmers. Their death is not from a lack of resistance, but from an industrial system that is built around tempering resistance, and ensuring resistance is not realised in the era of biocapital (Kowalczyk, 2014).

Where heteroromantic and familial structures are upheld as primary dependencies (hooks, 2000), the role of friendship in making and sustaining politics, culture and society is largely seconded to these other kinds of relationships. The refusal of friendship in more explicit animal rights activism has been related to masculinisation and 'pussy panic' of activists and scholars (Fraiman, 2012). Approaching in friendship might be understood as a resistance to the masculinisation of the subject, and as part of elucidating a different kind of politics informed by feminist practices. Friendship of these forms is not limited to the human (Oliver, 2021) and Scotton (2017) has argued that humans have a duty to socialise with animals. In the chicken barn, there are multiple registers of potential friendship: between humans, between humans and chickens, and between chickens.

Source: Catherine Oliver (2022).

Figure 3.3   A group of ex-commercial hens awaiting being collected to go to their new domestic homes

At around 5 am, a van filled with empty crates is loaded up to travel a couple of hours to a chicken farm. Two or three people accompany the van and, when they arrive at the farm, they have a short time frame to empty the barn of chickens. These chickens are around 18 months old, at the end of their 'productive' lives. Despite space and time restrictions, the goal of the activity is to leave no hen behind. With hens screeching in fear, they desperately try to escape the clutches of these unknown humans, but are backed into the corners of the barn. When the van arrives back at the sanctuary, crates of a dozen birds are counted out into another barn, albeit one that is light-filled and spacious. From here, it is our role to soothe the birds, to check their health, and once they are settled, to show them the sun and grass for the first time, before packing them neatly into the cars of people rehoming them. In our attempts to befriend and settle the hens, we handle the birds in ways they do not want us to. A swift flap in the face from a sharp featherless chicken wing is the most physically painful effect of their resistance, but their frightened huddles and shrill screams of confusion are haunting.

Friendship has been conceptualised as 'so tightly linked to the definition of philosophy ... that without it, philosophy would not really be possible' (Agamben, 2009). For Foucault (1997), friendship can be an approach – a way of life – that attempts to be outside of exploitative hierarchy (Foucault, 1997, 137), but friendship is not simple, nor should it be without difficulties. Friendship does not require unquestioning faithfulness, but difficult decisions and negotiations, and when complicated by a species barrier, approaching in friendship can be misunderstood (Oliver, 2021). In the chicken barn, the myriad relationships of friendship and resistance pulse beneath the catching, petting, feeding of rehoming. These relations extend beyond the barn, bringing different assemblages of subjects together in this messy work, month after month, year after year.

As I corner another a chicken to head off to a new home, I am struck by the question: how can a chicken distinguish the hand that reaches out in friendship from the one that reaches to harm (Wadiwel, 2016)? Encounters with animals in these liminal spaces of 'rescue' are encounters with life and death: a mode of 'carrying-on' (Emmerson, 2019). When these chickens are rehomed, and diverted away from death and towards life, they are removed from (but still connected with) hidden sites of violence (Morin, 2018), and engaged instead in orientations of friendship. In this sweaty, loud, overwhelming barn, escaping the clutches of the unknown is the order of the day. Rather than convincing other humans that these chickens are friends, our role is to convince these chickens that we are their friends, that it is safe(r) here. In the concluding section of this chapter, I contrast these different modes and spaces of resistance by, with and for animals, asking how friendship creates a geography of resistance.

CONCLUSION

Animal resistance does not look like human resistance, but this does not mean that it cannot be interpreted through the modes of empathy and reciprocity that animal studies scholars have developed over decades (see Meijer, 2019). Yet, claims of anthropomorphism are easily directed at claims of animal resistance. After all, why would humans domesticate and enclose animals that fought back? But, as Dinesh Wadiwel (2018, 528) writes:

> There is a curious instability in how we understand the concept of the 'domesticated animal' who, it is assumed through generations of training, habituation, body modification, reproductive controls, and enclosure, occupies some sort of position of docility or beneficent relationality with respect to humans and, through a kind of failure of resistance, is imagined as 'not wild' or 'not belonging in the wild.'

Research on chickens, for example, has largely been undertaken through the frame of agricultural science. Intimate and expansive knowledge of their relationships, behaviours and biology have been put to work in making them more efficient labourers (see Davis, 2009). Animals are not, however, passive objects in this scene: they resist capitalist violence (Kaarlenkaski, 2020), although not always in ways that humans recognise.

The academic frame for understanding animals relies on knowledge founded on their being 'less-than-human'. As such, their resistance is understood within an anthropocentric framework which is obscured by dominant epistemological assumptions about animals, one clearly put to work in 'friends, not food' campaigns at the opening of this chapter. However, those who live closely with animals know that they enact resistance at different scales. But, as Giraud (2013) argues, these animal intimacies without an activist praxis can make animals 'legitimately exploitable'. In this landscape, animal activists and advocates have become interpreters for animals and representatives of their resistance (Corman, 2016), leading to campaigns with greater and lesser degrees of success. In this chapter, I have shown how some of these campaigns rely on interspecies friendship to enact resistance. Friendship becomes, in different ways, a resistant ethic to dominant social structures. Through friendship, political subjects protect, organise and resist both on behalf of, and with, friends. Friendship, then, might be the grounds for a political, social and cultural geographical concept of resistance that is in solidarity with those made 'less-than-human' (Philo, 2017).

Friendship's destruction of strangeness is deployed in animal activism as an approach of resistance, aiming to unsettle resistance as an inherently human individual or collective action. In this chapter, I opened by offering a challenge to more-than-human geographies, building on critical animal studies work that resists the flattening and homogenisation of the world beyond the human. Then, I exemplified how human advocates have used friendship in activism to reframe animals who are traditionally eaten into animals who are loved. This category-shifting work is further theorised in the following section to entangle the material politics of the gut with collective political action for animals. Following these two seections on human-focused resistance on the behalf of animals, I move to consider the resistance of animals themselves: first, by considering animal resistance's legibility to human observers; then considering how more-than-human friendship can be understood as a form of resistance.

In the 'more-than-human' resistance imagined in this chapter, I have unsettled the subject of resistance between and beyond the human and the animal (see also Oliver, 2022), to disrupt predetermined, often binary, understandings of resistant subjects and objects. The field of more-than-human geographies often attends to animals as nodes or locations in a homogenised landscape of material actors. Approaching instead through a lens of friendship, more-than-human geographies' depoliticising tendencies towards non-human life can be unpicked. Friendship beyond the human as a form of resistance is not only the result of resistance by humans to normative ideologies, nor of animals to the conditions of the industrial farm (although it might also be these things), but a space where resistance coalesces, can be tried out and played with, allowing us new insights into these spaces where resistance and friendship intermingle.

NOTES

1. This chapter draws on both vegetarian and vegan campaigns which differently engage the animal but are both ethically motivated movements. While vegetarians do not eat animal flesh, vegans refuse any animal products. In the past, veganism has been viewed as the strictest subset of vegetarianism (see Povey et al., 2001), but veganism has a broader ethical and political project – a philosophy – against animal exploitation. Despite their differing views of un/acceptable animal use, veganism and vegetarianism have a shared history and overlapping campaigns drawing on the same evocative tactics drawn on in this chapter.
2. The image of a dog on a dinner plate pictured in Figure 3.2 was produced by the Vegetarian Society. It was a standalone image sold as an A4 poster, advertised in *The Vegetarian* magazine. Affectionately known as 'Puppy on a Plate', it inspired a 2010 campaign image, the 'Butcher's Cat', which pictures a cat whose body is sectioned into ribs, shank, brisket, and round, and asks, 'why do we make pets out of some animals and mincemeat out of others?' Thank you to Susan Furmage and the Vegetarian Society for sharing information about these campaigns with me.

REFERENCES

Agamben, G. (2009) *What is an Apparatus?* Stanford, CA: Stanford University Press.
Alter, L. (2018) 'Why love one but eat the other' ads stir controversy in Toronto subway system. *Treehugger*. https://www.treehugger.com/why-love-one-eat-other-ads-stir-controversy-toronto-subway-system-4856680.
Animal Aid (2010) Dog meat now promoted at UK farmers markets. https://www.animalaid.org.uk/dog-meat-now-promoted-uk-farmers-markets/.
Animal Clock (2021) https://animalclock.org/uk/.
Avieli, N. (2012) Dog meat politics in a Vietnamese town. *Ethnology: An International Journal of Cultural and Social Anthropology*, 50(1), pp. 59–78.
Blattner, C.E., Donaldson, S. and Wilcox, R. (2020) Animal agency in community. *Politics and Animals*, 6, pp. 1–22.
Cherry, E. (2006) Veganism as a cultural movement: a relational approach. *Social Movement Studies*, 5(2), pp. 155–170.
Cole, M. and Stewart, K. (2014) *Our Children and Other Animals: The Cultural Construction of Human–Animal Relations in Childhood*. Farnham: Ashgate Publishing.
Colling, S. (2020) *Animal Resistance in the Global Capitalist Era*. East Lansing, MI: Michigan State Press.

Corman, L. (2016) The ventriloquist's burden: animal advocacy and the problem of speaking for others. In J. Castricano and L. Corman (eds), *Animal Subjects 2.0*. Waterloo, ON: Wilfrid Laurier University Press, pp. 473–502.

Davis, K. (2009) *Prisoned Chickens, Poisoned Eggs*. Summertown, TN: Book Publishing Company.

Emmerson, P. (2019) From coping to carrying on: a pragmatic laughter between life and death. *Transactions of the Institute of British Geographers*, 44(1), pp. 141–154.

Flynn, C.P. (2000) Woman's best friend: Pet abuse and the role of companion animals in the lives of battered women. *Violence against Women*, 6(2), pp. 162–177.

Foucault, M. (1997) *Friendship as a Way of Life, Ethics: Subjectivity and Truth*. New York: New Press, pp. 135–140.

Fraiman, S. (2012) Pussy panic versus liking animals: tracking gender in animal studies. *Critical Inquiry*, 39(1), pp. 89–115.

Giraud, E. (2013) 'Beasts of burden': productive tensions between Haraway and radical animal rights activism. *Culture, Theory and Critique*, 54(1), pp. 102–120.

Giraud, E. (2019) *What Comes After Entanglement? Activism, Anthropocentrism and an Ethics of Exclusion*. Durham, NC: Duke University Press.

GoVegan (2019) 'Friends not Food' national vegan campaign arrives in Milton Keynes. *MKFM*. https://www.mkfm.com/news/local-news/friends-not-food-national-vegan-campaign-arrives-in-milton-keynes/.

GoVeganWorld (2019) Go Vegan World launches massive Christmas & New Year Campaign in Ireland & the UK. https://goveganworld.com/go-vegan-world-launches-massive-christmas-and-new-year-campaign-in-ireland-and-the-uk/.

Haenfler, R. (2006) *Straight Edge: Clean-Living Youth, Hardcore Punk, and Social Change*. New Brunswick, NJ: Rutgers University Press.

Herzog, H. (2010) *Some We Love, Some We Hate, Some We Eat*. New York: HarperCollins.

Hobson, K. (2007) Political animals? On animals as subjects in an enlarged political geography. *Political Geography*, 26(3), pp. 250–267.

Hocknell, S. (2019) CoPSE: a methodological intervention towards gentle more-than-human relations. *Area*. https://doi.org/10.1111/area.12593.

hooks, b. (2000) *All about Love: New Visions*. New York: HarperCollins.

Hovorka, Alice J. (2015) The Gender, Place and Culture Jan Monk Distinguished Annual Lecture: Feminism and animals: exploring interspecies relations through intersectionality, performativity and standpoint. *Gender, Place and Culture*, 22(1), pp. 1–19.

Hribal, J.C. (2007) Animals, agency, and class: writing the history of animals from below. *Human Ecology Review*, 14(1), pp. 101–112.

Hribal, J. (2010), *Fear of the Animal Planet: The Hidden History of Animal Resistance*. Petrolia and Oakland, CA: CounterPunch and AK Press.

Hughes, S.M. (2016) Beyond intentionality: exploring creativity and resistance within a UK immigration removal centre. *Citizenship Studies*, 20(3–4), pp. 427–443.

Hughes, S.M. (2020) On resistance in human geography. *Progress in Human Geography*, 44(6), pp. 1141–1160.

Isaacs, J.R. (2020). More-than-human geographies. In D. Richardson, N. Castree, M.F. Goodchild, A. Kobayashi, W. Liu and R.A. Marston (eds), *International Encyclopaedia of Geography*. https://doi.org/10.1002/9781118786352.wbieg2041.

Jones, P. (2014) *The Oxen at the Intersection*. New York: Lantern Books.

Kaarlenkaski, T. (2020) Man, cow and machinery: technological animal husbandry has long roots. *Ilmiö: Sosiologinen Media Kaikalle*. https://ilmiomedia.fi/artikkelit/

ihminen-lehma-ja-koneet-teknologisoituneella-karjanhoidolla-on-pitkat-juuret/?fbclid=
IwAR2NCL6jPHMPKd331sxB94n3SG-Z7_EjrxSry4vT83RX_Ie7qVEGovmv7TY.
Kowalczyk, A. (2014) Mapping non-human resistance in the age of biocapital. In N. Taylor and R. Twine (eds), *The Rise of Critical Animal Studies: From Margins to Centre*. London and New York: Routledge, pp. 183–200.
London Greenpeace Group (1986) *What's Wrong with McDonald's?* https://www.mcspotlight.org/case/pretrial/factsheet.html.
Markley, H. (2021) Gut sympathy: anthropomorphism and disgust in Whiting's Memoirs of a Stomach. *Configurations*, 29(1), pp. 1–23.
McFarland, S.E. and Hediger, R. (2009) *Animals and Agency: An Interdisciplinary Exploration*. Leiden: Brill.
Meijer, E. (2019) *When Animals Speak: Toward an Interspecies Democracy* (Vol. 1). New York: New York University Press.
Mol, A. (2008) I eat an apple. On theorizing subjectivities. *Subjectivity*, 22(1), pp. 28–37.
Mol, A. (2021) *Eating in Theory*. Durham, NC: Duke University Press.
Morin, K.M. (2018) *Carceral Space, Prisoners and Animals*. Abingdon: Routledge.
Mumby, D., Thomas, R., Seidl, D., Marti, I. (2017) Resistance redux. *Organization Studies*, 38(9), pp. 1157–1183.
Oliver, C. (2021) *Veganism, Archives and Animals*. Abingdon: Routledge.
Oliver, C. (2022) Animal-beings, animal-things. *Vegan Geographies*. Seattle, WA: Lantern Press.
Panelli, R. (2010) More-than-human social geographies: posthuman and other possibilities. *Progress in Human Geography*, 34(1), pp. 79–87.
Pedersen, H. (2011) Release the moths: critical animal studies and the posthumanist impulse. *Culture, Theory and Critique*, 52(1), pp. 65–81.
Philo, C. (2017) Less-than-human geographies. *Political Geography*, 60, pp. 256–258.
Philo, C. and Wilbert, C. (2004) *Animal Spaces, Beastly Places*. Abingdon: Routledge.
Pickett, E. (2018) New bus ad reminds us that animals are friends, not food. Vancouver Humane Society. https://vancouverhumanesociety.bc.ca/posts/govegbusad/.
Pointing, C. (2018) New vegan bus camp aign tells Vancouver residents that pigs are 'friends not food'. https://www.livekindly.co/new-bus-advertisement-campaign-go-veg-vancouver/.
Povey, R., Wellens, B. and Conner, M. (2001) Attitudes towards following meat, vegetarian and vegan diets: an examination of the role of ambivalence. *Appetite*, 37(1), pp. 15–26.
Ryder, R.D. (2010) Speciesism again: the original leaflet. *Critical Society*, 2, pp. 1–2.
Schroeder, T. (2012) Review: *Yuck The Nature and Moral Significance of Disgust* by Kelly, Daniel. *Ethics*, 122(2), pp. 430–434.
Scotton, G. (2017) Duties to socialise with domesticated animals: farmed animal sanctuaries as frontiers of friendship. *Animal Studies Journal*, 6(2), pp. 86–108.
Slicer, D. (2014) 'Joy', in C. Adams and L. Gruen (eds), *Ecofeminism*. New York: Bloomsbury.
Sokolowski, R. (2002) Phenomenology of friendship. *Review of Metaphysics*, 55(3), pp. 451–470.
Stroud, S. (2006) Epistemic partiality in friendship. *Ethics*, 116(3), 498–524.
Sutton, Z. (2019) Choreographing human–companion animal relationships. Unpublished PhD thesis, Flinders University, Adelaide.
Taylor, N. and Signal, T.D. (2009) Pet, pest, profit: isolating differences in attitudes towards the treatment of animals. *Anthrozoös*, 22(2), pp. 129–135.

Tidwell, C. (2009) 'Fish are just like people, only flakier': environmental practice and theory in *Finding Nemo*. *Americana: The Journal of American Popular Culture* (1900–present), 8(1). https://www.americanpopularculture.com/journal/articles/spring_2009/tidwell.htm.
Veggies (2010) 'Friend or food?' https://www.veggies.org.uk/2010/10/friend-or-food/.
Wadiwel, D. (2016) 'Do fish resist?' *Cultural Studies Review*, 22(1), pp. 196–242.
Wadiwel, D. (2018) Chicken harvesting machine: animal labor, resistance, and the time of production. *South Atlantic Quarterly*, 117(3), pp. 527–549.
Weisberg, Z. (2009) The broken promises of monsters: Haraway, animals and the humanist legacy. *Journal for Critical Animal Studies* 7(2), pp. 21–61.
Whatmore, S. (2002) *Hybrid Geographies: Natures, Cultures, Spaces*. London: SAGE.
Whatmore, S. (2006) Materialist returns: practising cultural geographies in and for a more-than-human world. *Cultural Geographies*, 13(4), pp. 600–610.
Wilbert, C. (2000) Anti-*this*-against-*that*: resistances along a human–non-human axis. In Sharp J., Routledge, P., Philo, C. and Paddison, R. (eds), *Entanglements of Power: Geographies of Domination/Resistance*. London: Routledge, pp. 238–255.
Wolch, J. and Emel, J. (1995) *Animal Geographies*. London: Verso.

4. Resistance without subjects: friction and the non-representational geography of everyday resistance

Sage Brice

INTRODUCTION

> 'Misfitting can be understood as generative precisely given it involves friction; when bodies do not fit seamlessly into space, things happen' (Ahmed, 2019, p. 224).

Casting resistance as an oppositional transaction between the sovereign subject and hegemonic structures of power reduces the fluidity of difference to the rigidity of identity. While identity has been crucial for the formation of liberatory movements in the last two centuries, it is also important to consider its limitations (Crenshaw, 1991). To understand resistance as spatial – as geographical – requires a loosening of the concept from lingering attachments to the notion of a pre-given, intentional subject as its principal site. Thinking spatially requires attending to the ontological vulnerability of identity, and suggests a politics rooted in relations of becoming rather than being. Where 'being' emphasises stasis and identity, 'becoming' emphasises transformation and difference (Braidotti, 2019). A politics of becoming recognises that power is not an edifice but a process; a deeply inequitable process. This is the principle at work when Eric Stanley (2021, p. vii and throughout) writes of 'structuring' rather than 'structured' violence.[1] Treating power as a process changes my understanding of what resistance is and does.

In her recent review article, Sarah Hughes (2020, p. 1141) notes that in geographical thought, resistance has conventionally been construed quite narrowly as 'organised opposition to a particular configuration of power relations'; a construction that emphasises structure and form over relational and processual dimensions. This preoccupation with the form of resistance has also meant that it is 'often conceptualised as a dualism; resistance is considered emancipatory and acts against the seemingly totalising force of hegemonic state power' (ibid., p. 1146). Hughes (2020, p. 1141) draws attention to the limitations of this framework in order to give context to her call for a more nuanced attention to the 'seemingly unremarkable practices' of everyday resistance in which 'intention', 'linearity' and 'opposition' are not necessarily the principal or definitive markers of political (in)action. Attention to the minutiae of the everyday is particularly crucial where erasure and denial (rather than subordination alone) is the threat that underpins a certain form of oppression. In these circumstances, creating a liveable sense of 'selfhood' and carving out spaces in which to do so can constitute vital and immediate forms of resistance that are not necessarily rooted in momentous oppositional events.

Theorising resistance as 'more than' opposition brings useful insight to a persistent difficulty in feminist, queer and trans approaches to theorising the political subject. In this context, a narrow understanding of resistance has at times produced a prescriptively normative approach that tries to delimit a 'proper' form for resistance to cis/hetero/patriarchal hegemonies (Berlin and Brice, 2022; Hines, 2019; Doan, 2010; Namaste, 2009).

For transgender, transsexual, non-binary and gender-variant (trans) people, in particular, resistance is not straightforwardly a liberatory force in quite the same way that feminist and queer theory and politics have traditionally imagined it. I write this not to undermine a queer/feminist politics of refusal whose values and approach I strongly resonate with, but in order to demand a more nuanced and less prescriptive approach to imagining and conceptualising what an inclusive feminist and queer resistance might look like in practice. Interrogating the concept of resistance without starting from a point of view that assumes its normative form and liberatory value makes it possible to ask how resistance figures in the lives of trans people as an ambiguous and ambivalent force.[2]

In this chapter, therefore, I examine the concept of resistance as both a practice oriented towards opening up space to thrive in the face of oppressive systems, and a force of opposition or obstruction to that practice: an opposition experienced in the everyday as a kind of 'friction'. Moreover, I advance the case that these two senses of resistance are neither mutually exclusive nor fully extricable. The everyday frictions of resistance both obstruct and enable the thriving of individuals and communities marked as 'different'. Strategies for thriving in these conditions – for resistance to oppression in the most conventional sense – necessarily involve working with that friction to reduce its negative impacts and activate its generative potential. This is resistance, rather than resilience, because thriving amid adversity can be expressive of a transformative, even a liberatory, impetus.[3] If this impetus goes unrecognised then an ethical and political commitment to liberation can too easily become a normative demand for opposition. In short, I argue that for trans people (and by extension also for other marginalised people), the path of least resistance is not necessarily synonymous with the path of conformity. Indeed, finding the path of least resistance sometimes constitutes a form of resistance.

In this chapter, I will therefore first develop an account of resistance as friction; friction that both enables and impedes liberatory or 'progressive' political change. Here resistance is conceived less as an act of diametric opposition to structural power, and more as a creative and critical engagement with that contradictory set of forces which friction activates. Where Hughes makes the important argument that resistance can be unintentional, emergent and entangled, my purpose in this chapter is somewhat different. I wish to explore – not without caution – the tensions that arise from a recognition that resistance and opposition can cut both ways. Specifically, I propose that in order to understand how resistance factors in the lives of trans people, it is necessary to consider resistance as a multiplicity; something that both enables and inhibits, and which cannot be straightforwardly accounted for through the model of resistance as opposition to structural power.

Crucially, resistance that impedes or constrains trans lives, and resistance that enables them, cannot be neatly disentangled into two opposing forces: 'for' and 'against'. Rather, when understood as friction, the forces of resistance can be seen to be relational, so that it is sometimes by avoiding, adapting to, or pre-empting resistance – reducing friction – that trans people resist coercion and constraint. Equally, trans people can find that they bump up against – experience friction from – conflicting and contradictory challenges. This is perhaps most self-evident in Julia Serano's (2007) example of the transmisogyny double-bind, whereby transfeminine people are accused of either being insufficiently feminine or conforming to prescriptive ideas of femininity (or sometimes both), leaving no acceptable path of transfeminine presentation and self-expression. The double-bind here is indicative of the ways in which friction can sometimes operate as a trap, but I want to foreground also the more mundane ways in which friction shapes habits and practices of doing gender in the everyday.

I next discuss the possibility that thinking of resistance as something more than straightforward opposition entails different activist possibilities which may be useful in challenging particular forms of oppressive politics, particularly those that are embedded and entangled within avowedly liberatory movements. Here activism is understood as a mode of resistance involving organised or targeted action for social change. Specifically, I reflect on my experiences working with the Dandelion Collective to run workshops addressing underlying causes of transphobia within feminist and environmental activist communities in the United Kingdom (UK). These workshops were not conceived or carried out as fieldwork, but took place in parallel with my academic studies in non-representational geographies and process ontologies more widely; studies which deeply informed my experimental approach to the transphobia work. Since the workshops were not conceived as research at the time, discussion in this chapter is limited to critical reflection on my own practice, in discussion with my workshop partners, rather than an empirical examination of the workshop content and process.[4]

THE DISCOMFORT OF FRICTION

Perhaps it is best to begin by saying that I write this entire chapter from a place of ambivalent unease. The work it discusses was uncomfortable work that walked a fine and troubled line between the politics of conciliation and refusal. The theoretical argument it advances – that resistance is not adequately accounted for as dualistic opposition – issues a gentle challenge to the politics of refusal, and in doing so, comes close to making an argument for recognition and inclusion as political goals. My aim, however, is not to propose a 'middle way' between these apparent poles, but rather to argue something which I think resonates most strongly with abolitionist and revolutionary critiques of the totalising forces of capitalism and the state. That 'something' is the contention that so-called identity is not a property of the individual, but a problem of the collective. More specifically, my argument is that resistance should be theorised not as a transaction between the individual and fixed, hegemonic structures of power, but as a mode of relation through which individuals (taken together) navigate, challenge, transform and survive the violent structuration of their (our) lives within organising fields of persistent and uneven power relations.

'The concept of everyday resistance', Rae Rosenberg (2021, p. 1398) notes, 'encapsulates the mundane and often invisibilised acts of living that [contribute] to the construction of activist subjectivities'. Writing on Black queer and trans young people in an urban gay village, Rosenberg highlights a critical dimension in the resistance of marginalised and excluded communities: the art of surviving and thriving in small ways. For those who experience intersecting marginalisations, this may involve navigating contradictory, non-linear terrains wherein varied assortments of solidarities and oppressions sit awkwardly side by side in each available space, rather than a dualistic opposition between hegemony and liberation (Boussalem, 2021). The pervasiveness of racism in queer circles is one example of how self-consciously liberatory spaces can also be exclusionary and oppressive (Puar, 2007).

For Priyanka Jindal (2008, p. 46), the critical distinction between queers of colour and the largely white 'mainstream' of queer culture is that for people of colour 'resistance is not necessarily about choice, it's about survival'. Jindal is writing of racism in queer spaces, an enduring concern which I do not wish to subsume into a generalised equivalence with other forms of oppression. Gender- and race-based oppressions should not be conflated. At the same time, it makes little sense to speak of them as entirely independent, given the intimacy with which racialisation and the enforcement of binary gender are bound up in colonial systems of knowledge production (Schuller, 2017; Snorton, 2017). The key insight which I draw on here – that resistance and agency are about more than choice and self-expression – also holds true for most multiply marginalised groups. One part of this argument is the assertion that resistance carries more material urgency for racialised queers and that often this entails a deeper political commitment to revolutionary change (see also Davis, 1992), but there is also an ontological claim here about the nature of resistance and agency, and therefore about the nature of political subjectivity (see also Mahmood, 2011). Without playing down the importance of a radical commitment to opposition in liberatory politics, my aim here is to attend to the ways in which resistance is not always and only dualistic and oppositional.

To do this, I develop the idea of resistance as friction. Anthropologist Anna Lowenhaupt Tsing (2004) uses 'friction' to complicate the idea of the culture clash. She demonstrates that, far from presenting a smooth and orderly frontal opposition, resistance to globalised environmental extraction emerges in a zone of awkward engagement characterised by misunderstandings and messy alliances across difference, which are nevertheless sometimes generative and productive of desired outcomes. For Tsing, the metaphor of friction appeals as a counter to the neoliberal ideal of a new and unimpeded global 'flow' under global capitalism. Tsing (2004, p. 5) insists that 'motion does not proceed this way at all'; in fact, motion across the globe's surface necessarily requires friction in order to have traction. Like railway tracks, that friction imposes directions and constraints as well as enabling movement. What is more, the friction of encounter across difference is potentially transformative:

> a study of global connections shows the grip of encounter: friction. A wheel turns because of its encounter with the surface of the road; spinning in the air it goes nowhere. Rubbing two sticks together produces heat and light; one stick alone is just a stick. As a metaphorical image, friction reminds us that heterogeneous and unequal encounters can lead to new arrangements of culture and power. (Tsing, 2004, p. 5)

It is worth noting that for Tsing (2004, p. 6), 'friction is not a synonym for resistance'; this is because 'hegemony is made as well as unmade with friction'. Thus, on the face of it, Tsing might seem to reject my proposed model of resistance as friction. Yet Tsing's use of the word 'resistance' here refers specifically to the concept of resistance as diametric opposition to structures of power; a definition which I aim to unsettle. With this caveat taken into account, there are two ways in which her conceptualisation of friction is useful to my project. First, Tsing contends that it is through friction that generalised political structures become effective: 'friction gives purchase to universals, allowing them to spread as frameworks for the practice of power' (ibid., pp. 8, 10). In other words, friction is what occurs when individual lives bump up against structural oppositions to difference. Importantly, however, 'engaged universals are never fully successful in being everywhere the same because of this same friction' (ibid., p. 10). Friction is thus also what produces the specificities and singularities of particular encounters; the 'awkward, unequal, unstable, and creative qualities of interconnection across difference' (ibid., p. 4).

The second insight is that 'these kinds of 'friction' inflect motion, offering it different meanings' (Tsing, 2004, p. 6). In other words, friction is a force which affects how particular bodies and lives move through space and time and are given meaning. This is both a constraining and an emancipatory force: friction contains the possibilities of rupture, transformation and dissent, as well as the limits by which structural inequalities can impose upon lives and communities marked as 'different'.

Like Tsing, Cresswell (2014) develops the concept of friction as a framework for thinking about differential mobility: how some bodies move, or are impeded in moving, through space. This concept has been further elaborated by crip/disability scholars (Hall and Bates, 2019; Hamraie, 2017). Hall and Bates employ Creswell's framework to explore geographies of anxiety and precarity in the lives of adults with learning disabilities, observing that 'people feel social and embodied "friction" as they move, and choose routes to reduce or avoid such constraints' (Hall and Bates, 2019, p. 105). While Creswell's account draws on the example of war and military planning, and Hall and Bates emphasise the dimension of choice, both accounts also draw attention to the material, contingent and relational nature of frictions which often escape or exceed the domain of cognitive intentionality. In other words, friction names not only conscious responses to structural inequalities, but also the affects and atmospheres with which non-representational geographies are concerned.

GENERATIVE FRICTION

I, too, first began to think with the concept of friction when trying to articulate an aspect of my (trans) experience which I felt was not fully accounted for by logics of choice, representation and self-expression. I have written briefly elsewhere on this idea, exploring what it might mean to understand trans experiences of transphobia and dysphoria, including my own, as a kind of friction. I drew this conceptual analogy from the experience of shaving my face as a transfeminine person and, together with my colleague Sam Berlin, developed the argument that difference should be understood not as the fixed property of a body but as emerging 'within and through a body's relations' (Berlin and Brice, forthcoming, p. 1).

Friction, in that chapter, named a number of things: the physical abrasiveness of the blade against agitated skin and stubble; the dysphoria induced by daily close engagement with a 'sexed' bodily feature (facial hair); and the cumulative impacts of regular misgendering on the business of everyday life. These are various kinds of friction that inflect everyday experience of living whilst trans. My habits of shaving or not shaving – not wholly determined by self-expression and/or intent – are also directed by these differential frictions. Thus, for example, prior to transition I kept my beard trimmed rather than shaving it, as this was the lowest-maintenance and hence least dysphoric option open to me: the option which generated least 'friction'. After transition, I began instead to remove my facial hair, because the relative balance between different frictional forces shifted. My habits reoriented to what was now the 'less abrasive' option. In either case, questions of representation and self-expression were secondary to more material considerations of how it feels to move through spaces and relate to both my own embodied experience and my encounters with/in a wider social world (Salamon, 2010).

The two key points which friction helped us to articulate in that chapter were, first, a sense that practices of gender are informed not only by 'choice' and 'self-expression' but by a more distributed field of forces, material affects and relational possibilities; and second, that this recognition requires a politics that is not too firmly attached to the idea of individual sovereignty as a mode of opposition to societal norms. Following Butler (2011), we argued that norms are not merely prescriptive but are also necessary enabling constraints in the articulation of liveable and liberatory practices of gender. We drew on the work of Deleuze and Guattari (2004) to bring together these two points, arguing for a 'trans-individual' politics that foregrounds vitality rather than opposition.

What this telling left somewhat under-developed, however, was a sense of friction as a generative and potentially desirable mode of engagement and connection. In describing my changing habits as a seemingly 'natural' tendency towards the path of 'least friction', I missed an opportunity to fully realise the ways that friction in fact underscores our wider argument: the argument that identity and/or difference is not an individual characteristic, but a relational field. Friction is relation and encounter, and as such, friction is not only a source of discomfort but also a space of transformative possibility.

The kind of ambivalent frictions I am pointing to here find a clear and evocative articulation in Harlan Weaver's (2014) analysis of Leslie Feinberg's landmark novel *Stone Butch Blues*. The novel's protagonist, Jess Goldberg, navigates a troubled path through the zone of indeterminate masculinity, experimenting with masculinising hormones and with 'passing' as a man before settling for a less socially acceptable, but more connected and ultimately more tolerable state of 'in-betweenness'. Weaver (2014, p. 88) contrasts the abrasive emotional landscape of Jess's misfit life with the 'lack of friction' experienced by the heteronormative subject whose shape 'meets but does not rub up against' the world through which they move.

Weaver here is building on Sara Ahmed's (2014, p. 148) contention that 'heteronormativity functions as a form of public comfort by allowing bodies to extend into spaces that have already taken their shape'. Indeed, Ahmed (2019, p. 41) has since also used the concept of friction to (re)articulate this observation:

> Friction is the resistance the surface of an object encounters when moving over another. The more people travel on a path, the flatter and smoother the surface becomes. When something is smoother, it is clearer; the more a path is followed, the easier it is to follow. Once something has become used, you are encouraged to go in that direction: your progression would be eased.

Friction in this account names the discomfort of not fitting in with familiar pathways, and the pressures which come to bear on bodies and lives which fail to follow them. However, this does not translate into a simple formula in which friction is a purely inhibitory constraint. For Feinberg's Jess, the absence of friction did not equate to comfort so much as a state of loneliness, disconnection and invisibility. Friction offered instead a way of being connected, in relation to and with a social world that is necessary to thriving.

Considering resistance as multi-directional also raises the question of who is envisioned doing the resistance. For example, what is the difference between saying that trans bodies resist categorisation, and that trans persons resist prescriptive gender assignments? How does each of these formulations position trans subjectivities and identities? When a person experiences dissonance and incongruence in relation to their own body, that body might be simultaneously resistant to social expectations attached to sex and gender, and also to an individual's desire for congruence. Resistance as opposition reinforces a Cartesian concept of the thinking, experiencing self as somehow separate and distinct from their body; whereas friction emphasises instead the condition of becoming-in-relation.

In conclusion, the work that friction does here is threefold. First, it draws attention to the ways that structural attitudes and inequalities impinge upon individual lives through forces of abrasion and drag; forces not always necessarily best accounted for through major incidents or momentous events. Second, its analogy to the materiality of bodies in relative stasis and motion emphasises that friction operates as a force, influencing the flow and arrangement of 'seemingly mundane, habitual and non-reflexive practices' (Hall and Wilton in Hall and Bates, 2019, p. 1010) in ways that may not be fully conscious and considered, or indeed may never register as a discernible effects, but nevertheless profoundly influence the paths that lives follow. Third, and most importantly for my argument here, it replaces the model of resistance as opposition with the idea of resistance as a relational mode of encounter which produces diverse strategies for surviving and thriving.

ACTIVATING FRICTION

In this section, I explore the implications of 'resistance as friction' for developing a process-based activist approach to combating transphobia in feminist spaces, particularly within environmental and anti-capitalist communities.

As noted above, this section draws on my work with the Dandelion Collective, a small group of feminists of various genders with a background in facilitation and a desire to address the schisms opened up by unaddressed transphobia in our activist communities.[5] Before discussing the work of the group in more detail, I want to contextualise the problem. At a theoretical level, we were informed by the idea that gender is best understood not as the property of an individual, but as a collective problem which we all navigate in relation. The struggle for trans liberation therefore involves not only a contestation over individual rights, but also a deeper intervention into the texture of this collective problem, facilitating a shift in the field of gendered possibilities. This idea aligns philosophically with my interest in process ontologies, and more specifically with non-representational theories in geography, in that it seeks to attend to difference as a process of becoming rather than a relationship between fixed states of being (Brice, 2020; Anderson and Harrison, 2010; Thrift, 2008). Thinking in terms of process and not identity suggests 'an alternate politics, one grounded not in the indeterminacy of transgender bodies, but rather in the indeterminacy of the social' (Weaver, 2014, p. 86).

This approach was also informed by the recognition that oppositional resistance can be mobilised in either direction: as a liberatory or a counter-liberatory opposition. This is seen, for example, in the increasingly effective adoption, by reactionary forces on the right, of concepts and discourses which originated with liberatory movements (Ahmed, 2016; Butler et al., 2016). As Catherine Nash and Kath Browne (2020) have observed, resistance to lesbian, gay, bisexual and trans (LGBT) equality can also take on an activist orientation, and indeed exists as a significant organised resistance to a perceived hegemonic LGBT order threatening an imperilled heterocentric way of life or set of values. While this inverted model of power and resistance can be a purely strategic or rhetorical move by those dedicated to opposing equality, it can also manifest as a sincerely felt anxiety among people who see themselves as committed to ideals of social justice and equality. In particular, anti-trans campaigns frequently construe themselves – not always disingenuously – as defending imperilled minorities against a range of perceived threats including 'lesbian erasure', '"transing" of young girls' (or children more widely), invasion of 'single-sex spaces', erosion of 'sex-based rights', and so on (Pearce et al., 2020; Armitage, 2020; Faye, 2021).

My aim here is not only to affirm that resistance, as others have rightly pointed out (e.g. Sharp et al., 2000), is usually – if not always – entangled with power in complex and messy ways (and is indeed a force or movement of power in its own right), and that resistance is therefore not solely or necessarily oppositional. More specifically, I argue here that the model of resistance which assumes opposition as its definitive characteristic also produces an overly simplistic set of normative assumptions about how marginalised lives are shaped by oppression, as well as what resistance can and should look like. To argue this line is tricky, because it comes uncomfortably close to arguing for a politics of moderation or a 'middle path'. Relinquishing the moral certainty of opposition can feel like compromise; like capitulation or conciliation. This is decidedly not my intention. My proposition here is therefore conditional upon maintaining an explicit and sustained commitment to the principle that there is no place for compromise or 'debate' between two propositions where there exists a stark asymmetry of power and harm. That is, where one side exclusively seeks to deny the dignity, integrity and basic human needs of the other. Friction, here, names something distinct from compromise: it is the possibility for generative and transformative encounter that emerges when difference comes into contact. Friction incorporates, but crucially is not limited to, the force of opposition (in technical terms: 'normal force', which is the net force compressing two surfaces together). In addition to normal force, friction activates both drag and traction; forces which both inhibit and enable movement.

The Dandelion Collective emerged in response to growing frictions in feminist and anti-capitalist spaces of which members were part; tensions which came to a head during the UK government's extended public consultation on reform of the Gender Recognition Act 2004 (GRA). The proposed procedural reform was intended to make legal registration easier and less discriminatory for trans people seeking a gender certificate for purposes such as marriage and taxation (Pearce et al., 2020). The protracted consultation provided fertile ground for a well-resourced campaign against trans inclusion[6] in 'single-sex spaces', whose primary legislative target was not the GRA itself, but the wider rights and protections afforded to trans people under the Equalities Act 2010. The UK saw a huge rise in largely negative media coverage of trans people during this period, and a corresponding rise in public attention to trans issues[7] (Armitage, 2020; Independent Press Standards Organisation, 2020).

Over a period of two years, the collective delivered a small number of workshops at community centres and festivals in England and Wales, in which we explored fears and concerns arising from this increased attention to questions of trans recognition and inclusion. The majority of participants in these workshops identified (in good faith) as feminists,[8] and all evidenced demonstrably high levels of commitment to ethical and political practices in their daily lives. All, however, situated themselves somewhere on a spectrum from confusion to outright opposition, regarding at least some aspects of trans recognition and inclusion.

We devised our workshop methods from the shared perception that pervasive doubts and concerns about trans recognition and inclusion stem at least in part from attachment to specific 'survival stories' about the nature of sex and gender; stories developed by feminists as a defensive reaction to the impacts of misogyny and patriarchy. Increasingly, over the course of our work, we came to think of these attachments as embodied and traumatic as well as ideological. As such, we felt that simply attempting to shut down those doubts and fears, or to reason against them – though justified in principle – was likely to compound rather than address the problem. We believed that this was specifically and perhaps exceptionally the case with regard to combating transphobia, because of the specific ways in which sex and gender identity figure in feminist liberatory epistemologies. We were not entirely convinced by the liberal-progressive narrative that sees resistance to trans inclusion as simply bigotry; that is, as the next in a series of frontiers inexorably following on from civil rights and LGB struggles (which, of course, also have yet to be won). In essence, this meant that we saw more reason than usual to be optimistic about the possibility of transforming rather than shutting down oppositional feelings.

We saw our approach as one option among a number of valid activist/ pedagogical approaches to tackling transphobia. For example, during the same period I attended a workshop detailing the significant parallels between anti-trans and fascist tactics and ideologies. The analysis was rigorous and informative, and concluded by advancing a case for applying established anti-fascist principles (such as no-platforming and exclusion from communal and organising spaces) in order to uproot transphobia from within the anarchist/anti-capitalist movement. This approach could be seen as antithetical to the one our collective adopted, which necessarily entailed holding space open for participants to explore potentially transphobic feelings and ideas. The danger of seeming to legitimise or facilitate those feelings and ideas by adopting a somewhat conciliatory approach is one that I was painfully aware of throughout our workshops. The feeling stayed with me despite having the explicit blessing of trans friends who had themselves adopted more uncompromising positions and commitments to oppositional action. I understood this discomfort as inherent to the kind of encounter- and process-based work we were trying to do. As such, it was not only a sacrifice or a necessary 'price to pay' for reaching a wider potential pool of people, but also an integral part of the friction of encounter across difference which we considered necessary to transformative change.

Indeed, though we did not frame it this way at the time, friction was in some senses the guiding force that informed the experimental development of our workshop methods. Friction worked in these workshops in four key ways. First, by welcoming awkwardness into the space. At the start of each workshop I explicitly acknowledged the discomfort, as a trans person, of seeming to tacitly condone positions which I perceive to be causing material harm to myself and to my trans siblings. Naming the discomfort became a part of the transformative impetus of the workshops, because my shared vulnerability effectively demanded a reciprocal level of integrity and openness from participants. The welcome ritual we used[9] was extensive, designed to open up a space where participants felt able to show up in their entirety, including with doubts, uncertainties and conflict.[10]

Second, by alleviating friction in a number of important ways. A significant portion of the workshops was dedicated to 'container building': addressing some of the potential barriers and creating a sense of safety, trust and clear boundaries. Participant feedback indicated that this profoundly influenced the dynamic of the workshop. Using techniques such as body awareness and grounding exercises, humour, and careful sharing of vulnerabilities, we worked to elicit a shift of atmosphere and disposition among participants, thus enabling a more open flow of ideas and feelings and an easing of oppositional positionality.

Third, through heightening friction where this felt necessary. By insisting on examining the composition of trans-facing fears or concerns in very high resolution, we forced a slowing down and invited a closer, more intimate engagement with participants' fears. One way in which we did this was through an adaptation of the classic 'fishbowl' exercise. In this exercise, members of a minority group form an 'inner circle' to engage in active discussion of a matter that affects them, while their peers or colleagues form an 'outer circle' who only listen and observe. This technique enables groups to examine issues that disproportionately affect their minority members, without majority perspectives dominating or derailing the discussion. Our use of the technique was slightly recalibrated: the team of three gender-diverse facilitators used the space to engage in depth with example fears and concerns sourced from previous participants. In a sense, the fishbowl was turned inside out so that it was the majority group whose experiences were placed under scrutiny, though the power dynamic of whose voices were centred remained consistent with the original design.

The process was carried out in two rounds, with workshop participants having an opportunity to process together in pairs between each round, but maintaining the separation between fishbowl and listeners. In the first round, we as the facilitators spent time working with a single fear or concern, trying to imagine and understand what might be at stake for the concerned individual, and to piece together a detailed picture of the imagined scenarios that might inform that fear. For example, when exploring the fear that young women might be pressured to transition in order to escape misogyny, we took time to explore who was envisioned as experiencing that pressure, what forms societal pressure might take and from where, and how transition might be imagined in this situation as a means of escape. We floated the idea that the concerned individual might themselves identify in some ways with the young women in this imagined scenario, and speculated about the kinds of feelings that this could give rise to. In the second round, we tried to imagine what might be missing from that picture; not only information, but also alternative imagined scenarios. In this instance, we discussed barriers that young people experience to transition, and noted the kinds of advice which we have seen given to young people in trans spaces (never to rush; not to seek immediate answers). We also looked at the ways in which gatekeeping can inadvertently have the opposite of a deterrent effect, if it denies young people the chance to safely explore uncertainty. The sheer weight of detailed attention and care which we as facilitators brought to each round of the activity produced its own forms of drag and traction. Creating a separation between the performing/listening space and the processing space meant that there was little opportunity to be reactive.[11] Instead, participants reported deep surprise at discovering how much there was to consider in relation to issues that they might previously have held reactive positions on.

Fourth, by valuing encounter and difference, we were able to elicit the generative buzz that comes from bringing unfamiliar or incompatible perspectives together in one space. Refusing to adopt an oppositional stance – while remaining clear about our own boundaries and principles – opened up a space to engage differently. Attending to friction becomes transformative, because friction is where the force of resistance is situated and expressed. This is unusual in a culture that tends either to stifle opinion in order to avoid conflict, or to approach conflict as an oppositional dualism (right/wrong, good/bad, and so on).[12] Such a limiting framework can shut down the possibility for transformative change, since friction is a necessary condition of movement.

CONCLUSIONS

In conclusion, friction offers a way of conceptualising resistance that does not assume a dualistic oppositional form as its prerequisite for politics. Through analogy to the physics of normal force, drag and traction, the concept of friction encompasses both the inhibitive and the mobilising effects of resistance. The analogy enables a consideration of the ways in which resistance enables, or prevents, the relative freedoms of bodies moving through space; in other words, a consideration of resistance as a geographical force. This, in turn, informs a more nuanced reading of the ways in which resistance plays out in the lives of those for whom resistance is situated in the everyday business of surviving and thriving in the face of opposition, and for whom refusal is but one important strategy among many. Finally, this reading also suggests a particular kind of activist sensibility: one which utilises friction rather than opposition to create spaces of transformative possibility. As my brief case study of the Dandelion Collective elucidates, finding ways to work beyond friction here is not an alternative to opposition, but rather includes and also exceeds it. As a mode of resistance, friction is admittedly not a panacea, and notably comes at a cost that may sometimes be disproportionately met by the oppressed and marginalised. Nevertheless, I argue that conceptualising resistance as friction supports a more nuanced and complete picture of what resistance might look like in practice.

ACKNOWLEDGEMENTS

This research received no dedicated funding and no data was produced as part of this project. I give warm thanks to my colleagues in the Dandelion Collective, Scarlet Hall and Jay Wilkinson, for being creative and steadfast partners in this project. I am also grateful to those who participated in our workshops. Thank you to Ben Anderson, Samuel Berlin, Paul Harrison, Sarah Hughes, and my anonymous reviewers for comments which greatly improved this chapter.

NOTES

1. I have elsewhere used the term 'structuration' for the same reason (Brice, 2020).
2. Rather than imagine liberation as an absolute freedom from power relations entailing a dualistic opposition between power and freedom, 'liberation' here is understood as a dynamic and relational process; a movement towards relative freedom from violence, coercion and constraint.
3. On the relationship of resilience to a *status quo*, see Evans and Reid (2014).
4. The Ethics Committee at Durham University has confirmed that because the chapter is a reflective piece of work based on an experience where no data collection took place, and because the content of the chapter is primarily methodological, conceptual and auto-ethnographic in nature, this project falls outside the remit of formal research ethics protocols. Since the workshops were not intended as research activities at the time, there was no systematic collection of data; nor was consent sought from workshop participants to collect data for research purposes. This chapter therefore uses only auto-ethnographic material, and no identifying information or research data is included from individual participants. All members of the collective have given consent for this discussion of our work and methods.
5. I refer to the Dandelion Collective by name, with the consent of all members. While members have read and commented on this chapter, the argument which it

advances follows my own academic interests, and I alone am answerable for its flaws and limitations.
6. While I write here on resistance to inclusion, I do not hold inclusion itself as a political end goal. For incisive commentary on how 'inclusion' extends violence and coercion, see Ahmed (2012) and Stanley (2021).
7. After numerous delays and extensions, the Conservative government under Johnson eventually decided to disregard the outcomes of this consultation, and GRA reform was limited to a reduction in registration fees and a statement of intention to take the application process online.
8. One exception preferred to understand all struggle in terms of class, while a second felt more comfortable naming himself as an ally.
9. Modelled on a technique taught by the Training for Change collective.
10. There is of course a cost to the performative use of vulnerability by marginalised people to elicit learning and political transformation in members of the marginalising group; for example, trans people doing anti-transphobia work, black people or people of colour doing anti-racism work, disabled people doing anti-ableism work, and so on. A downside of our model as a collective was that we found it draining and exhausting (as well as exhilarating and rewarding) to organise and run the workshops. This, alongside the weight of multiple other commitments and our struggle to source adequate funding, was undoubtedly one of the reasons why the work of the collective has not so far become properly sustainable.
11. The highly structured and controlled environment we created, and which was necessary in this setting to prevent sliding off into opposition, also had its limitations. Given more time for trust to develop, this need for control might be gradually relinquished, thus deepening the transformation.
12. Working 'against the grain' of opposition took a lot of energy, however, because we continuously worked to accommodate the emotional processes of everyone in the space as well as our own. One member of the collective later reflected that this had been a classic example of a 'hardworking *femme*' project.

REFERENCES

Ahmed, S. (2012) *On Being Included*, Durham, NC, Duke University Press.
Ahmed, S. (2014) *Cultural Politics of Emotion*, Edinburgh, Edinburgh University Press.
Ahmed, S. (2016) 'An affinity of hammers', *TSQ: Transgender Studies Quarterly*, vol. 3, no. 1–2, pp. 22–34.
Ahmed, S. (2019) *What's the Use? On the Uses of Use*, Durham, NC, Duke University Press.
Anderson, B. and Harrison, P. (2010) *Taking-Place: Non-Representational Theories and Geography*, Farnham, Ashgate.
Armitage, L. (2020) 'Explaining backlash to trans and non-binary genders in the context of UK Gender Recognition Act reform', *INSEP – Journal of the International Network for Sexual Ethics & Politics*, vol. 3. https://www.budrich-journals.de/index.php/insep/article/view/35949 (accessed 20 July 2021).
Berlin, S. and Brice, S. (2022) 'The Ontopolitics of Gender as Transindividual Relation', in Cremin, C. and Buchanana, I. (eds), *Deleuze, Guattari, and the Schizoanalysis of Trans Studies*, London, Bloomsbury, pp. 9–34.

Boussalem, A. (2021) 'When the spotlight is always on the neighborhood: LGBTQ people from a Muslim background deconstructing imagined borders in Brussels, Belgium', *Sexualities*. DOI: 10.1177/1363460720986932.

Braidotti, R. (2019) *Posthuman Knowledge*, Medford, MA, Polity Press.

Brice, S. (2020) 'Geographies of vulnerability: mapping transindividual geometries of identity and resistance', *Transactions of the Institute of British Geographers*, vol. 45, no. 3, pp. 664–677.

Butler, J. (2011) *Bodies That Matter: On the Discursive Limits of Sex*, Abingdon, Routledge.

Butler, J., Gambetti, Z. and Sabsay, L. (2016) *Vulnerability in Resistance*, Durham, NC, Duke University Press.

Crenshaw, K. (1991) 'Mapping the margins: intersectionality, identity politics, and violence against women of color', *Stanford Law Review*, vol. 43, no. 6, pp. 1241–1299.

Cresswell, T. (2014) 'Friction', in Adey, P., Bissell, D., Hannam, K., Merriman, P., & Sheller, M. (eds), *The Routledge Handbook of Mobilities*, Abingdon, Routledge, pp. 127–135.

Davis, A.Y. (1992) *If They Come in the Morning: Voices of Resistance*, New York, Third Press.

Deleuze, G. and Guattari, F. (2004) *A Thousand Plateaus: Capitalism and Schizophrenia* (trans. B. Massumi), London, Continuum.

Doan, P.L. (2010) 'The tyranny of gendered spaces – reflections from beyond the gender dichotomy', *Gender, Place and Culture*, vol. 17, no. 5, pp. 635–654.

Evans, B. and Reid, J. (2014) *Resilient Life: The Art of Living Dangerously*, Cambridge, Polity.

Faye, S. (2021) *The Transgender Issue: An Argument for Justice*, London, Allen Lane.

Hall, E. and Bates, E. (2019) 'Hatescape? A relational geography of disability hate crime, exclusion and belonging in the city', *Geoforum*, vol. 101, pp. 100–110.

Hamraie, A. (2017) *Building Access: Universal Design and the Politics of Disability*, Minneapolis, MN, University of Minnesota Press.

Hines, S. (2019) 'The feminist frontier: on trans and feminism', *Journal of Gender Studies*, Routledge, vol. 28, no. 2, pp. 145–157.

Hughes, S.M. (2020) 'On resistance in human geography', *Progress in Human Geography*, vol. 44, no. 6, pp. 1141–1160.

Independent Press Standards Organisation (2020) 'New research on reporting of trans issues shows 400% increase in coverage and varying perceptions on broader editorial standards'. https://www.ipso.co.uk/news-press-releases/press-releases/new-research-on-reporting-of-trans-issues-shows-400-increase-in-coverage-and-varying-perceptions-on-broader-editorial-standards/ (accessed 20 July 2021).

Jindal, P. (2008) 'Sites of resistance or sites of racism', in Sycamore, M.B. (ed.), *That's Revolting*, New York, Soft Skull Press, pp. 39–46.

Mahmood, S. (2011) *Politics of Piety: The Islamic Revival and the Feminist Subject*, Princeton, NJ, Princeton University Press.

Namaste, V. (2009) 'Undoing theory: the "transgender question" and the epistemic violence of Anglo-American feminist theory', *Hypatia*, vol. 24, no. 3, pp. 11–32.

Nash, C.J. and Browne, K. (2020) *Heteroactivism: Resisting Lesbian, Gay, Bisexual and Trans Rights and Equalities*, London, Zed Books.

Pearce, R., Erikainen, S. and Vincent, B. (2020) 'TERF wars: an introduction', *Sociological Review*, vol. 68, no. 4, pp. 677–698.

Puar, J.K. (2007) *Terrorist Assemblages: Homonationalism in Queer Times*, Durham, NC, Duke University Press.

Rosenberg, R.D. (2021) 'Negotiating racialised (un)belonging: Black LGBTQ resistance in Toronto's gay village', *Urban Studies*, vol. 58, no. 7, pp. 1397–1413.

Salamon, G. (2010) *Assuming a Body: Transgender and Rhetorics of Materiality*, New York, Columbia University Press.

Schuller, K. (2017) *The Biopolitics of Feeling: Race, Sex, and Science in the Nineteenth Century*, illustrated edition, Durham, NC, Duke University Press Books.

Serano, J. (2007) *Whipping Girl: A Transsexual Woman on Sexism and the Scapegoating of Femininity*, New York, Seal Press.

Sharp, J., Routledge, P., Philo, C. and Paddison, R. (2000). 'Entanglements of power: geographies of domination/resistance'. In R. Paddison, C. Philo, P. Routledge and J. Sharp (eds), *Entanglements of Power*, Abingdon, Routledge.

Snorton, C.R. (2017) *Black on Both Sides: A Racial History of Trans Identity*, Minneapolis, MN, University of Minnesota Press.

Stanley, E.A. (2021) *Atmospheres of Violence: Structuring Antagonism and the Trans/Queer Ungovernable*, Durham, NC, Duke University Press.

Thrift, N.J. (2008) *Non-Representational Theory: Space, Politics, Affect*, International library of sociology, London, Routledge.

Tsing, A.L. (2004) *Friction: An Ethnography of Global Connection*, illustrated edition, Princeton, NJ, Princeton University Press.

Weaver, H. (2014) 'Friction in the interstices: emotion and landscape in Stone Butch Blues', *Emotion, Space and Society*, vol. 12, pp. 85–91.

5. Towards a more-than-human theory of resistance: reflections on intentionality, political collectives and opposition

Carlotta Molfese

INTRODUCTION

Resistance is a key subject area in human geography, being central to many debates in political geography and contributing to the development of critical perspectives and methodologies within the discipline (Routledge, 1996; Sparke, 2008). However, as Hughes (2020) has observed in a recent intervention, the concept of resistance itself has been little examined over the last decades, despite a number of theoretical turns within the discipline.

This chapter engages one such turn that has partly emerged as a critique to anthropocentrism: posthumanism (Braun, 2004). At its core, it challenges the passivity traditionally ascribed to non-human others and foregrounds their 'livingness' (Whatmore, 2006, p. 602) and interconnectedness with human societies. This focus upon the 'vitality' of the non-human challenges some of the basic ontological assumptions of traditional conceptualisations of resistance (Hughes, 2020, p. 1143). This chapter reflects specifically on notions of intentionality, political collectives and opposition, and considers how more-than-human perspectives can assist in developing a non-anthropocentric framework of resistance in critical geography.

It aims to do so for two inter-related reasons. First, while the hybrid and lively character of a more-than-human world is being increasingly recognised, questions still remain regarding the potential for posthumanist thinking to contribute to critical scholarship (Diener, 2020). Developing a non-anthropocentric conceptualisation of resistance can assist in the formulation of an 'insurgent posthumanism' (Papadopoulos, 2010, p. 134) that can contribute to emancipatory and grassroots projects seeking radical social and ecological change. Second, and relatedly, a critical perspective must address the human exceptionalism inherent in many of geography's theoretical tools, including notions of resistance, because they perpetuate human–non-human hierarchies and injustices. A critical geography of resistance can not stop at the boundary of the human, and not simply because this boundary is ever more porous, but also because it is a geographical and historical product that has caused the subjugation and marginalisation of human and non-human communities around the world.

The human-centred focus of conceptualisations of resistance is not surprising given the anthropocentrism of orthodox political philosophies (Bennett, 2010; Whatmore, 2002). Non-humans – be they animals, plants, viruses, technologies, elements, whole ecosystems – have no 'voice', so how could they effectively engage in politics? The interests of some can and have been represented politically by different human collectives, and some successes have been achieved through conventional political processes and fora. However, this approach of 'politicising ecology' (Hinchliffe et al., 2005, p. 650) leaves non-humans as objects of political processes and deliberations. In the case of non-human animals, they are mostly 'passive recipients of human attention, either for being the receptacles of suffering or the bearers of rights' (Driessen, 2014, p. 90); while the great majority of non-human others are mere resources or tools that bear instrumental value to human actors (Braun and Whatmore, 2010). Thinking non-humans as political subjects is another project altogether: one of 'ecologising politics' (Hinchliffe et al., 2005, p. 650).

This chapter does not aim to reconcile the varied ways in which politics is being reworked in more-than-human terms, nor to develop an explicit and unified posthuman political theory. The aim is more modest and the focus more restricted: it brings together the emerging literature that has begun to take seriously the agency of non-humans in political theory, to explore its significance and potential contribution to critical (non-anthropocentric) conceptualisations of resistance. After an introduction to the more-than-human turn and a brief evaluation of resistance relationship to more-than-human perspectives, it examines the ways in which political subjectivity and power are being reworked in more-than-human terms. This chapter finally builds upon these theoretical developments, delineating some of the tensions that must be navigated and advancing a number of suggestions for developing and pursuing a non-anthropocentric conceptualisation of resistance.

THE END OF NATURE AND ITS POLITICS: RELATIONAL ONTOLOGIES

Over the past two decades there has been a growing body of literature within geography – variously termed 'hybrid' (Whatmore, 2002), 'multinatural' (Lorimer, 2012), 'vitalist' (Greenhough, 2010) – that recognises the agency and interconnectedness of the non-human world with human societies, and studies their dynamic co-constitution. These 'more-than-human' geographies have a diverse theoretical lineage (Greenhough, 2010), but have more broadly emerged from a sustained critique of the Nature–Society dualism that underpins the 'modern constitution' of Western society (Latour, 1993, p. 29). This ontological dualism is not a simple affirmation of difference between the natural and social world, but a hierarchical relationship where Nature is defined as the 'Other' of the Human, and therefore as an inanimate and inferior world to that of human societies. This ontological binary has not only generated a deterministic and mechanistic view of the natural world that has promoted its manipulation and exploitation, but has also allowed the unfolding of a series of interlinked dualisms (mind/body, reason/emotion, masculine/feminine, objective/subjective, native/non-native, civilised/wild) that have contributed to processes of 'othering' in human societies too (Plumwood, 1993).

Human geographers have critiqued the Nature–Society dichotomy from many critical perspectives, revealing the power relations hidden in its social construction and material production and exposing its spatial and political consequences. For instance, Marxist geographers and political ecologists have demonstrated how the ideological separation of nature and society has been key to capitalist relations of production, processes of environmental degradation and animal exploitation (Smith, 1984; Blaikie and Brookfield, 1987; Philo, 1995). Similarly, feminist and decolonial geographers have shown how cultural representations of Nature as wild, passive and inferior have contributed to the othering and subjugation of particular social groups within society presumed to be closer to the natural world, including women and indigenous people (Rose, 1993; Anderson, 1997).

More-than-human geographers add to these critiques and challenge binary framings directly by employing a relational ontology that describes the world in its hybrid form, as made up of historically contingent and heterogeneous networks or assemblages of human and non-human actors. As Lorimer (2012, p. 595) explains it: 'Nature, Society and other identities have been rethought as relational achievements, power-laden constructions emergent from "assemblages" of interacting "actants" – not all of whom are human or alive'.[1] In these more-than-human assemblages, no subject or quality precedes the relations but is emergent within the process of relating. Hence agency, or the capacity to act, is not a pre-existing and exclusively human property based on reason, will or intentionality, but it is emergent from and distributed across relations. A more-than-human perspective, then, recognises non-humans – be they animals, plants, objects, technologies, elemental forces – as co-participants in the making of worlds.

With this reformulation of form and agency, more-than-human perspectives have since their inception raised important ethical and political concerns. Above all, in their 'flattening out of agency' (Laurier and Philo, 1999,

p. 1047) they have made questions of difference, power and accountability difficult to address, so their take-up has been slower in more human-centred sub-disciplinary fields such as political geography.

RESISTANCE IN MORE-THAN-HUMAN WORLDS

Conceptualisations of resistance in human geography have been developed to examine and understand the ways in which difference and inequalities are created and contested in the production of space, place and nature (Katz, 2008). However, nature has traditionally been conceived either as a resource and cultural symbol for which struggles are fought, or alternatively as a static, homogenous and passive background against which which they take place; not as being able to shape, or being itself an active agent of, resistance. This is because traditional conceptualisations of resistance rely upon modernist notions of political subjectivity and power that tie resistance to humans, their intentionality and oppositional forms (Hughes, 2020). Such exclusive focus is problematic because it dismisses or excludes non-humans from accounts of resistance based on their (assumed) lack of agency and intentionality, and because it ignores political activities embedded in everyday life.

For instance, while animal geographers have long recognised the entanglement of non-human animals in social networks and practices that exclude and/ or exploit them, attempts at theorising their resistance have been few and far between (Wilbert, 2000; Gillespie, 2016). Instead, geographers such as Philo (1995, p. 656) have preferred using the term 'transgression' to describe the acts of animals violating and challenging the boundaries and categorisations allotted to them by humans in city spaces. The reason being that attributing agency and intentionality to non-human others, as it is conventionally done to humans, runs the risk of anthropomorphism: 'interpreting nonhuman beings through the lenses of what goes on in the human world' (Philo, 1995, p. 656). However, such framings are unnecessarily exclusionary and anthropocentric as they deny non-humans, and particularly animals, diverse capacities and sensibilities, or define them according to human standards.

Similarly, in traditional political ecology accounts, social movements' struggles are often framed in terms of inequalities over access and distribution of natural resources, or between competing environmental discourses and imaginaries (Peet and Watts, 1996). However, as de la Cadena (2010) observes in the case of indigenous politics, while such interpretations are not incorrect, they also tend to occlude or marginalise the relational worlds of indigenous populations which do not ascribe to Nature–Culture binaries. She argues that their resistance against corporate and state exploitation, and destruction of forests, mountains and livelihoods associated with them, is about more than natural resources and 'cultural beliefs', and it involves more than public contestation. They are struggles for a different ontological reality populated by a multiplicity of agentic Earth-beings, spirits and human practices of respect and care, and they take place as much in protests as in everyday life.

Following the more-than-human turn, some political geographers such as Routledge (2008) and McFarlane (2009) have examined resistance in its networked spatiality and more-than-human composition. However, notwithstanding a turn to metaphors of networks, they have paid scant attention to questions of non-human agency, how it may shape or limit resistant practices and networks, or influence the decisions and intentions of resistant subjects (for an exception, see Featherstone, 2004, 2007). For instance, Routledge (2008) has examined the political associations constituting the global network of grassroots peasant movements People's Global Action (PGA) by following humans, non-humans and their relations across the network. However, he concludes that 'it is not the computers, boats, airplanes, etc that direct the work of actor networks, but the social relations – the human *intentionality* – of enacting and embodying the network ... The nonhuman actors, while important to the association ... remain insufficient by themselves' (Routledge, 2008, p. 215). And yet, being a peasant network, it is surprising to see that he only considers those non-humans (mostly technologies) that allow for transnational meetings and connections to occur. Besides some passing references to peasants' livelihoods being intertwined with rivers, cattle, fields, monsoons, and so on, he does not consider how these may have contributed to the formation of the network in the first place, or indeed to human intentionality.

Taking non-human agency seriously in theories and accounts of resistance is about more than adding a neglected technical dimension to political activity. As Hughes (2020, p. 1143) observes, a 'focus upon the vitality of the non-human can serve to displace intention, which is a pivotal component of how resistance is determined in many dominant geographical accounts'. Moreover, thinking in terms of relations rather than entities, and agency as effect rather than a property of individual beings, raises a number of important conceptual questions for resistance: Who/what constitutes a resistant subject? What happens to intentionality? And what forms might resistance take?

Addressing these questions is important not just to theoretically advance critical conceptualisations of resistance. Forms of oppression, exclusion, exploitation, appropriation and commodification are often mediated by the material world, and they extend to and intersect with non-human animals, plants, landscapes and ecosystems (Buller, 2014; Gibbs, 2021). Remaining within an anthropocentric framework that denies non-humans any agency and overlooks how the lives and vulnerabilities of humans, animals and ecosystems are materially mediated and inter-related, reduces political possibilities and can therefore undermine efforts to contest injustices and build more emancipatory worlds.

TOWARDS A MORE-THAN-HUMAN POLITICAL THEORY

Almost two decades ago, critical geographers espoused the need for 'a new "political theory of nature" that can reconceptualise the means and ends of politics in an increasingly hybrid world' (Castree, 2003, p. 203). While this is in no way a *fait accompli*, there is a growing literature in geography that has begun to consider the implications of more-than-human perspectives for political theories, concepts and practices. However, with the diversity of sub-disciplinary interests, theoretical inspirations and empirical examples, these works are disturbingly varied and fragmented. The range of designations used to describe such novel analyses and approaches – 'material politics' (Barua, 2014), 'ontological politics' (Whatmore, 2013), 'cosmopolitics' (Hinchliffe et al., 2005) – is exemplary of this proliferation and confusion. Similarly, empirical examples stretch from large megafauna and inhospitable flora (Hobson, 2007; Sundberg, 2011), to elemental forces (Whatmore, 2013), infrastructures and mundane objects (Hawkins, 2010; Meehan, 2014).

Despite this diversity, these studies do speak to similar concerns and share some common features. Above all, they recognise that politics can not be separated from the myriad of things and beings that constitute our common world, so they turn their attention, quite literally, to the 'stuff' of politics: the material and affective relations between humans, objects, technologies, organisms and ecologies. In doing so, they also enrich traditional political registers based on discursive, representative and procedural terms with practices, arrangements and affects. Most importantly for conceptualisations of resistance, these studies have been reworking notions of political subjectivity and power to account for non-humans and their agency.

Political Subjectivity

Modern notions of political subjectivity originate in Enlightenment thinking that posits a self-conscious and autonomous (human) individual that possesses reason, intentionality and other deliberative capacities necessary to institute a social contract and contribute to a polity (Whatmore, 1997). The ability to speak, in particular, is what has conventionally defined a political subject, because through speech a person is believed to manifest will and intentionality (Driessen, 2014). However, this has resulted in the privileging of defined and contained political spaces, scales, actors and processes in political geography, including 'the false distinctions between the global and public ("Politics"), and the local and private ("politics")' (Hobson, 2007, p. 253).

Over the last two decades, this ontology of the subject has been thoroughly problematised in geography from many critical perspectives (Simpson, 2017). There is now a broad recognition that subjects are not only produced by deeply structured historical processes (political economy, colonialism, patriarchy, and so on) and social mechanisms (language, culture, discourses, knowledge, and so on), but also emerge from embodied experiences and 'encounters with various more-than-human others/alterity' (Simpson, 2017, p. 2). When it comes to political subjectivity, a number of interventions have already begun to foreground the importance of emotions and affects in the formation of political identities and networks (Bosco, 2007; Sziarto and Leitner, 2010). More-than-human scholars add to this literature by foregrounding the ways in which non-humans have the capacity to 'spark new publics into being' (Braun and Whatmore, 2010, p. xxvi) and generate new forms of knowledge and action.

For instance, in her seminal paper that calls for enlarging political geography's ambit to include animals as political subjects, Hobson (2007) examines the politics surrounding the Asiatic black bear, its bile farming networks and conservation groups as they emerge in relation to the bears' own history, ecology, behaviour and physiology. She argues that the bears are not just objects of global capitalist networks, and animal welfare and conservation groups, but active agents in their formation and operation. More specifically, she reveals how through their charismatic appeal, physiological amenability and behavioural placidity, the bears became constituted in and constituted the networks of care and politics surrounding them: 'whilst their ability to be farmed in the first place constituted the bear bile farming trade, their ability (and perhaps willingness?) to be healthy, happy and active once freed has constituted a driving force in the regions [sic] animal welfare debates' (Hobson, 2007, p. 263).

Besides large charismatic animals, Hawkins (2010) has also demonstrated how plastic bags can both trigger and disrupt the formation of new ethico-political subjects and everyday actions depending on their web of associations. In its entanglement with environmental campaigns, the destructive and toxic materiality of a plastic bag has the capacity to generate environmentally aware subjects and new forms of everyday conduct; but in the mundane relations of domestic spaces, its humble practicality as a cheap and convenient waterproof container for everyday use can also disturb the development of more virtuous identity and habits. Another way in which the political agency of non-humans is being foregrounded is through knowledge controversies in which particular non-human entities or phenomena force thought, attachments and associations, turning 'matters of fact' to 'matters of concern'. For instance, Whatmore (2013, p. 36) has argued for the 'earthly powers' of floods as affective events that can force thought in those affected by them, and create new knowledge polities and civic associations that can challenge established practices and claims around flood risk and management.

However, it is also important to note that there has been little consideration so far of whether certain affects, (dis)attachments and encounters with non-humans are unequally distributed along axes of social difference (gender, class, race, sexuality, and so on), and how these can contribute to the (un) making of political subjectivities by hindering or enhancing the affective and political capacity of non-humans.

Power

More-than-human scholars have also built upon Foucauldian notions of biopower and biopolitics to take seriously 'the entanglement' of humans and non-humans in forms of power and governance (Rutherford and Rutherford, 2013). In these perspectives, power is no longer understood as a reified and unified totality, but as a 'relational effect' (Allen, 2004, p. 19) emerging from assemblages of human and non-human beings and forces. Hence, non-humans are not just subjects or tools of power, but they are constitutive of it: they can act as catalysts or 'power-brokers' (Meehan, 2014, p. 217) with the capacity to mediate, produce and reconfigure political arrangements, practices and orders.

For instance, in her study of the water infrastructures of Tijuana, Mexico, Meehan (2014) examines objects not just as 'tools' of states, but as conduits of power that help to produce, arrange and consolidate state authority. Hence, the complex assemblage of laws, engineers, scientific data, dams, rivers, aqueducts and pumps that went into constituting the municipal water infrastructure materially reconfigured the hydrosocial cycle of the city, paving the way for capital accumulation and federal state control, while cultivating people's dependency on a distant and centralised water source. At the same time, though, she notes how the 'raw empirics of water – its divisibility, flow regime, and weight', in conjunction with household objects such as rain barrels, cisterns and buckets, 'permit alternative infrastructural and institutional configurations to proliferate alongside and in spite of state control' (Meehan, 2014, p. 222). Hence, different more-than-human configurations allow for different worlds to exist and be enacted, and some are more just than others.

More recently, animal geographers have begun to engage critically with non-human animals not just as subjects of (in)justice, but also as beings whose action and entanglement within particular multi-species networks and socio-economic arrangements have justice implications for other forms of life (Hovorka, 2019). For instance, Margulies and Karanth (2018) have examined the entangled geographies of humans–cattle–carnivores in India, taking into considerations not just social structures but also the role of cattle as an intermediary animal in human–wildlife conflicts. They note how state-enforced economic and spatial rearrangements of these rural landscapes, through new wildlife conservation laws and the use of hybrid races of cattle, have created new spaces of encounter and conflict between farmers and tigers. More specifically, because of their higher economic value and biological sensitivity than traditional races, hybrid cattle are grazed near farmers' homes and have shifted human–wildlife conflicts from forests to villages. Similarly, but in the context of pig factory farming in North Carolina, Stoddard and Hovorka (2019) consider the role of farmed pigs as vulnerable beings, but also active agents that can influence and shape others' vulnerabilities in the face of global environmental change. They demonstrate how pigs' lives, health and wellbeing are compromised within intensive farm animal production, but also how these conditions render farmers, local communities and surrounding ecosystems more vulnerable to extreme storms and flooding by exposing them to anxiety, illnesses, economic losses and environmental pollution. Most importantly, by considering non-human agencies in their entanglement with specific socio-economic systems and agrarian practices, both of these studies show how 'the vulnerabilities of animals, humans, and ecosystems are necessarily interconnected and interdependent' (Stoddard and Hovorka, 2019, p. 153).

To summarise, more-than-human reconsiderations of political subjectivity and power recognise non-humans as political subjects, not in the rationalist sense of entities capable of participating in institutionalised decision-making processes or simply as subjects deserving rights, but as active agents of political life. Through their relational affectivity and enrolment in particular relations and practices, they have the capacity to bring concerned publics into being, create new forms of knowledge and action, mediate power relations and vulnerabilities, and reconfigure practices and orders. However, non-humans are not political in themselves: their material and affective agencies are the outcomes of specific relations and arrangements. Their political capacities are thus normatively variable: they can open up as well as constrict political opportunities (Braun and Whatmore, 2010).

FOR A NON-ANTHROPOCENTRIC CONCEPTUALISATION OF RESISTANCE

The works reviewed go beyond the anthropocentrism of modern political theories that consigns non-humans to a state of passivity, as either instruments of humans or recipients of their attention and compassion, by demonstrating how they have the capacity to affect our social and political worlds. However, they do not explicitly address how such reframing can contribute to more just and emancipatory political trajectories. Developing a non-anthropocentric conceptualisation of resistance can advance such efforts, but a number of inter-related theoretical tensions related to how resistant subjects and power have been traditionally theorised must be navigated first.

The most significant incongruity lies in a broad reliance upon humanist frameworks of intentionality, which are closely tied to modernist ideas of political subjectivity that negate or dismiss non-humans and their agency. In conjunction with more-than-human perspectives, a post-phenomenological reading of subjectivity, such as that advanced by Ash and Simpson (2016), can assist in reconceptualising intentionality in non-anthropocentric terms. As they argue: 'rather than suggesting that human life and agency be considered in a hierarchical relationship against the non-human, we would argue that the appearance of human life and agency is only ever an outcome gifted to us through a relationship with non-human objects' (Ash and Simpson, 2016, p. 55). Hence, such reframing would not deny human intentionality within resistant acts, but it would account for the role that non-humans play in the formation of resistant subjects and their intentionality. Put differently, with intentionality reconceived as 'an emergent relation with the world, rather than an a priori condition of experience' (Ash and Simpson, 2016, p. 48), a non-anthropocentric conceptualisation of resistance would recognise that non-humans 'have the capacity of *making others act*' (Rodríguez-Giralt et al., 2018, p. 260) by shaping their affective dispositions, identities and intentions.

Examples of such capacities are most developed in the literature on environmental and animal rights activism. For instance, in the Chilean mobilisation against the destruction of a wetland ecosystem investigated by Sepùlveda-Luque (2018, p. 335), it was the agency of swans, and in particular their suffering, that turned out to be 'the most agentive force within the struggle, displaying a capacity to "move" all sorts of actors to "do" things in response'. Similarly, Armiero and Fava (2016) tell the tragic, yet also transformative, tale of how a dying shepherd and his sheep living and working in the toxic landscapes of the periphery of Naples, Italy, contributed to the formation of a local and regional environmental justice movement. Here, in the corporeal experiences of and encounters with contaminated environments, human and non-human bodies had 'transformative power, contributing to uncovering the unjust distribution of environmental burdens and converting victims into activists' (Armiero and Fava, 2016, pp. 67–69). Hence, rather than conceiving non-humans as passive beings and assuming intentionality to be pre-existing within resistant subjects, a non-anthropocentric framework pays attention to how resistant subjects are enrolled by non-human others, how their intentionality emerges from their embeddedness within particular socio-material contexts and more-than-human affective encounters and relations. Uncovering and taking seriously these bodily and affective connections is not just a theoretical exercise. As Armiero and Fava (2016, p. 69) argue, placing humans and their bodies within more-than-human ecologies can make visible the histories and systems that exploit both humans and non-humans, and 'lead to a quest for a more-than-human emancipatory project'.

Moreover, while it is difficult to think of non-humans as having intentionality in the conventional (humanist) sense, a post-phenomenological reframing of intentionality as 'practical consciousness' (Wilbert, 2000, p. 250) can also assist in recognising acts of resistance of non-human animals as more than mere transgressions. For instance, when farm animals repeatedly escape, kick, bite and refuse to eat and work, they may not be reflexively thinking about and conceptualising their plans, but they are taking action against the anthropocentric systems that makes them subordinate and exploitable as it manifests through the material conditions of their existence, including their everyday spatial and bodily management (Gillespie, 2016). This is intentionality of a 'non-reflexive kind' (Wilbert, 2000, p. 250), but purposive action nonetheless. Again, reframing intentionality in non-anthropocentric terms in order to recognise animals' own efforts to resist oppressive relations is not just theoretically significant: it forces us to recognise animals as autonomous subjects, and therefore the possibility and significance of 'interspecies alliances' to address animal oppressions and their intersections with human societies (Gillespie, 2016).

But why stop at animals? Building upon more-than-human reconceptualisations of power that recognise the capacity of non-humans to mediate and reconfigure power relations, a non-anthropocentric framework of resistance can expand the subjects of resistance to include a variety of non-human allies and attend to the ways in which 'more-than-human collectives' can disrupt political regimes and practices. Within the social movement literature, Galis and Summerton (2018) have examined the 'cyber-material alliances' of activists and counter-technologies in Sweden to subvert immigration control on public transport; while Sepúlveda-Luque (2018) has foregrounded the power of citizens/swans associations to address and reconfigure destructive environmental practices. Within geography, Featherstone (2004, 2007) has long argued for the importance of material arrangements and strategic interventions in the configuration of human and non-human relations for subaltern political struggles. For example, the political activity of the 18th century Irish peasant movement the Whiteboys, against land enclosures and unjust market and labour relations, was enacted and constituted through experimental collaborations and active interventions in the configurations of associations between cottiers, land, animals, potatoes, ditches, fences, middlemen and landlords (Featherstone, 2007).

However, as Hughes (2020) has noted, bringing non-humans and their vitality into conceptualisations of resistance also means that the forms which resistance may take cannot be predicted in advance in terms of intentionality and opposition, but must be traced in their emergence and potentiality. This is because through their circulation and associations with other materials and/or subjects, non-humans 'may exceed the apparent intentions of human subjects' (Hughes and Forman, 2017, p. 675). This in turn entails the need to go beyond the more familiar alliances and 'tools' that are (intentionally) enrolled into practices of resistance (banners, computer technologies, disruptive artwork), and to consider more ordinary or even unintentional associations and doings that have the potential to disrupt power in its multiple forms and more-than-human configurations. For instance, Rezvani (2022, p. 1600) has analysed the cultivation, care and breeding of open-pollinated crops by peasants as a form of 'interspecies resistance' against industrial monocultures and agribusiness control. However, neither peasants nor plants are intentionally resisting industrial agricultural practices and corporate seed monopolies, nor is their resistance oppositional in form. What constitutes resistance here is the 'relations of response-ability and relational freedom between crop plants and farmers', enacted through everyday tinkering, caring, growing and pollinating, because they create the material conditions for small-scale, agroecological peasant farming system to exist and persist (Rezvani, 2022, p. 1600). Hence, a non-anthropocentric conceptualisation of resistance also attends to those experimental practices and modes of doing in relation with non-human others that disrupt the certainty of established political regimes and practices, and keep the future open by creating the conditions for alternative and more just socio-material orderings to emerge. Attending to heterogeneous associations engaged in such 'world-building activities' (Featherstone, 2007, p. 303) offers resources for thinking about political identities and agencies which have often been ignored or dismissed by theories of resistance relying upon subjects' intentionality and opposition, and opens up new political possibilities.

Perhaps, with its experimental ethos and focus upon the construction of alternatives within, beyond and against hegemonic regimes and orders (Pickerill and Chatterton, 2006), the anarchist concept of prefiguration could be a potential resource to enrich a non-anthropocentric conceptualisation of resistance and explore its experimental and multiple, situated forms. However, like conceptualisations of resistance, it has so far been little scrutinised, and remains within modernist dichotomies that privilege social (as in human-to-human) relations. More work is therefore needed to theorise and engage with experimental more-than-human collectives 'which are more equal, less riven by unequal geographies of power, less ecologically wasteful and damaging than the collective experiments of neoliberal globalisation' (Featherstone, 2007, p. 303).

CONCLUSION

This chapter has begun to consider the implications of more-than-human perspectives for conceptualisations of resistance. It has argued that traditional conceptualisations of resistance rely upon anthropocentric framings that are unnecessarily exclusionary: they not only deny non-humans any capacity to act, and neglect how choices and actions may be limited or shaped by them, but they also reduce political possibilities. Indeed, this residual anthropocentrism is not only theoretically inadequate, but also politically problematic because it hinders a better appreciation of how social and natural worlds are interconnected, and therefore how struggles are or may be engaged in. By building upon work that is revising two important categories of political thought, this chapter has highlighted some of the tensions that more-than-human perspectives bring to traditional conceptualisations of resistance, and has put forward ways to navigate them in order to develop a non-anthropocentric framework of resistance.

It has advanced a post-phenomenological reading of intentionality that does not deny its significance within resistant practices, but acknowledges non-human agency in its formation and allows geographers to recognise non-human animals' acts of resistance. However, such a redistribution of agency and intentionality also destabilises and multiplies the traditional (human) subjects of resistance, requiring an expansion of what a political collective is, how it comes into being and the political work it does. Indeed, by shifting attention to more-than-human collectives a non-anthropocentric conceptualisation of resistance also extends beyond oppositional forms to consider mundane, (un)intentional practices and arrangements that do not necessarily oppose hegemonic regimes, but create the conditions for alternative worlds to emerge. In light of this, the chapter has also suggested a potential avenue for future work in the anarchist concept of prefiguration.

Overall, this chapter has argued for the development of a non-anthropocentric conceptualisation of resistance not only to address the residual humanism of geographical theories, but also in order to develop a more insurgent posthumanism that is able to recognise and engage with resistant forms and actors that are fighting against injustices and are attempting to build more liveable more-than-human worlds.

NOTE

1. The concepts of 'assemblage' and 'actant' originate from different theoretical sources but they are related in their endeavour to reframe both agency and form in relational terms. More specifically, 'actant' is a modification of the term 'actor' devised to include non-humans and their relations as sources of action. Similarly,

'assemblage' is the English translation of the French term '*agencement*' and it relates agency with the coming together or the 'gathering' of different entities and beings.

REFERENCES

Allen, J. (2004), 'The whereabouts of power: politics, government and space', *Geografiska Annaler, Series B: Human Geography*, Vol. 86 No. 1, pp. 19–32.
Anderson, K. (1997), 'A walk on the wild side: a critical geography of domestication', *Progress in Human Geography*, Vol. 21 No. 4, pp. 463–485.
Armiero, M. and Fava, A. (2016), 'Of humans, sheep, and dioxin: a history of contamination and transformation in Acerra, Italy', *Capitalism Nature Socialism*, Vol. 27 No. 2, pp. 67–82.
Ash, J. and Simpson, P. (2016), 'Geography and post-phenomenology', *Progress in Human Geography*, Vol. 40 No. 1, pp. 48–66.
Barua, M. (2014), 'Volatile ecologies: towards a material politics of human-animal relations', *Environment and Planning A*, Vol. 46 No. 6, pp. 1462–1478.
Bennett, J. (2010), *Vibrant Matter: A Political Ecology of Things*, Duke University Press, Durham, NC.
Blaikie, P.M. and Brookfield, H.C. (1987), *Land Degradation and Society*, Routledge, London.
Bosco, F.J. (2007), 'Emotions that build networks: geographies of human rights movements in Argentina and beyond', *Tijdschrift Voor Economische En Sociale Geografie*, Vol. 98 No. 5, pp. 545–563.
Braun, B. (2004), 'Querying posthumanisms', *Geoforum*, Vol. 35 No. 3, pp. 269–273.
Braun, B. and Whatmore, S.J. (2010), *Political Matter: Technoscience, Democracy, Public Life*, University of Minnesota Press, Minneapolis, MN.
Buller, H. (2014), 'Animal geographies I', *Progress in Human Geography*, Vol. 38 No. 2, pp. 308–318.
de la Cadena, M. (2010), 'Indigenous cosmopolitics in the Andes: conceptual reflections beyond 'politics'', *Cultural Anthropology*, Vol. 25 No. 2, pp. 334–370.
Castree, N. (2003), 'Environmental issues: relational ontologies and hybrid politics', *Progress in Human Geography*, Vol. 27 No. 2, pp. 203–211.
Diener, S. (2020), 'New materialisms', *The Year's Work in Critical and Cultural Theory*, Vol. 28 No. 1, pp. 44–65.
Driessen, C. (2014), 'Animal deliberation', in Wissenburg, M. and Schlosberg, D. (eds), *Political Animals and Animal Politics*, Palgrave Macmillan UK, London, pp. 90–104.
Featherstone, D. (2004), 'Spatial relations and the materialities of political conflict: the construction of entangled political identities in the London and Newcastle port strikes of 1768', *Geoforum*, Vol. 35 No. 6, pp. 701–711.
Featherstone, D. (2007), 'Skills for heterogeneous associations: the Whiteboys, collective experimentation, and subaltern political ecologies', *Environment and Planning D: Society and Space*, Vol. 25 No. 2, pp. 284–306.
Galis, V. and Summerton, J. (2018), 'We are all foreigners in an analogue world: cyber-material alliances in contesting immigration control in Stockholm's metro system', *Social Movement Studies*, Vol. 17 No. 3, pp. 299–317.
Gibbs, L. (2021), 'Animal geographies II: Killing and caring (in times of crisis)', *Progress in Human Geography*, Vol. 45 No. 2, pp. 371–381.

Gillespie, K. (2016), 'Nonhuman animal resistance and the improprieties of live property', in Braverman, I. (ed.), *Nonhuman Animal Resistance and the Improprieties of Live Property*, Routledge, pp. 117–132.
Greenhough, B. (2010), 'Vitalist geographies: life and the more-than-human', in Anderson, B. and Harrison, P. (eds), *Taking-Place: Non-Representational Theories and Geography*, Taylor & Francis, New York, pp. 37–54.
Hawkins, G. (2010), 'Plastic materialities', in Braun, B. and Whatmore, S.J. (eds), *Political Matter: Technoscience, Democracy, and Public Life*, University of Minnesota Press, Minneapolis, MN, pp. 119–138.
Hinchliffe, S., Kearnes, M.B., Degen, M. and Whatmore, S. (2005), 'Urban wild things: a cosmopolitical experiment', *Environment and Planning D: Society and Space*, Vol. 23 No. 5, pp. 643–658.
Hobson, K. (2007), 'Political animals? On animals as subjects in an enlarged political geography', *Political Geography*, Vol. 26 No. 3, pp. 250–267.
Hovorka, A.J. (2019), 'Animal geographies III: species relations of power', *Progress in Human Geography*, Vol. 43 No. 4, pp. 749–757.
Hughes, S.M. (2020), 'On resistance in human geography', *Progress in Human Geography*, Vol. 44 No. 6, pp. 1141–1160.
Hughes, S.M. and Forman, P. (2017), 'A material politics of citizenship: the potential of circulating materials from UK Immigration Removal Centres', *Citizenship Studies*, Vol. 21 No. 6, pp. 675–692.
Katz, C. (2008), 'Social systems: thinking about society, identity, power and resistance', in Clifford, N., Holloway, S.L., Rice, S. and Valentine, G. (eds), *Key Concepts in Geography*, SAGE Publications, London, pp. 236–250.
Latour, B. (1993), *We Have Never Been Modern*, Harvard University Press, Cambridge, MA.
Laurier, E. and Philo, C. (1999), 'X-morphising: review essay of Bruno Lafour's Ariimis, or the Love of Technology', *Environment and Planning A: Economy and Space*, Vol. 31, pp. 1047–1071.
Lorimer, J. (2012), 'Multinatural geographies for the Anthropocene', *Progress in Human Geography*, Vol. 36 No. 5, pp. 593–612.
Margulies, J.D. and Karanth, K.K. (2018), 'The production of human–wildlife conflict: a political animal geography of encounter', *Geoforum*, Vol. 95, pp. 153–164.
McFarlane, C. (2009), 'Translocal assemblages: space, power and social movements', *Geoforum*, Vol. 40 No. 4, pp. 561–567.
Meehan, K.M. (2014), 'Tool-power: water infrastructure as wellsprings of state power', *Geoforum*, Vol. 57, pp. 215–224.
Papadopoulos, D. (2010), 'Insurgent posthumanism', *Ephemera: Theory and Politics in Organization*, Vol. 10 No. 2, pp. 134–151.
Peet, R. and Watts, M. (eds) (1996), *Liberation Ecologies: Environment, Development, Social Movements*, 2nd edn, Routledge, London and New York.
Philo, C. (1995), 'Animals, geography, and the city: notes on inclusions and exclusions', *Environment and Planning D: Society and Space,* Vol. 13 No. 6, pp. 655–681.
Pickerill, J. and Chatterton, P. (2006), 'Notes towards autonomous geographies: creation, resistance and self-management as survival tactics', *Progress in Human Geography*, Vol. 30 No. 6, pp. 730–746.
Plumwood, V. (1993), *Feminism and the Mastery of Nature, Environmental Values*, Vol. 6, Routledge, New York. https://doi.org/10.1016/0743-0167(96)82231-5.

Rezvani, L. (2022), 'Cultivating response: peasant seed and plant–human collaboration in an agro-industrial heartland', *Environment and Planning E: Nature and Space*, Vol. 5 No. 3, pp. 1597–1617.

Rodríguez-Giralt, I., Marrero-Guillamón, I. and Milstein, D. (2018), 'Reassembling activism, activating assemblages: an introduction', *Social Movement Studies*, Vol. 17 No. 3, pp. 257–268.

Rose, G. (1993), *Feminism and Geography*, Polity Press in association with Blackwell Publishing, Cambridge.

Routledge, P. (1996), 'Critical geopolitics and terrains of resistance', *Political Geography*, Vol. 15 No. 6–7, pp. 509–531.

Routledge, P. (2008), 'Acting in the network: ANT and the politics of generating associations', *Environment and Planning D: Society and Space*, Vol. 26 No. 2, pp. 199–217.

Rutherford, S. and Rutherford, P. (2013), 'Geography and biopolitics', *Geography Compass*, Vol. 7 No. 6, pp. 423–434.

Sepúlveda-Luque, C. (2018), 'Bringing animals within political communities: the citizens/swans association that fractured Chile's environmental framework', *Social Movement Studies*, Vol. 17 No. 3, pp. 333–352.

Simpson, P. (2017), 'Spacing the subject: thinking subjectivity after non-representational theory', *Geography Compass*, Vol. 11 No. 12, pp. 1–13.

Smith, N. (1984), *Uneven Development: Nature, Capital and the Production of Space*, Blackwell Publishing, Oxford.

Sparke, M. (2008), 'Political geography – political geographies of globalization III: resistance', *Progress in Human Geography*, Vol. 32 No. 3, pp. 423–440.

Stoddard, E.A. and Hovorka, A. (2019), 'Animals, vulnerability and global environmental change: The case of farmed pigs in concentrated animal feeding operations in North Carolina', *Geoforum*, Vol. 100, pp. 153–165.

Sundberg, J. (2011), 'Diabolic caminos in the desert and cat fights on the Río: a posthumanist political ecology of boundary enforcement in the United States–Mexico Borderlands', *Annals of the Association of American Geographers*, Vol. 101 No. 2, pp. 318–336.

Sziarto, K.M. and Leitner, H. (2010), 'Immigrants riding for justice: space-time and emotions in the construction of a counterpublic', *Political Geography*, Vol. 29 No. 7, pp. 381–391.

Whatmore, S. (1997), 'Dissecting the autonomous self: hybrid cartographies for a relational ethics', *Environment and Planning D: Society and Space*, Vol. 15 No. 1, pp. 37–53.

Whatmore, S. (2002), *Hybrid Geographies: Natures Cultures Spaces*, SAGE Publications, London.

Whatmore, S. (2006), 'Materialist returns: practising cultural geography in and for a more-than-human world', *Cultural Geographies*, Vol. 13, pp. 600–609.

Whatmore, S.J. (2013), 'Earthly powers and affective environments: an ontological politics of flood risk', *Theory, Culture and Society*, Vol. 30 No. 7–8, pp. 33–50.

Wilbert, C. (2000), 'Anti-this–against-that: resistances along a human—non-human axis', in Sharp, J.P., Routledge, P., Philo, C. and Paddison, R. (eds), *Entanglements of Power: Geographies of Domination/Resistance*, Routledge, London, pp. 238–255.

6. Activism and resistance: activist dispositions and the hidden hierarchies of action

Charlotte Lee

INTRODUCTION

'Activism' and 'resistance' are often conflated and used interchangeably within geographical literature, meaning that the assumptions around activism are similar to those around resistance, such as 'intentionality' and 'form' (Hughes, 2020). For example, of a Washington, DC Women's March in 2017, Hughes (2020: 1141) writes: 'The form of this protest – a march – aligns with a conventional conceptualisation of resistance within geography: organised opposition to a particular configuration of power relations.' Here, arguably, 'activism' could just as easily be substituted for 'resistance'. Martin and Pierce (2013: 63) observe that the '[u]se of one term or another tends to signal orientation to different scholarly audiences' rather than any substantial differentiation between the terms. Furthermore, Martin et al. (2007: 81) describe how a resistance lens to activism is constricting: 'resistance to power is not necessarily the main purpose of creating change in one's community, nor does the concept of resistance adequately capture the full scope of the outcomes of activism'. Such an ingrained association therefore limits how activism is enacted, perceived and researched, influencing what is valued and counted, and what actions and actors are enabled or hindered.

In particular, such conflation reproduces assumptions around what 'counts' as activism (Martin et al., 2007), who counts as an activist, and what impact such acts can produce. In addition to Martin et al. (2007), I draw here on Thrift's (1996: 2) division in his explanation of agency, 'understood as both the production of action and of what counts as action (and of actors and of what counts as actors)', to help unravel this entangled relationship between resistance and activism and the effects on geographies of activism. Firstly, such an association implies that activism is always an oppositional and confrontational act, which in turn is imbued with assumptions around intentionality and power

(Bayat, 2000; Hughes, 2020). Secondly, and perhaps more importantly, it implies a hierarchy of actions, with more dramatic acts being of greater importance and having greater potential of outcome, in turn implying assumptions around scales of effect. Thirdly, these are not merely theoretical concerns: they are enacted in the everyday, and create a privileged and exclusionary identity of the 'activist' (Chatterton and Pickerill, 2010; Maxey, 1999). Therefore, there is an equal need to rethink activism separately from our rethinking of resistance; as Ruddick writes: 'the meaning, content and context of our activism has changed over time and must continue to change' (Ruddick, 2004: 230), especially due to the increasing prevalence of activism in a multitude of forms. Resistance, I argue, should be considered a *disposition* present in some activism, rather than the sum total of activism. In my use of 'disposition', I draw on Jullien's (1995) phrasing around the 'disposition of things', and therefore not necessarily simply a human disposition, as well as Horton and Kraftl (2009: 19) 'tentatively label[ling] as a kind of activist disposition' their interviewees' 'collective inclination towards frustration and an implicit feeling that something should/could be done'. Furthering both, I argue that such dispositions are only one element amongst many that make up the 'conditions for action' in activism (Lee, 2013), and that our focus needs to shift more towards the conditions from which activism can and does emerge, rather than our current emphasis on the acts themselves.

In embarking on this chapter I realised that as an activist researcher,[1] in particular of global north climate activism, I considered resistance to be a form of activism, that is, activism which seeks to explicitly resist something; whereas many resistance researchers may consider the reverse, that is, activism is a particular form of resistance, the extreme end of a spectrum of resistance from everyday subtle acts to what we may typically think of as activism, namely 'direct'[2] actions such as protests, marches, and so on. Both are of course the consequence of 'habits' of thinking, as Bennett (2010)[3] would say, and the need to arrange our understandings into groupings and hierarchies, but they also reflect our personal relationships with the terms. My own experience is one in which 'activism' has always more accurately captured what I, and those I acted with, practised through actively striving to act on a particular issue rather than simply halt or oppose something. 'Resistance' has additionally always implied a more combative approach. In both cases there are implicit gendered implications behind the terms. Chatterton and Pickerill (2010: 478), for example, write of the association of 'resistance' with the 'great man of history', 'the militant figure who is dedicated to revolutionary change and detached from the mundanity of everyday reality'. Similarly, Brown and Pickerill (2009: 27) observe that in the 'direct' action often associated with activism, 'masculine gendered performances can abound, as activists compete with each other to see who can be most daring'. They note that 'this macho heroism is not only performed by men' (ibid.), but their observations highlight that these hierarchies of activism are also gendered such that the default activist is assumed to be male or to embody masculine qualities.

With a view to countering the implicit hierarchies of activism, we might ask why subtler acts of resistance, such as those referred to in this book, cannot instead count as acts of activism. Such questions should not be considered foreclosed by this book, and indeed have already been posed within broader activism literature (e.g. Martin et al., 2007), and more recently in 'implicit' (Horton and Kraftl, 2009), 'quiet' (Askins, 2014, 2015; Bayat, 2000; Pottinger, 2017) and 'slow' (Murrey, 2016) activism literature, but arguably not explicitly in relation to 'resistance' and without consideration of whether a prefix such as 'quiet', 'implicit' or 'slow' fully moves forward our assumptions of activism. The very fact that geographers have this choice of terminology, 'activism' and 'resistance', demonstrates the current lack of clarity. Nearly two decades after Ruddick (2004: 230) wrote of 'the conflicted nature of the meanings generally ascribed to the term', we are still not always explicit in our use of 'activism', and it is often positioned as inherently in opposition to that which is 'passive' and inactive (ibid.).

This chapter largely approaches activism from the perspective of global North activism literature;[4] however, the literature upon which I draw comes from a range of empirical settings, for example, from childcare centres in the global North to practices of informality in the global South, demonstrating that activist assumptions cut across a range of acts and spaces. While this chapter is largely theoretical, it is inevitably informed by my personal and academic experience. Climate activism is increasingly prominent in broader society and academic literature; this is both heartening and frustrating, especially when there is not always acknowledgment of how long activists have been acting on the climate crisis prior to the more recent Fridays for Future and Extinction Rebellion. Such activism, while welcomed by established activists and researchers, does to an extent reproduce some of the assumptions highlighted above. This chapter therefore seeks to think through our assumptions around 'activism' and 'resistance', and doing so is about, as Horton and Kraftl (2009: 22) write, 'broadening the debate about what constitutes activism and what activism can do'. The central thread is the hierarchies of action implied by this association, exploring in turn 'direct' action, everyday activism, and the expansion of literature around differently named and more specified activism, that is, quiet, implicit and slow, before concluding with the start of a way forward, namely a consideration of resistance as simply one among many *dispositions* present within activism.

HIERARCHIES OF ACTION

Direct Action

The language that geographers tend to associate with activism, not only 'resistance' but equally specific terms such as 'direct' action, 'protest', 'mobilisation' and 'social movements', often leads to the assumption that activism is inherently collective and combative, often phrased as a group 'struggle' or 'fight' against something (Anderson, 2004; Chatterton and Pickerill, 2010; Pickerill and Chatterton, 2006). Of course, part of our inseparable view of activism and resistance is tied up with the history of activism as we generally conceive it, namely our association of the terms with prominent and large-scale (and generally Western) social movements with clear intentions and oppositions; for example, the suffragettes, civil rights movement, nuclear disarmament, environmental movement, and so on. Such prominent historical movements involved mass numbers of people being mobilised against a clearly defined issue, and were often to an extent successful, suggesting that only similarly scaled actions can be effective and produce similar effects. Additionally, as Horton and Kraftl (2009) note, such historical and ingrained associations lead us to associate activism with key famous figures and particular 'isms' (for example, feminism, environmentalism, and so on).

More recently, 'direct' action came to prominence in the United Kingdom (UK) through the anti-roads protest movement[5] of the 1990s, which arguably account for at least part of the roots of current UK climate activism. Such environmental direct action is described by Jon Anderson (2004) as encompassing:

> the use of traditional spaces of political protest (for example public inquiries, high court actions or public petitions), more radical spaces of action (for example street demonstrations, illegal land occupation), and the invention of new spaces of protest (for example cyber-activism, shareholder protests, and 'subvertising') (ibid.: 107)

Here 'direct' action is perceived as taking the 'fight' directly to the perpetrators or the specific space being contested; therefore, intentionality is nearly always assumed. Furthermore, not only is 'direct' action often the default type of action with which the term 'activism' refers to, but in turn, it is often seen as the pinnacle of activism, as the prominent activist geographer Pickerill (2008) writes:

> It is only in recent years that I have realised how blinkered I was. The notion of what constituted activism had become fixed, bound up in radical environmental rhetoric that direct action was not just the best tactic but a life choice. As a result, anything less felt ineffectual. (ibid.: 484)

Similarly, in Chatterton's (2006) article 'Give up activism', it is really 'direct' action which is being given up. While Chatterton rightly points to the disempowering and dividing work of activist versus non-activist identities, and 'the need to transcend activist spaces and identities, to seek creative alliances' (ibid.: 260), here activism is imagined as 'environmental direct action (EDA)', epitomised by the blockade of an oil refinery which forms the focus of Chatterton's article.

'Direct' action, and its association with resistance, 'impl[ies] intention – purposeful action directed against some disliked entity with the intention of changing it or lessening its effect' (Cresswell, 1996: 22); it is assumed that 'direct' action, like resistance must be explicitly and intentionally directed towards something. Rather than 'resistance', Cresswell prefers the term 'transgression', which 'in distinction to resistance, does not, by definition, rest on the intentions of actors but on the *results* – on the "being noticed" of a particular action' (ibid.: 23). However, transgression equally implies that such action must be 'noticed' to count, much like highly visible acts of 'direct' action. Additionally, the emphasis placed on the results implies such acts must have a clear and immediate tangible effect to count, even if that effect was not necessarily sought or intended.

Despite Cresswell's critiques of resistance, we still see the interchangeable use of 'activism' and 'resistance' in the activism literature. Prominent activist geographers, such as Pickerill and Chatterton, tend towards 'resistance' in their labelling of activism, though with some clauses and conditions: 'The kinds of activism that we explore ... identify more complex forms of contention and resistance politics that are not simply oppositional but simultaneously interweave "anti-", "post-" and "despite-" capitalisms' (Chatterton and Pickerill, 2010: 476). Here, while the precise form of activism's opposition is complicated, there are still oppositional implications, just not necessarily always directly oppositional.

More recently, in the work of Chatterton (e.g. Chatterton et al., 2013) and the prominent activist scholar Routledge (2017), activism is nearly always in 'direct' action or protest form. In Chatterton and Heynen (2011), 'resistance', 'collective social action' and 'activism' are used simultaneously and largely interchangeably, and here the empirical example is one of typical 'direct' action in the form of 'climate disobedience' on a train carrying coal to a power station in England. Similarly, Routledge (2004, 2010, 2017) has repeatedly written of the emblematic activism of the counter-globalisation Clandestine Insurgent Rebel Clown Army. More recently, Routledge (2017) continues to focus on highly visible forms of 'direct' action, within both the global North and South, which are intentionally and overtly directed towards clearly defined opponents, meaning that understandably here 'resistance' is often used interchangeably with 'activism'. However, less spectacular and more 'everyday' forms of activism are gaining increasing attention within geographical literature, perhaps partly as a response to the increased notice now given to the everyday, embodied, emotional and affective within geography more broadly.

Everyday Activism

The empirical focus of much activism research, namely its preoccupation with intentional, dramatic 'direct' acts of activism, has hindered the ability of other less visible and less overtly intentional forms of activism to permeate activism literature and '(re)produce[d] a particular version of activism' (Horton and Kraftl, 2009: 16). Horton and Kraftl (2009: 16) observe that activism is often positioned as outside or in opposition to the 'mainstream' and 'everyday', with activist researchers 'often foregrounding autonomous spaces of/for radicalism and opposition'. Here 'autonomous spaces' refers to academics such as Pickerill and Chatterton (2006) who call for greater attention to more mundane and everyday acts of activism, because '[p]eak moments of resistance rest upon the often hidden but vital support structures where resistance is defined and planned' (ibid.: 738). Pickerill and Chatterton's call is situated within the growth of interest in 'the everyday' more broadly, rather than actually problematising the assumptions of activism. Indeed, to some extent Pickerill and Chatterton (2006) further reinforce the prominence of 'direct' action (that is, the 'peak moments') by arguing for the need to explore everyday activism precisely *because* of the way in which they contribute to 'direct' action: 'Most importantly, we explore the role of everyday practices in these movements' constitution, as they work alongside – indeed comprise vital building blocks for – mass protests' (ibid.: 731)

While Chatterton and Pickerill (2010) broaden this argument later, framing such actions as building blocks towards activist aims in themselves – 'everyday practices are used as building blocks to construct a hoped-for future in the present' (ibid.: 476) – there is still a sense in which everyday actions only count insofar as they contribute to definite and tangible goals. Moreover, the concern is still with overtly intentional and collective acts; for example, activist meetings within a social centre enacted by a self-identified group of activists. Individual and less explicit forms of action are overlooked and implied to not count.

Conversely, the everyday activism within Horton and Kraftl's (2009: 21) research is 'the everyday against which activisms are typically figured; or they are the everyday which goes completely unwritten in accounts of the "everyday" of activism'. Therefore, attention to everyday activism in Pickerill and Chatterton's case is to the 'everyday' within 'recognisable activisms', and not 'the banal activisms momentarily and modestly enmeshed in everyday lives' (Horton and Kraftl, 2009: 21). Such resistance-orientated activism literature, therefore, still reproduces a hierarchy of actions in which 'direct' action is considered the central focus of activism. For example, Routledge (1996), prior to and like Chatterton and Pickerill, situates 'direct' acts as central, but simply assembled from the everyday: 'terrains of resistance ... are assembled out of the materials, practices, becomings and knowledges of everyday life' (ibid.: 517). The everyday is portrayed as revolving around activism, rather than activism revolving around or being inseparable from the everyday. Routledge, like Pickerill and Chatterton, is interested in intentional acts enacted by those easily labelled as activists. More recently, Routledge (2008) highlights the mundane and administrative acts which are enacted in an activist network, such as 'attending meetings and conferences, and performing coordination tasks' (ibid.: 201). For Routledge, the acts which count are those which intentionally attempt to contribute to the maintenance and construction of this broader collective network.

In some of Routledge's most recent work (Routledge, 2017), 'everyday activism' often refers to mundane acts of reproduction within 'direct' action spaces. For Routledge, such acts are only worthy of consideration as activism in themselves in exceptional spaces; for example, 'in Palestine, everyday activities can themselves constitute resistance' (ibid.: 37), or the Occupy movement in 2011, where at the protest camps 'the reproduction of everyday life was also a form of political activism' (ibid.: 56). There is a sense here, and in Pickerill and Chatterton above, in which literature on everyday activism feels the need to justify itself by situating it within larger or longer-term frameworks of 'direct' action, in particular collective acts by an easily identifiable activist organisation or group. Arguably, here there are underlying gendered associations in which acts of reproduction are automatically deemed lesser, despite the increasing valuing of reproductive acts and practices of care more broadly in geography (Hall, 2020).

The expansion of literature on everyday activism often appears to be about acknowledging that more mundane acts contribute to seemingly more important elements, which in Chatterton and Pickerill's case is often 'direct' action and tangible activist goals, and for Routledge the building and sustaining of explicit and overt activist networks, which themselves often practice 'direct' action. In both cases, such acts only count if the contribute to intentional collective action, a term in itself often used interchangeable with 'activism' and 'resistance' (e.g. Chatterton and Heynen, 2011). Where this is the case, it further reinforces the hierarchies of action present within activism discourse, as such acts are not considered worthy of attention in their own right, nor of having transformative and productive effects in themselves.

Part of the reason for this privileging of 'direct' action is arguably assumptions around scales of effect, in which more dramatic and mass actions are assumed to have the potential for more significant effects and on a larger scale.

More mundane, easily overlooked, or individual acts are assumed to have a lesser potential of effect, and even then only on a small and more immediate scale, that is, it is assumed that they cannot have effects of the same magnitude as mass dramatic acts. Though this assumption appears logical, outcomes are not always logical and scale does not always work in this way: in the words of Latour, 'A giant in a story is not a bigger character than a dwarf, it just does different things' (Latour, 1988: 30 cited in Bingham and Thrift, 2000: 286); a point which, in turn, can be read from Thunberg's (2019) book title, *No One is Too Small to Make a Difference*. Assuming these scales of effect both discourages smaller or individual acts which are not necessarily any less productive of change, and places too much pressure on larger or group acts to deliver significant and tangible outcomes. There are clearly also gendered dimensions to these scale assumptions, not least the implication that the personal scale is not relevant to activism or an effective form of activism, something which feminists have long demonstrated to be far from the case (Hanisch, 1970).

From a feminist perspective, Martin et al.'s (2007) pivotal paper argues for attention to what Horton and Kraftl (2009) might term 'banal' everyday activism, for example, 'small acts of social networking or social change' (Martin et al., 2007: 78), and for an opening up of the 'category of activism' 'to consider actions and activities that, because of their limited geographic reach, normally are considered too insignificant to count as activism' (Martin et al., 2007: 79). As Martin et al. argue, such banal acts can produce change, but in their work the scale of such change is assumed, like the acts themselves, to be small. Therefore, while their focus is not on the centrality of 'direct' action or typical spaces of activism, there are still assumptions around the potential scale of effect of such action. In turn, therefore, there is still the implication of a hierarchy of acts, as it is considered that such banal acts 'may not in themselves create direct political action but that foster the social relationships that may enable future political action or organizations' (Martin et al., 2007: 78). Martin et al. (2007: 80) ultimately 'situate [such] activism as a potential precursor to formal movement', suggesting a hierarchy in which a full social movement should always be considered the ultimate goal and the most effective form of action.

Indeed, as Martin et al. (2007) go on to state, they aim to 'move, explicitly and theoretically, "down" the political action hierarchy to conceptualize the nascent stages of political action and movement formation' (ibid.: 81). While they problematise the downward hierarchical scale there is still the implication of a linear scale. Similarly, later Martin et al. discuss how in one of their examples 'an individual has moved further along the political-action hierarchy by mobilizing others in her social network to address a problem within the community' (ibid.: 90). Like the terms I discuss in the next section, Martin et al. similarly prefix their type of activism with 'embedded', implying a differentiation from typical and singular 'activism'. However, their writing makes important and impassioned arguments for making visible acts which were previously largely invisible and overlooked, which is likewise an aim of the literature I discuss in the following section.

Quiet, Implicit and Slow Activism

While researchers are increasingly turning their attention to 'quiet' (Askins, 2014, 2015; Bayat, 2000; Pottinger, 2017), 'implicit' (Horton and Kraftl, 2009) and 'slow' (Murrey, 2016) activism, such language still implies a hierarchy of action, as though such acts cannot simply be termed 'activism' and instead must be prefixed with a proviso. Present within these prefixes is the assumption that activism *is* and *should* normally be loud, visible, explicit, overt, fast-acting and immediate, in turn implying 'masculine gendered performances' (Brown and Pickerill, 2009: 27). We might argue that the majority of activism is quiet, implicit and slow, suggesting that what we consider the norm is simply the most visible and obvious forms of activism.

In what can be considered a pivotal article on the rethinking of activism (alongside Martin et al., 2007), Horton and Kraftl (2009) offer multiple critiques of preceding activism literature and several ways in which activism conceptions can and should be broadened and rethought. Fittingly, Horton and Kraftl's radical theoretical critiques are, like their participants' activism, put forward with 'little fanfare' or 'fuss'. However, in prefixing the activism they describe taking place 'from *within* the social spaces of the post-welfarist, neo-liberal state' (ibid.: 17) with 'implicit', they still imply that the 'norm' of activism is explicit and overt. Similarly, in their discussion, they often refer to their chosen activism as 'discrete modes of activism' (ibid.: 21), and as involving a 'banal activist disposition' (ibid.: 19), likewise implying that activism is and should normally be more visible and extraordinary, or at the very least that the norm is activism which is less modest and which does involve a fanfare.

In a similar vein, in her research around a refugee befriending scheme in England, Askins (2014: 354) puts forwards what she terms a 'quiet politics' – 'an unassuming praxis of engaging with others, in which new social relations are built in/through everyday places, relationally connected across a range of geographies' – but contrasts this to Horton and Kraftl's 'implicit activism': 'These relationships are explicit, there is a political *will to engagement* that requires commitment' (Askins, 2015: 476). For Askins, there is no less will to such 'unassuming' actions; however, there is still the sense that such acts, like implicit activism, are positioned along a linear scale of action or continuum: 'Recent work on activism in geography has been unpicking the everyday activities in quotidian spaces which are part of a broader continuum of movements for change' (Askins, 2015: 475). Quiet politics, which is arguably quiet activism,[6] is positioned as 'fragile' (ibid.: 354), implying a contrast to the presumably 'stronger', and by implication more masculine, forms of action that we typically associate with activism.

Drawing on Horton and Kraftl, Askins, and Martin et al. (alongside Hackney, 2013), Pottinger (2017: 216), in her research around gardening and seed saving, argues for an explicitly 'quiet activism', which she likewise describes using feminine qualities, as 'characterised by qualities of gentleness, slowness, subtlety and subversion', again implying a contrast to less gentle 'direct' action. However, contrary to previous literature, 'direct' action is positioned as ineffective by both Pottinger and her participants, and almost childish in its 'demands to be seen and heard': 'the quietness of gardeners' practice is often conceived in contrast to discursive, demonstrative forms of action (shouting, arguing, protesting, placard-waving) that demand to be seen and heard' (ibid.). Here, there is a reversing of the hierarchy of actions in terms of their assumed effects, which could partly be attributed to the unreasonable expectations made of typical forms of activism to fully resist and initiate change, and less attention or worth given to smaller, less tangible and longer-term effects of 'direct' action. Pottinger justly argues that quiet activism should be considered no less worthy of attention or effecting change. Quiet and noisy (that is, 'direct') activism are also contrasted by Pottinger in terms of the speed of their approach to action, including the stillness of quiet activism versus the presumed rapid movement of 'direct' action. Like more typical forms of activism, quiet activism is positioned as 'purposeful' and contrasted with an implied lesser form of more 'passive' action: 'Gardeners' practices ... represent a purposeful rather than passive expression of quietness' (Pottinger, 2017: 217). Activism, for Pottinger, must be assertive, active and intentional, even if quietly and slowly so.

Furthermore, the perpetuating of the activism norm, implicit in even the above work, also privileges a generally Western and white activism in which there is less fear of repercussions, as Murrey's (2016: 226) rightly points out in her research on 'slow dissent' in relation to the Chad–Cameroon oil pipeline: 'Politico-ethnic affinities and a fear of the repercussions of resistance actions are two factors that restrict imaginaries of possible action.' In Murrey's work, such slow dissent is positioned alongside 'quiet' forms of action, and there is understandably an underlying assumption that the dissent here *should* be louder. While in Pottinger's case quietness is an active choice for her participants in terms of the type of activism they choose to practice, in Murrey's case slowness is born of necessity.

Similarly, and prior to all of the above work, sociologist Bayat (2000) put forward the concept of 'quiet encroachment'[7] to understand the gradual everyday acts subaltern of the global South to improve their lives, in particular through practices of informality. Like Murrey's work, the subtle and incremental process implied by Bayat's phrase is a product of constrained conditions and 'driven by the forces of necessity, the necessity to survive and improve a dignified life'; however, such acts are performed 'not as a deliberate political act' (Bayat, 2000: 547). Further, Bayat offers an in-depth critique of the assumptions of resistance literature long before our more recent re-engagement with it as geographers, including highlighting the lack of a clear conception of resistance, and the assumed intentionality and oppositional nature of such acts. Additionally, Bayat argues that within resistance literature there is an overestimation of the potential of everyday acts and an underestimation of systems of power, namely state power, meaning that such acts often 'float around aimlessly in an unknown, uncertain and ambivalent universe of power relations' (Bayat, 2000: 544), and, in turn, there is a lack of theorising of such acts' broader conditions within resistance literature.

Bayat's discussion rightly signals the need for greater distinguishment in what we mean by 'activism' and 'resistance', and what such acts are trying to do: for example, to defend an existing condition or claim, or to extend or 'encroach' new claims and conditions. 'Quiet encroachment', therefore, demonstrates the strength of a clearly defined and specified naming of acts, and the importance of understanding and theorising the specific conditions from which such acts emerge. More recent literature posits whether activist dispositions can in fact also be imbued in apparent inaction (Wilkinson and Ortega-Alcázar, 2019) in which there is a 'passive dissent' in the 'right to be weary' (ibid.: 164) and a right to not explicitly or implicitly 'resist'. We could see Wilkinson and Ortega-Alcázar's interviewees, young people experiencing some of the worst effects of UK austerity, as advancing or 'quietly encroaching' in their claims for a right to inaction, a right to not have to be the quintessential energetic activist in the face of adversity, where an improvement of their lives must be (at least for now) an apparent halting of action.

Subtler prefixes such as 'quiet', 'implicit' and 'slow' do at least counter assumptions around the type of actions that count as activism, who counts as an activist (even if only as quiet, implicit or slow activists), and the temporal and spatial scale on which such actions can occur. In turn, such literature is paving the way for a dismantling of the engrained association of activism and resistance. Alongside these theoretical developments, the empirical focus of such research is shifting and moving beyond spaces, acts and actors typically associated with resistance. However, there are still ingrained assumptions around what effect these different forms of activism can produce, and the implication of a hierarchy of actions in which 'direct', collective and masculine-style acts still reside at the top.

ACTIVIST DISPOSITIONS

Previously (Lee, 2013) I have reflected on waiting to become an activist and to practice 'real' activism through the act of waiting for a climate march to begin. Similarly, during the height of the Covid-19 pandemic, myself and fellow members of a climate choir had been waiting to practice our activism in the form of singing with local youth strikers. Our activism, it seemed, was on pause and in limbo, and our fortnightly online rehearsals were about staying in a constant state of readiness for such action. Our regular online meetings and communication did not count in our eyes as activism in itself. As we have seen, even prior to our recent predicament, such activism has often gone unacknowledged and uncelebrated as activism; and while now gaining increasing attention, this is often made provisional through prefixes of 'quiet, 'implicit' or 'slow', suggesting only a partial acknowledgment of the ways in which these acts and actors count (Martin et al., 2007) as activism. Arguably, a large part of the problem is the ingrained assumptions that we hold around activism, and the seemingly inseparable and interchangeable way in which we often talk about activism and resistance.

Resistance should be considered a *disposition* to some, but not all, acts of activism. Some activism is of course actively and explicitly resisting, but even within such explicitly resistant activism other inclinations and desires are present. Perhaps the most obvious counter to a resistance disposition is a creative one, as other activist scholars have noted (e.g. Pickerill and Chatterton, 2006), and such activism can have a subtly creative disposition to 'rework' or 'reconfigure' (Martin et al., 2007: 81) existing relations, actions and spaces. However, such creative dispositions and potentials are often, like resistance, assumed to require an intentional 'creating', and positioned as always occurring alongside or simultaneously to the more important work of resistance. Equally, other forms of activism may be more concerned with maintaining or try to enable things to '*continue as normal*' (Horton and Kraftl, 2009: 22) or to simply 'survive' in the face of adversity (Wilkinson and Ortega-Alcázar, 2019). Here we can also look to Katz's (2001) conceptions of 'resistance', 'resilience' and 'reworking' as signally different activist dispositions.

Within resistant, creative and survival (or 'reworking' and 'resilience') dispositions of activism, so-called quiet, implicit and slow approaches can additionally be considered specific 'activist dispositions' (Horton and Kraftl, 2009), rather than how we come to fully define and label such activism. In other words, seeing such leanings as part of the 'conditions for action' (Lee, 2013) within these activisms, as signalling a particular relationship with the space, action, moment and the associated assumptions around 'activism'. For example, Horton and Kraftl (2009: 20) ask why their participants felt that they must proceed with 'not too much fuss', and suggest that 'the styles of activism experienced by individuals like Sure Start users are constrained by multiple manifestations of (working) classed and gendered assumptions'. This is not to say that Horton and Kraftl's participants *should* be practising more explicit activism, but rather that we as researchers *should* take seriously the conditions for action in all forms of activism, with the ultimate aim of fostering the potential for open and uninhibited – though not necessary resistant – activist dispositions. Future research could, for example, seek to understand why such actions were pursued, what constraints or assumptions may have inhibited such actions, and how actors can be supported or encouraged to pursue further actions. Like Bayat (2000), we should seek more specific ways of naming and describing the acts we research, resisting (ironically) the urge to fall back on 'activism' or 'resistance', even with prefixes or provisos, and understand the conditions of power from which such acts emerge and are constrained. By acknowledging activism assumptions and the ways in which they contribute to the broader agency of activism, and 'restrict imaginaries of possible action' (Murrey, 2016: 226), we should seek to counter, or at least not reproduce, the hidden hierarchies of action with activism.

NOTES

1. Here meaning someone who both practices and researches activism.
2. I use quotation marks here to unsettle the notion that such forms of action are more *direct* than others.
3. Drawing on Bennett's (2010) phrasing of 'habit' but in a broader sense, who in turn draws on Ranciere: 'partition of the sensible' (ibid.: vii)
4. This is clearly a limitation and unintentionally reproduces the dominance of this literature; however, arguably it is important to unpack such literature precisely because of its dominance and sway in academic activism discourse.
5. Preceded by Earth First! in the United States, and Reclaim the Streets after and alongside the anti-road protest movement (McKay, 1996, 1998).
6. For example, one of the ways in which Askins (2015: 474) describes the befriending scheme as political is the way in which 'these relationships are about remaking society at the local level'.
7. Fittingly, Bayat (2000: 548) also refers to such acts as a 'quiet direct action', and in some ways acts such as those to which he refers are arguably more direct than more typical 'direct' action.

REFERENCES

Anderson, J. (2004). Spatial politics in practice: the style and substance of environmental direct action. *Antipode* 36(1): 106–125.
Askins, K. (2014). A quiet politics of being together: Miriam and Rose. *Area* 46: 353–354.

Askins, K. (2015). Being together: everyday geographies and the quiet politics of belonging. *ACME: An International E-Journal for Critical Geographies* 14: 470–478.

Bayat, A. (2000). From 'dangerous classes' to 'quiet rebels': politics of the urban subaltern in the Global South. *International Sociology* 15(3): 533–557.

Bennett, J. (2010). *Vibrant Matter: A Political Ecology of Things*. London: Duke University Press.

Bingham, N., Thrift, N. (2000). Some new instructions for travellers: the geography of Bruno Latour and Michel Serres. In M. Crang, N. Thrift (eds), *Thinking Space*. London: Routledge.

Brown, G., Pickerill, J. (2009). Space for emotion in the spaces of activism. *Emotion, Space and Society* 2(1): 24–35.

Chatterton, P. (2006). 'Give up activism' and change the world in unknown ways: or, learning to walk with others on uncommon ground. *Antipode* 38(2): 259–281.

Chatterton, P., Featherstone, D., Routledge, P. (2013). Articulating climate justice in Copenhagen: antagonism, the commons, and solidarity. *Antipode* 45(3): 602–620.

Chatterton, P., Heynen, N. (2011). Resistance(s) and collective social action. In V.J. Del Casino Jr, M. Thomas, P. Cloke, R. Panelli (eds), *A Companion to Social Geography*. London: SAGE

Chatterton, P., Pickerill, J. (2010). Everyday activism and transitions towards post-capitalist worlds. *Transactions of the Institute of British Geographers* 35: 475–490.

Cresswell, T. (1996). *In Place/Out of Place*. London: University of Minnesota Press.

Hackney, F. (2013). Quiet activism and the new amateur: the power of home and hobby crafts. *Design and Culture* 5: 169–193.

Hall, S.M. (2020). The personal is political: feminist geographies of/in austerity. *Geoforum* 110: 242–251.

Hanisch, C. (1970). The personal is political. In S. Firestone, A. Koedt (eds), *Notes from the Second Year*. New York: Published by the editors.

Horton, J., Kraftl, P. (2009). Small acts, kind words and 'not too much fuss': implicit activisms. *Emotion, Space and Society* 2(1): 14–23.

Hughes, S.M. (2020). On resistance in human geography. *Progress in Human Geography* 44(6): 1141–1160.

Jullien, F. (1995). *The Propensity of Things: Towards a History of Efficacy in China*. New York: Zone.

Katz, C. (2001). On the grounds of globalisation: a topography for feminist political engagement. *Signs: Journal of Women in Culture and Society* 26(4): 1213–1234.

Latour, B. (1988). *The Pasteurization of France (with Irreductions)*. Cambridge, MA: Harvard University Press.

Lee, C. (2013). The energies of activism: rethinking agency in contemporary climate change activism. Unpublished PhD. http://etheses.dur.ac.uk/6953/.

Martin, D.G., Hanson, S., Fontaine, D. (2007). What counts as activism? The role of individuals in creating change. *Women's Studies Quarterly* 35(3/4): 78–94.

Martin, D.G., Pierce, J. (2013). Reconceptualizing resistance: residuals of the state and democratic radical pluralism. *Antipode* 45(1): 67–79.

Maxey, I. (1999). Beyond boundaries? Activism, academia, reflexivity and research. *Area* 31(3): 199–208.

McKay, G. (1996). *Senseless Acts of Beauty: Cultures of Resistance since the Sixties*. London: Verso.

McKay, G. (ed.) (1998). *DiY Culture: Party and Protest in Nineties Britain*. London: Verso.

Murrey, A. (2016). Slow dissent and the emotional geographies of resistance. *Singapore Journal of Tropical Geography* 37: 224–248.

Pickerill, J. (2008). The surprising sense of hope. *Antipode* 40(3): 482–487.

Pickerill, J., Chatterton, P. (2006). Notes towards autonomous geographies: creation, resistance and self-management as survival tactics. *Progress in Human Geography* 30(6): 730–746.

Pottinger, L. (2017). Planting the seeds of a quiet activism. *Area* 49(2): 215–222.

Routledge, P. (1996). Critical geopolitics and terrains of resistance. *Political Geography* 15(6/7): 505–531.

Routledge, P. (2004). Reflections on the G8 protests: an interview with general unrest of the Clandestine Insurgent Rebel Clown Army (CIRCA). *ACME: An International E-Journal for Critical Geographers* 3(2): 112–120.

Routledge, P. (2008). Acting in the network: ANT and the politics of generating associations. *Environment and Planning D: Society and Space* 26: 199–217

Routledge, P. (2010). Major disasters and general panics: methodologies of activism, affinity and emotion in the Clandestine Insurgent Rebel Clown Army. In D. Delyser, S. Herbert, S. Aitken, M. Crang, L. McDowell (eds), *The SAGE Handbook of Qualitative Geography*. London: SAGE.

Routledge, P. (2017). *Space Invaders: Radical Geographies of Protest*. Radical Geography Series. London: Pluto Press.

Ruddick, S. (2004). Activists geographies: building possible worlds. In P. Cloke, P. Crang, M. Goodwin (eds), *Envisioning Human Geographies*. London: Arnold.

Thrift, N. (1996). *Spatial Formations*. London: SAGE.

Thunberg, G. (2019). *No One is Too Small to Make a Difference*. London: Penguin.

Wilkinson, E., Ortega-Alcázar, I. (2019). The right to be weary? Endurance and exhaustion in austere times. *Transactions of the Institute of British Geographers* 44: 155–167.

7. Making space: relational ethnography and emergent resistance
Sarah Zell and Amelia Curran

INTRODUCTION

I walked through inner-city and suburban areas in Winnipeg, Canada, to community centres, church basements and school gymnasiums. During these trips I did not encounter gang territories; their boundaries, which I surely crossed, went unnoticed. Later, when I knew where gang territories were, at least in a 'regional' sense (for instance, when I knew that crossing Portage Avenue took me from one territory into another), these spaces continued to exist beyond my reach. But young people in these areas were accessing, and making, gang territories as spaces they could see, feel, experience; spaces they brought into being.

In Mexico City, I found myself entering what looked like a regular home in an unassuming, middle-class neighbourhood, and sitting on an uncomfortable plastic chair in a makeshift waiting area. It was hidden away, and there was no signage. Another woman was beside me, nervously twitching her leg and reviewing paperwork. As the labour recruiter who I was meeting eventually led me into a non-descript boardroom, I realized that this was where migrant applicants also waited for an interview, their performances determining whether they would gain admission to her agency's labour pool, and the Canadian jobs on the other side. This was a space of the border: not the formal, territorial border, but an important front-end border in a labour migration journey.

These reflections on geography emerged during our respective fieldwork; each of us was studying different spaces: gang territories in the inner city of Winnipeg, Canada, and the recruitment process and the Canadian border for Mexican migrant workers. We each experienced challenges 'locating' these spaces: they existed in ways that differed from expectations of territory as regionally situated and accessible. They were, in a sense, spaces that resisted identification through conventional research methods which assume that geographies can be accessed by crossing their boundaries and learning what is contained therein. We discuss here how a relational ethnographic orientation allowed us to approach these spaces in assemblage: not as regionally defined locales, but as spaces that emerge through various material practices. In doing so, we were able to recognize these geographies, and also instances of resistance, in new ways.

We bring these cases together not because of their empirical content, but because we adopted a similar methodological approach to studying space, one which allowed each of us to encounter (unexpected, emergent) spaces that came alive in practice, irrespective of their regional coordinates. As the above fieldnotes reflect, we found that our sites defied expectations of spaces as being 'there': they resisted preconceived forms. In one case, gang turf came to be not only as a regional territory, but also as an embodied, mobile space. In the other case, a border space emerges thousands of miles away from its presumed territorial location. While neither of us set out explicitly to research 'resistance', we found that our approaches to studying space offered the possibility of: (1) seeing spaces as emergent forms of resistance; and (2) recognizing (more-than-human) actors and practices that may be resisting (intentionally or not).

In this chapter, following a brief framing of resistance in geographical literature, we discuss how our methodological approach helped us to shift from thinking about resistance in space, to space as resistance. Reflecting on our fieldwork on the boundaries of gang territories and the borders of labour migration, we discuss how a materialist orientation focused on practices helped us to encounter elusive spatial forms, and concomitantly, emergent and seemingly unremarkable instances of resistance. We close with a reflection on the implications of studying resistance as emergent, and our own position as scholars within a 'research-assemblage'.

FRAMINGS OF RESISTANCE IN GEOGRAPHY

Resistance is often conceived of in opposition to power, with intentional human subjects countering the coercive or oppressive exercise of power, and acts of resistance often taking anticipated forms. Within the discipline of geography, Hughes (2020) traces two dominant framings of resistance: as oppositional to power, and as entangled with power. The first includes approaches to resistance rooted in a 'structural shared sense of counter-movement from below' (p. 1145). Much work adopting this framing is informed by the influential work of Katz (2001), in which resistance is distinguished from 'reworking' or 'resilience' through its oppositional consciousness. Recent examples include work on activism and the quotidian tactics of oppressed groups (e.g., Gill et al., 2013; Pottinger, 2017). These studies offer insights into forms of resistance to oppressive or hegemonic power, though they have been critiqued for their foundational assumption of a dualism between power and resistance.

A second framing sees resistance as intimately entangled with power. Much work in this vein draws on Foucauldian-inspired theorizations that refute the separation of power and resistance; resistance is never external to the relation of power (see, especially, Sharp et al., 2000; and the review in Sparke, 2008). There is a rich literature in political geography, in particular, demonstrating the diffusion of sovereign power through an array of actors and entities, including boundaries and borders (e.g., Boyce et al., 2015; Johnson et al., 2011; Jones et al., 2017). In practice, though, many studies still isolate 'forms' of resistance for analysis, and implicitly privilege human subjects, reinforcing resistance as intentional and directed at a 'target' (Hughes, 2020, p. 1147; Alldred and Fox, 2017). Hughes (2020) does note some recent exceptions in urban geography (e.g., McFarlane, 2011; McGuirk et al., 2016). For example, Wideman and Masuda (2018) argue that conceiving of the city through an assemblage approach helped them to recognize the unanticipated ways that planning and place-naming processes stimulated resistance through anti-gentrification activism and the formation of unlikely alliances. While studies informed by relational and assemblage approaches may illustrate how non-human material entities motivate or influence acts or forms of resistance, few show how those entities or boundary spaces themselves become agentic.

Moreover, within both of these framings of resistance, Hughes (2020) argues, geographers tend to engage with resistance in ways that rest on a priori assumptions about forms of resistance, of what can be considered resistance. Instances of resistance that do not take predetermined forms may be overlooked or erased entirely. Hughes (2020, p. 1141) asks, 'how can geographers also account for the seemingly unremarkable practices' which may not cohere to expectant forms of resistance (for example, activism, protest marches, subversive tactics, and so on), but which nevertheless contribute to conditioning possibilities for future claims? She calls for geographers to engage with resistance in emergence.

Encountering Resistance in Emergence

An alternative approach to encountering resistance comes from a rich body of work in political geography conceiving of power as dispersed through multiple actors. Geographical works drawing on performativity, actor network theory and assemblage thinking conceive of power as plural and diffuse, and attend to the ways in which entities, including subjects and spaces, are made through practice and emerge out of relational encounters. This move reflects a broader materialist turn in geography (Anderson and Tolia-Kelly, 2004; Whatmore, 2006). Challenging matter as inert and passive, new materialist approaches 'affirm matter's immanent vitality', an ontological stance which asserts that matter is both made and contributes to the making of realities (Coole and Frost, 2010, p. 8). This position emphasizes radical relationality in which entities – objects, texts, institutions, humans – have no inherent qualities but instead take form through their relations with other entities (Law, 1999). It thus challenges traditions that privilege a conception of human agency as an essential characteristic of the rational subject, instead seeing the self as emerging out of relational encounters (e.g., Brice, 2020).

Understanding human and non-human entities as emergent has implications for how resistance is conceived. If agency is not an innate characteristic of a solitary, often human, entity, but produced through sociomaterial assemblages, the notion of resistance becomes untethered to an intentional autonomous self. This has two implications. The first is an expansion of the category of who or what constitutes resistance: resistance does not reside solely in the domain of the human subject, and other, non-human entities also have emergent capacity to act as quasi agents and forces of their own (Bennett, 2010). Second, acts or events can emerge as resistant even if not intended: recognizing the vibrant materiality of entities in assemblage 'destabilises intention as a criterion for determining resistance a priori' (Hughes, 2020, p. 1148). Resistance is not necessarily oppositional, nor necessarily intentional. Recent work in geography suggests the importance of seeing resistance (and conditions for resistance) through the emergent, non-intentional, material and non-human (Brice, 2020; Hughes, 2020). We assert that a relational, materialist methodological orientation is one way to do this.

RELATIONAL, MATERIALIST METHODOLOGICAL APPROACHES

Materialist perspectives shift the focus for inquiry to how relational assemblages come to be, but many of the main theoretical texts do not provide recommendations for research practices themselves. Also, a new materialist ontological stance raises questions about 'conventional' research practices, which are often designed with predetermined subjects and objects. In many cases, researchers have turned to experimental, mobile and performative ways of 'doing' research (e.g., Dolphijn and van der Tuin, 2012; Vannini, 2015). This has led to diverse and eclectic research processes, including the incorporation of drawing, photography, movement, sound or story-telling alongside more traditional qualitative methodologies (Fox and Alldred, 2015); multi-sensory collaborations with artists or ecological activities (e.g., Renold and Ivinson, 2014); or novel approaches such as diffraction, encountering research data to see how something 'comes to matter' when approached from various angles (e.g., van der Tuin, 2014).[1]

A growing number of researchers argue that adopting an ontological approach based in new materialism does not necessarily mean doing away with more 'traditional' methods developed through other epistemological frameworks, but prompts their reframing. Fox and Alldred (2015), for example, propose the 'research-assemblage', which comprises all components of the research process: all the bodies, things and abstractions that get caught up in it, including the researcher, data, methods and contexts. This approach reconfigures 'traditional' case studies (Andersson et al., 2020) that identify a predetermined case, or object of inquiry, and then use 'ready-made' methods to examine it. If we use this approach to rethink resistance, we need to consider, first, that resistance may not emerge exclusively through predetermined or expected forms. Keeping the object of research open may reveal emergent instances of resisting. For us, this has meant shifting away from predefined study objects toward practice and performativity.[2]

In our respective projects, we both engaged in multi-sited, relational ethnography. A relational approach focuses on processes, and 'gives ontological primacy not to groups or places, but to configurations of relations' (Desmond, 2014, p. 554). It shifts the focus from asking what or where gang territories or borders are, or what is happening at or in them, instead exploring how they come together through various actors and practices. While critical of its foundations, ethnography's emphasis on immersiveness and fieldwork, of being-in-the-world, was helpful to us. Ethnography allows for flexibility and creativity in combining methods, and promotes attention to the everyday. Also, ethnography fosters an attitude of openness to 'surprise', and careful reflexivity on the part of the researcher, which aligned with the feminist methodological approaches that also informed our research training. This orientation helped us to encounter elusive and emergent spatial practices and relations, and as such, offers new avenues for seeing instances of resistance in our research.

CASE STUDIES

Drawing on examples from our own fieldwork on studies of spaces – gang territories in Winnipeg, Canada, and the borders of labour migration to Canada – we reflect on the methods we used that helped us to: (1) see spaces as emergent forms of resistance; and (2) recognize alternative instances of resistance beyond the intentional or expected.

Elusive Gang Spaces: Amelia's Case

In my work on gang territories as urban spaces, one of the issues that I contend with is their invisibility. Most people have come to know gang territories through media and popular culture; we think of certain blocks or parts of neighbourhoods that are claimed, marked by graffiti, and defended by gang members. Through these images, gang territories seem obvious as places. However, as a research location they are stubbornly difficult to locate. They lack conventional identifying landmarks: there are no walls or obvious signs distinguishing gang territories from their corresponding neighbourhoods, and graffiti is too widespread across urban landscapes to play this role. This tends to be dealt with in two ways. The first is to conceptualize gang territories as 'symbolic spaces', discussed in terms of what they mean to those who are gang-affiliated (Decker, 1996; Horowitz, 1983; Papachristos et al., 2013; Venkatesh, 1997). However, while gang spaces may be invisible to some, they are not immaterial, and foregrounding their symbolic properties can eclipse their materiality. Others focus on their origins, understanding gang territory as resulting from violent predator–prey like interactions occurring between a gang and its rivals (Brantingham et al., 2012); or consider the effects of these boundaries, such as the spatial distribution of violence within and around gang turf (Valasik and Tita, 2018).

Yet the meaning, origins and effects of gang spaces all elide what gang spaces are made of: what makes these spaces material? Reflecting on Mol's (2002) ethnography of a hospital in *The Body Multiple*, I strained to see the equivalencies: she found microscopes and X-rays as the material practices of the body; what were the material practices of gang territories? Without conventional, representational markers, I turned instead to the ways that gang spaces are made material through mobile, expressive and affective bodies that have been overlooked as material, as practices, and as space (Cadman, 2009; Thrift, 2008). Remaining open to the ways gang space might be made, I turned my attention to the movement of bodies through these areas: young people walking, playing, travelling in groups; neighbourhood residents standing together in small groups outside restaurants, smoking, talking on cell phones; people crossing streets, dodging traffic on their way to the corner store. I asked: what distinguished these, as spaces of the inner city, from spaces of gang territories?

In the central Canadian city of Winnipeg, a diverse inner-city community called West Broadway coexists with B-side gang territory. Members of the Indigenous B-side gang wear prominent tattoos with their gang name and images across their bodies. As Brittany, an ex-semi-affiliated B-side gang member describes:

> The most recognizable [gang members] are the ones with the tattoos. You can tell by certain tattoos. Some people have them on their face, their hands, their necks. A whole lot of the B-side have the face tattoos. Most of them are a big 'B'. Some of them have 'WB', it looks like the Warner Bros. logo. Some of them have them on their necks or their arms. But a lot of the really deep-in B-siders have 'B's on their faces and their necks.

While these observations (my own and those of area residents) can be interpreted as the presence of gang members walking within their gang territories, a relational ethnography emphasizes people's everyday actions, activities and behaviours, beyond a description of the practices of an already established space or people. As Desmond (2014) explains, relational ethnography 'takes as its scientific object neither a bounded group defined by members' shared social attributes nor a location delimited by the boundaries of a particular neighborhood or the walls of an organization but rather processes involving configurations of relations among different actors or institutions' (p. 547). Applied to gang territories, we begin to see that the tattoos of B-side members perform a mobile space: as gang members move through B-side regional territory, their tattoos provide a visual spatial materialization of this otherwise difficult-to-see space. Through repeated sightings, the presence of gang tattoos traces this space and its boundaries in an embodied form. As 15-year-old Jordan tells me:

> I've seen people just walking around. You see someone fuzzy walking around, you know? 12-years-old and I'm not going to just keep walking, I'm crossing the road and walking on the other side. Yeah, you can tell, especially with B-siders, B-siders wear Brooklyn Nets and they have tattoos all over their necks. So I just caught on within myself, I'm good, I'll stay away from that side.

As the flow of gang bodies outlines and fills in these areas, their repetitive movements create an inscription that throws into relief a gang space differentiated from surrounding areas. We can think of these tattoos – found on faces, necks and hands – as embodied maps (Kitchin and Dodge, 2007) that slowly, through movement and over time, rematerialize municipally established boundaries of the West Broadway neighbourhood as B-side.

This is more than a regional enactment of territory. B-side tattoos bring depth to the gang space interior; if certain areas are in use more often or in more concentrated ways, these tattoos map not just area but also density as gang bodies congregate or disperse. These embodied maps also show when territory spreads beyond the regional boundaries of West Broadway. As we looked at photos of the B-side gang, an officer of the Organized Crime Unit and Gang Expert Program explained:

> This is [the B-side gang] back at the Community Centre, they're all posing here. They're a little older here. So, they do stuff like this, they return back here to show where they're from, and their territory being West Broadway, this is the area they carved out. And the tattooing has become really big within this group. This particular group has managed to use symbolism associated with West Broadway and they have basically spread it throughout the city.

As these embodied maps extend outward, gang territory follows. The B-side tattoos perform space through the body in real time and in ways that make territory mobile and inhabited. B-side embodied inscriptions and movements map territory as differentially populated and active within boundaries that exist both regionally and as the body.

In this example, we can see space of gang territory resisting dominant spatial forms. It is perhaps easiest to see B-side, as an Indigenous gang, resisting settler-colonial practices of space that have tried to evict Indigenous bodies from these lands (Wolfe, 2006) that are now Winnipeg, Canada. This is indeed what we expect, often, from an understanding of resistance as intentional opposition. It seems reasonable that Indigenous youth would reclaim these regionally designated municipal spaces from which they have been excluded, either by force or through a variety of systemically discriminatory practices. I do not discount nor underestimate the importance of this form of resistance.

However, recognizing a material, embodied version of space reveals other forms of resistance as well. As embodied maps, B-side tattoos join an assemblage of bodies that resist not only whose space this is (resistance in space, over space), but what space is. An assemblage of bodies – human and non-human – materialize a new space, one which resists, or emerges to be other than the dominant (settler-colonial) conception of this space as a defined city neighbourhood. Gang space is made here in form other than colonial staked regionality, and it is made in addition to it: here B-side is not superseding the Broadway neighbourhood, nor is it simply a new way of experiencing it. It performs a space that is multiple, and thus resists the model of territory as a singular, tractable space. In other words, gang spaces do space differently: they are multiple, unclaimable and ephemeral, and as such offer daily possibilities to subvert the power that colonial space exerts. As my fieldnote at the start of this chapter suggests, while these were spaces that I found difficult to access, attending to their embodied practices helped me to recognize their alternative geography: an enactment of territory that resists settler-colonial models of space. This version of territory, however, is lost from view through conventional methods which assume that going to where a space is located is synonymous with access.

This example also illustrates how resistance is not always intentional. B-side emerges in multiple forms, some of which resist traditional Western conceptions of spatiality. But who means to do this? Practices of resistance emerge out of an assemblage of actants: tattoos, items of clothing, colours, gang members, mobility, to name a few. While no one actor meant to achieve this alternative spatiality, it emerges in resistance to dominant understandings of space. This is not to say that an emergent resistance forsakes the role of human intention. Instead, understanding the world as made in assemblage reconfigures agency, and thus resistance, in ways that encourage a relational ethics of accountability between bodies, practices and place. While connections between race, space and crime are often naturalized, understanding gang space as enacted through the embodied material practices of many provides an alternative way to think through, trace and resist these associations. And as I encountered and spoke with gang-affiliated research participants, or police officers, or discuss my findings with others in the academy, I am aware that my own engagement with and framings of these spaces sets conditions for altering them, for various entities involved in their enactment to do them differently.

Labour Migration and Embodied Bordering: Sarah's Case

In recent work on labour migration, I was initially focused on the process of recruitment of migrant workers, including from Mexico, for low-wage jobs in Canada (Zell, 2018). Labour recruiters became a point of entry, and as I remained open to the various actors and entities engaged in recruitment, the border emerged as a spatial concept of emphasis. While traditional conceptions of borders understand them as static and physical territorial lines, theorizing on borders has grown increasingly relational, seeing them as dispersed spatial assemblages, enacted and experienced at myriad sites and by a host of 'unconventional' actors (see reviews in Johnson et al., 2011; Jones et al., 2017). Scholars have come to understand borders as mobile, provisional and performative (Amilhat-Szary and Giraut, 2015; Paasi, 2012; Salter, 2011). A relational ethnographic approach foregrounds the processes and practices of bordering. Paying attention to the various practices of recruiters – as illustrated in my fieldnote at the start of this chapter – I witnessed a Canadian border, emerging through assemblage, thousands of miles away from its presumed territorial location.

I was interviewing a bureaucrat in Mexico City involved in recruiting and processing migrant worker applications. The room felt heavy with stacks of cardboard banker boxes filled with applications, which lined the wall of her small office. I glanced at them several times, and following the movement of my eyes she shook her head at one point, nodding toward the boxes and noting, 'Many of these were rejected because their English is not good enough.' The boxes themselves affected my gaze, which shifted our conversation (and allowed for a 'case-assemblage' to emerge; see Andersson et al., 2020). We began to speak about the role of English language schools and testing regimes, integral to identifying candidates for migration to work in the hospitality sector in Canada. Language assessments can vary widely, with the same individual receiving a different score depending on who conducts the assessment. To standardize and streamline the process, she had contracted one local English instructor whom she trusted.

Following from that conversation, I went to interview the instructor. Entering a house with no markings other than the number, I was a little surprised to be meeting the instructor, José, in his living room. He greeted me and said, '*Voilà*', sweeping his hand around the room. 'This is where the decisions are made.' The interview was long, and at one point, to simulate the assessment process, we were acting out conversations, pretending we were at a restaurant. José explained that he created his own test, specific to the service sector, which involves a written component, an oral component and a role-play scenario. Based on the encounter he has with an applicant, he issues a letter with a score and explanation of their language ability, which is attached to the government application. The performance of a would-be migrant worker is judged by José, often in his living room, where a discretionary decision based on unwritten rules plays out in a space and time, as he put it, 'prior to you ever even going to the "official" border' of the state.

As recruiters construct labour pools for interactive service positions in Canada, a candidate's English competence is often the first factor in deciding someone's admissibility. Third-party recruiters in Mexico City indicated that they first administer (often unannounced) a pre-screening phone call or video interview, and terminate applications if they feel that potential candidates cannot converse sufficiently in English. Some also require language test scores. One recruiter explained:

> The government doesn't believe anything [applicants] say about their English skills until they see the IELTS [International English Language Testing System] results, so we're the same way – send me the results and then I'll talk to you about English, because it's a waste of everybody's time. Of course everybody's gonna say 'my English is perfect.'

Recruiters act as a 'first border' agent. They impose pre-screening requirements just as the government would, and indeed they often do so on behalf of the Canadian government, to make things easier down the road and not 'waste everybody's time'. Another described:

> We vet them ... this guy has a law degree and he wants to come work as a dishwasher? You have to get down to what's motivating them, you know, have they been unemployed a long time? ... Are they committed to the industry? If this guy's interviewed [by the Canadian Embassy], what are his chances of passing?

After English ability, he explained, he imposed an education level maximum (not exceeding high school) for Mexican workers applying for low-wage service jobs, as part of the pre-screening process. His presumption was that those with less human capital have a stronger orientation to low-waged work, and would demonstrate more loyalty to the industry.

Bordering practices can be revealed in particularly telling ways at the scale of the body: as an embodied process, bodies become sites upon which borders emerge as inscribed and embedded (Amoore, 2006; Mountz, 2004). Bordering is also embodied in its emergence through the practices of those performing it. These auditions for entry are bordering practices wherein unsupervised, discretionary decisions are made about who may enter transnational migration routes. Through my fieldwork, I came to realize that a key site of bordering emerged out of the relational encounters between recruiters and migrant applicants.

Like Amelia's case, above, this example illustrates how space itself can be resistant. The performance of space described here provides a counterpoint to a more static, authorized 'official' international border. Migrant bodies auditioning in a pretend living-room–restaurant, or engaging with recruiters through phone calls or digital space, join an assemblage of bodies that materialize a space of the border emerging as other than and in addition to the territorial, jurisdictional line of the Canadian border. Recruiters exercise a form of 'rogue' sovereign power; as I have argued, drawing on Butler (2004), they act as 'petty sovereigns', introducing biases and discriminating in extra-legal ways (Zell, 2018). Through these encounters, mobile and embodied border spaces, which are extra-territorial and extra-juridical, can be seen to emerge. These border spaces, and the sovereign power that inheres in them, resist a model of territory as a singular, hegemonic space. They are multiple, performed, and as such offer conditions for subverting the state power typically associated with nation-state borders and their enforcement.

When we think of resistance to state borders, migrant activist rallies or acts of graffiti on border walls may come to mind. These are intentional and relatively expected forms of resistance which stand in opposition to the assertion of state power that the border represents. However, the practices of recruiters, along with other entities involved in the recruitment process – language assessors such as José, but also migrants, government agents, travel agencies, doctor's offices, applications, websites, even cardboard banker boxes – create border spaces and generate pathways that make (certain) migration(s) easier and more efficient, but also route and delimit movement. While I was not specifically looking for resistance, mapping this case-assemblage through a relational ethnography, I began to recognise other, more mundane, sometimes fleeting instances of resistance.

Recruiters, for one, performed the border in ways that both asserted the sovereign power of the state but also, at times, resisted it. Though they did not necessarily intend to resist state power, through moments of coaching in language assessments, or through relationships of care for the migrants they shepherded through the process, there was the potential for doing the border differently. There were instances when performances might not go exactly as planned, or where recruiters and language assessors, as 'petty sovereigns', were in fact performing the border in ways that subverted state power: making decisions about who should gain access to the Canadian labour market that contradicted or pushed up against official government criteria. Each encounter carries with it the possibility of the border, understood as a sedimented and relational effect, failing to materialize as anticipated. Indeed, my work documented that recruiters at times acted with a humanitarian impulse, intervening to help, care for and protect migrant workers; disrupting and resisting neoliberal productions of migrants as (only) workers. Moreover, I was implicated in these bordering practices: José, for example, adjusted his language test based on my feedback and 'performance'. This case shows that moving away from predefined objects of study, and examining how things come to matter, can enable us to see entities that may be resisting even if they did not intend to, and/or do not fall into an expected form of what is conventionally considered 'resistance'.

DISCUSSION

Space as Resistance, and Seeing Resistance in Emergence

Western models of space, and many traditional methodological approaches to research, conceive of space in 'regional' ways, and tend to ascribe the production of space to a variety of human actors, such as government officials, lawmakers or cartographers (Law and Urry, 2004). An ontological commitment to studying the ways spaces are done changes the metrics between space and resistance. When agency is positioned as a collaborative effect of an assemblage, it unsettles the assumption that resistance is singularly within the domain of human intentionality. In addition to being an oppositional reaction to an outside power, it can also be processual, transitory and diffused (Alldred and Fox, 2017). Understanding spaces through assemblage, and conceiving of them as performed and emergent, means that entities involved in the making of space are becoming with each other (Braidotti, 2002; Haraway, 2008). Through the iteration of practices or performances, spaces can come to be seen or felt as fixed and real, but there is the ever-present possibility for emergent resistance, responses and counter-tactics. This shifts our view of space from being something resistance happens within or towards, to a resistance-generating entity. Just as it is possible for space to be an active force in the emergence and maintenance of colonial and state power and inequality, so it is possible for spaces to be agents of, or conditions for, resistance. Our examples go beyond illustrating how non-human material entities motivate or influence acts or forms of resistance; they also illustrate spatial alterities 'other' than colonial models emerging through an array of more-than-human practices.

If our methods assume that the geographies we study are preformed and accessible as static research locations, we fail to take note of their capacity to resist dominant spatial models in practice. Through our reflections, we show that one way of encountering resistance in emergence is through a relational ethnographic approach that focuses on material practices and processes. This and other materialist methodologies can bring to light the ways in which human and non-human bodies enact spaces that have otherwise been obscured or devalued through conventional understandings of space.[3] Studying space as made in practice not only forces us to refocus assumptions about who or what makes space, but also helps to reveal its emergent and contested nature, enabling us to see instances of resistance beyond the intentional or expected. Through methodological approaches that foreground practices and performativity, alternate resistances, or their potentialities, can be recognized. This approach also prompts us to reflect on our own position as scholars, and the possibilities of enacting resistance within a research-assemblage.

Making Space, and the Researcher's Role in Resisting

Bringing space into being through research entanglements has ethico-political implications, and offers another terrain for resistance. Viewing space as emergent and made through practice reorients the politics of research. It broadens our understanding of who or what is responsible for spaces; and this includes the practices that researchers use to become-with and know them. As researchers, we are not separate entities making decisions about objects or data under study, but are accountable for the spatial forms which we enact through our research practices. A process of inquiry informed by materialism generates not just representations, but configurations of onto-ethical relations with both human and non-human entities, producing 'genuinely new ways of being in the world' (Renold and Ivinson, 2014, p. 374). As part of a research-assemblage, the work of researchers does more than document the world: it materializes the world around them and brings certain spaces – and cases – into view, and into being.

A relational ethnographic approach, informed by a materialist orientation viewing spatial forms as agentic, can open up new lines of inquiry. Such an approach, one that inherently decentres human agency, involves openness and humility on the part of the researcher, who must be okay with letting go of predefined methodologies.[4] The researcher must be open to witnessing, and indeed taking part in, the (re)making of spaces. As such, it also offers potential for researchers to be resistant subjects. Through research practices, researchers can work to reduce, reprivilege or foster certain flows (Fox and Alldred, 2015); there is the possibility of spaces not coming to be in the same way. We are part of the environment we attend to; knowledge practices do not discover, but create the world. The boundaries of gang and border spaces in our work were co-fabricated and enacted in part through the material, theoretical and methodological orientations which we brought to those practices. The way that we bring these geographies into the academy, and beyond, in new ways, changes the ways in which they can be thought and practiced,[5] and can contribute to resisting previous ideas about what these spaces were and how they functioned. Emphasizing the materiality of space is to acknowledge a relational ethics of responsibility that offers the possibility, through practice, of resisting the ways things are in order to make it anew.

NOTES

1. Advocates of 'post-qualitative inquiry' have asked whether we should leave behind 'qualitative research' altogether, noting that each research entanglement creates 'something new and different that might *not* be recognizable in existing structures of intelligibility' (St Pierre, 2019 in Thorpe et al., 2020, p. 35).
2. This approach also prompts us to reflect on our own position as scholars and the possibilities of enacting resistance within a research-assemblage, a point that we return to in the 'Discussion' section below.
3. It is important to note that Indigenous and other non-white, non-Western scholars have long recognized and engaged with such spaces (e.g., Rosiek et al., 2020; Tuck and McKenzie, 2015; Watts, 2013).
4. Acknowledging non-human agency, 'humans need to be comfortable with, perhaps even seek out, a condition of being an instrument of another agency' (Rosiek et al., 2020, pp. 338–339).
5. This includes the liveliness of research stories told through us (Rosiek et al., 2020, p. 341): for example, interviews are brought to new life through testimonial theatre.

REFERENCES

Alldred, P., and Fox, N.J. (2017). Young bodies, power and resistance: a new materialist perspective. *Journal of Youth Studies*, 20(9), 1161–1175.

Amilhat-Szary, A.-L., and Giraut, F. (eds) (2015). *Borderities and the Politics of Contemporary Mobile Borders*. Palgrave Macmillan.

Amoore, L. (2006). Biometric borders: governing mobilities in the war on terror. *Political Geography*, 25(3), 336–351.

Anderson, B., and Tolia-Kelly, D. (2004). Matter(s) in social and cultural geography. *Geoforum*, 35(6), 669–674.

Andersson, Å., Korp, P., and Reinertsen, A.B. (2020). Thinking with new materialism in qualitative case studies. *International Journal of Qualitative Methods*, 19, 160940692097643.

Bennett, J. (2010). *Vibrant Matter: A Political Ecology of Things*. Duke University Press.

Boyce, G.A., Marshall, D.J., and Wilson, J. (2015). Concrete connections? Articulation, homology and the political geography of boundary walls: concrete connections? *Area*, 47(3), 289–295.

Braidotti, R. (2002). *Metamorphoses: Towards a Material Theory of Becoming*. Polity Press.

Brantingham, P.J., Tita, G., Short, M.B., and Reid, S.E. (2012). The ecology of gang territorial boundaries. *Criminology*, 50(3), 851–885.

Brice, S. (2020). Geographies of vulnerability: mapping transindividual geometries of identity and resistance. *Transactions of the Institute of British Geographers*, *45*(3), 664–677.
Butler, J. (2004). *Precarious Life: The Powers of Mourning and Violence*. Verso.
Cadman, L. (2009). Nonrepresentational theory/nonrepresentational geographies. In R. Kitchen and N. Thrift (eds), *International Encyclopedia of Human Geography* (pp. 456–463). Elsevier.
Coole, D., and Frost, S. (eds) (2010). *New Materialisms: Ontology, Agency, and Politics*. Duke University Press.
Decker, S.H. (1996). Collective and normative features of gang violence. *Justice Quarterly*, *13*(2), 243–264.
Desmond, M. (2014). Relational ethnography. *Theory and Society*, *43*(5), 547–579.
Dolphijn, R., and van der Tuin, I. (2012). *New Materialisms: Interviews and Cartographies*. Open Humanities Press.
Fox, N.J., and Alldred, P. (2015). New materialist social inquiry: designs, methods and the research-assemblage. *International Journal of Social Research Methodology*, *18*(4), 399–414.
Gill, N., Conlon, D., and Moran, D. (2013). Dialogues across carceral space: migration, mobility, space and agency. In N. Gill, D. Conlon and D. Moran (eds), *Carceral Spaces: Mobility and Agency in Imprisonment and Migrant Detention* (pp. 239–247). Ashgate.
Haraway, D. (2008). *When Species Meet*. University of Minnesota Press.
Horowitz, R. (1983). *Honor and the American Dream: Culture and Identity in a Chicano Community*. Rutgers University Press.
Hughes, S.M. (2020). On resistance in human geography. *Progress in Human Geography*, *44*(6), 1141–1160.
Johnson, C., Jones, R., Paasi, A., Amoore, L., Mountz, A., Salter, M., and Rumford, C. (2011). Interventions on rethinking 'the border' in border studies. *Political Geography*, *30*(2), 61–69.
Jones, R., Johnson, C., Brown, W., Popescu, G., Pallister-Wilkins, P., Mountz, A., and Gilbert, E. (2017). Interventions on the state of sovereignty at the border. *Political Geography*, *59*, 1–10.
Katz, C. (2001). On the grounds of globalization: a topography for feminist political engagement. *Signs*, *26*(4), 1213–1234.
Kitchin, R., and Dodge, M. (2007). Rethinking maps. *Progress in Human Geography*, *31*(3), 331–344.
Law, J. (1999). After ant: complexity, naming and topology. *Sociological Review*, *47*(1 suppl), 1–14.
Law, J., and Urry, J. (2004). Enacting the social. *Economy and Society*, *33*(3), 390–410.
McFarlane, C. (2011). *Learning the City: Knowledge and Translocal Assemblage*. Wiley-Blackwell.
McGuirk, P.M., Mee, K.J., and Ruming, K.J. (2016). Assembling urban regeneration? Resourcing critical generative accounts of urban regeneration through assemblage. *Geography Compass*, *10*(3), 128–141.
Mol, A. (2002). *The Body Multiple: Ontology in Medical Practice*. Duke University Press.
Mountz, A. (2004). Embodying the nation-state: Canada's response to human smuggling. *Political Geography*, *23*(3), 323–345.
Paasi, A. (2012). Border studies re-animated: going beyond the relational/territorial divide. *Environment and Planning A*, *44*(10), 2303–2309.

Papachristos, A.V., Hureau, D., and Braga, A. (2013). The corner and the crew: the influence of geography and social networks on gang violence. *American Sociological Review*, *78*(3), 417–447.

Pottinger, L. (2017). Planting the seeds of a quiet activism. *Area*, *49*(2), 215–222.

Renold, E., and Ivinson, G. (2014). Horse–girl assemblages: towards a post-human cartography of girls' desire in an ex-mining valleys community. *Discourse: Studies in the Cultural Politics of Education*, *35*(3), 361–376.

Rosiek, J.L., Snyder, J., and Pratt, S.L. (2020). The new materialisms and indigenous theories of non-human agency: making the case for respectful anti-colonial engagement. *Qualitative Inquiry*, *26*(3–4), 331–346.

Salter, M. (2011). Places everyone! Studying the performativity of the border. *Political Geography*, *30*(2), 66–67.

Sharp, J., Routledge, P., Philo, P., and Paddison, R. (eds) (2000). *Entanglements of Power: Geographies of Domination/Resistance*. Routledge.

Sparke, M. (2008). Political geographies of globalization III: Resistance. *Progress in Human Geography*, *P32*(3), 423–440.

Thorpe, H., Brice, J., and Clark, M. (2020). New materialist methods and the research process. In H. Thorpe, J. Brice and M. Clark, *Feminist New Materialisms, Sport and Fitness* (pp. 29–59). Springer International Publishing. https://doi.org/10.1007/978-3-030-56581-7_2.

Thrift, N.J. (2008). *Non-representational Theory: Space, Politics, Affect*. Routledge.

Tuck, E., and McKenzie, M. (2015). *Place in Research: Theory, Methodology, and Methods*. Taylor & Francis.

Valasik, M., and Tita, G. (2018). Gangs and space. In G.J.N. Bruinsma and S.D. Johnson (eds), *The Oxford Handbook of Environmental Criminology* (pp. 843–871). Oxford University Press.

van der Tuin, I. (2014). Diffraction as a methodology for feminist onto-epistemology: on encountering Chantal Chawaf and posthuman interpellation. *Parallax*, *20*(3), 231–244.

Vannini, P. (2015). *Non-Representational Methodologies Re-Envisioning Research*. Routledge.

Venkatesh, S.A. (1997). The social organization of street gang activity in an urban ghetto. *American Journal of Sociology*, *103*(1), 82–111.

Watts, V. (2013). Indigenous place-thought and agency amongst humans and non-humans (first woman and sky woman go on a European world tour!). *Decolonization: Indigeneity, Education and Society*, *2*, 20–34.

Whatmore, S. (2006). Materialist returns: practising cultural geography in and for a more-than-human world. *Cultural Geographies*, *13*(4), 600–609.

Wideman, T.J., and Masuda, J.R. (2018). Toponymic assemblages, resistance, and the politics of planning in Vancouver, Canada. *Environment and Planning C: Politics and Space*, *36*(3), 383–402. https://doi.org/10.1177/2399654417750624.

Wolfe, P. (2006). Settler colonialism and the elimination of the native. *Journal of Genocide Research*, *8*(4), 387–409. https://doi.org/10.1080/14623520601056240.

Zell, S. (2018). *Outsourcing the Border: Recruiters and Sovereign Power in Labour Migration to Canada*. University of British Columbia.

PART II

EMERGENT RESISTANCE: REFLECTIONS FROM THE FIELD

8. 'My existence is resistance': an analysis of disabled people's everyday lives as an enduring form of resistance

Angharad Butler-Rees

INTRODUCTION

'Caring for myself is not self-indulgence, it is self-preservation, and that is an act of political warfare' (Lorde 1988: 129). Resistance has traditionally been associated with masculine concepts of power, strength and defiance (Butler 2016). It is therefore perhaps unsurprising that disabled people have rarely been portrayed as political actors or as individuals capable of engaging in acts of political resistance. Instead, disabled people have regularly been perceived as a 'vulnerable' population group, who are in need of care and protection, as opposed to possessing any individual agency. Vulnerability, as Butler (2016: 1) argues, has long been understood as the opposite of resistance, 'impl[ying] the need for protection ... at the expense of collective forms of resistance and social transformation'.

Drawing upon the scholarship of Lorde (1988) along with other feminist scholars researching acts of 'quiet resistance' (Askins 2014, 2015; Pain 2014; Wilkinson and Ortega-Alcazar 2019), this chapter highlights how disabled people in the United Kingdom can be seen to engage in forms of resistance through their everyday existence and acts of self-care, in a society which honours certain ideal bodies (McRuer 2013) while shaming and dishonouring others which lie outside of this 'norm'. Moving attention away from 'the grandiose, the iconic, and the unquestionably meaning-ful' (Horton and Kraftl 2009: 14), this chapter considers how resistance may be inherent in (disabled people's) everyday quiet, often overlooked, hidden acts of survival and self-care. This chapter therefore helps geographers to extend understandings of resistance to consider wider and less overt or obvious practices.

Within this chapter, I draw on observations and findings from my doctoral research into disability activism in response to austerity. The research consisted of 27 biographical interviews with disability activists from across the United Kingdom (UK). Biographical interviews have been thought to have the potential to give voice to marginalised groups (Goodson, 2001) by placing individuals as experts in their own experiences. Further, they place the emphasis on participants' individual understandings, interpretations and experiences. Alongside this, participant observation was also conducted at 13 disability activist gatherings and events, including, for example, protest, direct action, art activist installations and meetings. The research findings make clear how everyday visibility and existence may serve as central to disabled people's resistance, particularly during times of crisis, where individuals' citizenship and personhood become increasingly under threat.

Disabled people's citizenship has been denied, challenged and contested throughout history. Those with disabilities have often been said to only have partial access to citizenship rights, depicted as 'shadow citizens' (Chouinard 2001: 188), an 'underclass' of failed citizens (Murray and Field, 1990), or even as 'absent citizens' (Prince 2009). While great gains have been made by the Disabled People's Movement over the years, such as the implementation of the 1995 Disability Discrimination Act (now called the Equality Act) and the flourishing of inclusive education, the past decade, with the onset of austerity, has made abundantly clear that disabled people are yet to be treated as full and equal citizens in UK society (Ryan 2019).

A small yet growing body of literature over recent years has sought to highlight disabled people making some inroads and achieving some success as political actors (Berghs et al. 2019; Pearson and Trevisan 2015; Williams-Findlay 2011). Disabled people have been responsible for bringing about a number of policy changes, including anti-discrimination legislation, access to inclusive education and the right to independent living (Berghs et al. 2019). As this small body of literature demonstrates, disabled people have a long and proud history of fighting for their rights. Literature to date, however, has focused predominantly on the more vocal, spectacular, antagonistic and public forms of protest undertaken by disabled people; see for example Campbell and Oliver (1996) on the early actions of the Disabled People's Direct Action Network, where disabled people chained themselves to public transport in an attempt to demand their right to equal access. This preoccupation with disabled people's public forms of protest has largely served to overlook the more private, mundane and everyday forms of resistance enacted by disabled people (see McRuer 2013 for an exception). These forms of resistance are arguably particularly critical under conditions of acute hardship such as that brought about by austerity.

The following section outlines disabled people's unequal treatment following the onset of the UK's austerity programme (2007–08 onwards) and how individuals have sought to resist the grave impacts of policy implementations through political acts of quotidian survival, solidarity and self-care.

EVERYDAY EXISTENCE/RESISTANCE IN THE WAKE OF AUSTERITY

Following the 2008 financial crisis, a programme of fiscal austerity measures was introduced across the United Kingdom, based upon the principle that economic difficulties had been caused by the state's overspending in the public sector (Clarke and Newman 2012). A programme of fiscal retrenchment and 'structural reform' was introduced in an attempt to reduce the debt, which was framed as if it were the only option (Clarke and Newman 2012). Austerity measures, however, were not felt equally across all echelons of society, with women, lone parents, disabled people, Black and minority ethnic, and working-class communities amongst those experiencing the ramifications more profoundly (Emejulu and Bassel 2015; Greer Murphy 2017; Moffatt et al. 2015). Disabled people were amongst those most affected by the measures, as some of the main users of social welfare and public services within our society. Austerity cuts therefore were a very direct attack on disabled people's lives, with, for example, the re-assessment and retrenchment of key disability welfare benefits, the withdrawal of the Independent Living Fund (ILF),[1] and reductions in social care provision as a result of diminished social care budgets.

An inquiry held by the United Nations Committee on the Rights of Persons with Disabilities (UNCRPD) in 2016 found that cuts to public services and social welfare by the UK government had led to 'grave and systematic violations' of disabled people's human rights. The Committee reported breaches under Articles 19, 27 and 28 of the UN Convention on the Right of Persons with Disabilities, however, the government took little action. This was further demonstrated in October 2018 when the Equality and Human Rights Consortium (EHRC), as part of its progress report on disability rights in the UK, noted that: 'The most recent evidence about disabled people's rights is deeply concerning ... across the UK they face serious regression of many of their rights ... Social protections have been reduced and disabled people and their families continue to be some of the hardest hit.'

It is difficult to convey quite how difficult some individuals' lives have become under austerity. During my doctoral research, I heard harrowing personal accounts of participants stuck in their homes, unable to leave, due to a lack of support or investment in accessible council housing. I also heard from individuals who had been forced to wear incontinence pads as a result of reductions to their social care; and those who were left fearful of the arrival of a brown envelope from the Department for Work and Pensions declaring them 'fit for work', withdrawing their access to critical finances and support. Anna, a woman in her forties with a physical impairment and a mental health condition, was one of the participants who relied on the out-of-work benefit, the

Employment and Support Allowance, for her everyday survival. Anna reports: 'You don't know where you are, you are [thinking] how am I going to survive if I don't get this and it's torture. It's PURE TORTURE! they put you through.'

The way in which austerity measures have disproportionately impacted upon the lives of disabled people in the United Kingdom has been seen to illustrate how certain lives within our society are demarcated as being of lesser value (Ryan 2019). As Rose (2001: 21) argues, 'the biological lives of individual human beings are recurrently subject to judgments of worth'. The lesser worth ascribed to the bodies and lives of disabled people has been said to be associated with disabled people's inability to contribute economically to capitalist society (McRuer 2006).

The hardship experienced by disabled people across the country over the past decade has left people decimated and devastated. The focus for many has become about mere survival. Engaging in resistance was framed by many participants as being a necessity, a matter of life and death. There was no alternative. Some participants reflected starkly upon how they would be unable to survive without access to their current level of support. Nathan[2] was one of these individuals, a 41-year-old man from Wrexham, North Wales, with a degenerative disease. The condition had led to him gradually becoming a wheelchair user and developing muscle weakness in his arms and legs. In 2018, at the time of this study, he had 86.5 hours of care a week paid for by the Welsh Independent Living Grant. Nathan's activism was predominantly driven by a sense of fear, hearing of the possible reduction to his number of allocated hours of care as a result of the proposed closure of the Welsh Independent Living Grant (WILG):

> In May 2015, I had a visit from a social worker. And she advised me that without the Welsh Independent Living Grant, my hours of care would be reduced from 86.5 hours a week to 31 hours a week. Now, I can't cope on 31 hours, so I was panicking ... I was in crisis ... I was thinking oh my god I've got to get myself involved in the community more so that I become integral to the community. Therefore, the council would find it more difficult to take hours off me because I could argue well, I need to do this and that. So that was sort of my trigger, all from fear and the reality of what would happen if they removed my support.

Nathan demonstrates how he found himself in a state of heightened anxiety, fearful of the future and what lay ahead. Here we might draw upon Horton's (2016) writing around 'anticipated futures', where he notes that the anticipation of funding cuts can be more troubling than the cuts themselves. For participants like Nathan, it was often the uncertainty of 'not knowing' which was most difficult to deal with. Nathan was of the view that he needed to become a more visible and prominent member of his local community in order to retain his level of care and support; he believed that in doing so, he would be able to gain greater public support and more people would be made aware of his situation. Nathan saw this as being 'the straw that broke a camel's back' in igniting his activism. While Nathan (along with others) had experienced adversity for some time (both prior to and after the onset of austerity), it was at this particular point in time that Nathan felt 'enough was enough', and decided to take action.

Nathan's account shows us how public visibility and occupying public space can in itself be perceived as a form of resistance amongst disabled people. Through simply being present and visible in society, and continuing with his everyday life as a disabled man, he saw himself as challenging ableist expectations and as actively refusing to be silenced or overlooked by the council, social services and indeed the wider community.

In this chapter, 'resistance' is defined as preserving oneself and one's self-worth by pushing back against oppression. Resistance is seen as a 'conscious practice intentionally designed to overcome or change some perceived effect of power' (Rose 2002: 385). Meanwhile, 'activism' is generally understood as everyday 'acts of defiance' (Baumgardner and Richards 2000: 283), having the capacity to act, along with the capacity to make or change history (Jordan 2002). Gitlin (2003: 5) notes how 'It reminds us that the world not only is, but is made'. In this chapter, the two terms are often used interchangeably, with participants frequently conflating them. With activism often heralded as being of greater significance than resistance, it was felt that by using both terms interchangeably, greater recognition could be given to what were seen as everyday political acts of survival.

While a number of participants became involved in anti-austerity campaign groups such as Disabled People Against Cuts[3] (Williams-Findlay 2011), the Broken of Britain[4] and Black Triangle,[5] others perceived their everyday endurance and survival as a form of resistance in itself. Resistance for some participants such as Nathan did not solely mean engaging in confrontational or oppositional acts, but was also demonstrated in making themselves visible, in their slow endurance and desire to keep on living despite experiencing extreme hardship and injustice.

Hedva (2016: 9) has noted how 'most modes of political protest are internalised, lived, embodied, suffering and no doubt invisible'. Here she refers to how marginalised groups within our society (for example, Black, disabled and transgender people), experience various forms of oppression that can cause great suffering. Individuals may as a result live out an embodied daily protest, as they seek to carve out a space for themselves within society. The account of another participant, Robert, largely echoes this experience of engaging in an embodied daily resistance.

Robert is in his early seventies, lives with his wife (who is also his carer) in a city in the South East of England. He became physically disabled during his early forties due to severe arthritis. For Robert, disability activism was much more than campaigning, raising awareness, and sharing views and opinions with others around disability rights. Battling the welfare system and holding onto his existing support had become a full-time job for Robert, as he was continually having to justify himself and his impairment to social services, the local authority and the wider public. He found himself living in a perpetual state of anxiety, with constant worry and fear for the future; a phenomenon associated with austerity more widely (Horton 2016). Robert explained how this had not prevented him from engaging in resistance, however, as he saw the very tasks of everyday endurance and his will to keep going in spite of ongoing pressures as a form of resistance in itself: 'It might be you as a disabled person at home getting on with your life when all the barriers are there to stop you, if that is your experience and you get on with your life. That actually is being an activist!'

We might draw here upon Wilkinson and Ortega-Alcázar's (2019: 157) recent concept of 'slow resistance', seeing Robert's actions 'as a form of politics that is not spectacular or public but instead often hidden, gradual and difficult to detect'. While relatively invisible, these acts of everyday survival are far from insignificant. In contrast to Wilkinson and Ortega-Alcázar's (2019: 164) use of the concept 'slow resistance' to refer to young people's active decision to 'retreat from the relentless drive to move forwards' under austerity, participants in my study saw their desire and tenacity to keep ploughing on, while maintaining a positive visible disabled identity, to be in itself a form of resistance.

Taking an interpretivist approach (Gray 2009) with participants seen as defining their own realities, I amplify their views and argue that endurance during a time of austerity can indeed be seen as a form of disabled people's (slow) resistance. By keeping on going and not giving in despite punitive welfare reforms (targeted largely at disabled people, and perceived as intentionally made to make them feel like a burden on society or as unworthy citizens), participants saw this as an act of slow resistance, not allowing reforms to knock them down or get the better of them.

Robert noted that while he did not seek to directly resist or challenge austerity and the micromanagement of the disabled and the poor, for example via the implementation of benefit sanctions and increased conditionality (DeVerteuil and Wilton 2009; Peck and Tickell 2002), he saw his will to 'keep on going' in spite of such dehumanising policies as a form of resistance in itself, as a refusal to be defeated. Such a viewpoint could be seen to challenge the conceptual binary between 'resilience' and 'resistance' (DeVerteuil and Golubuchikov 2016), by seeing them as inherently interconnected, with resilience (and being resilient) recognised as an important and necessary form of resistance. By engaging in endurance techniques such as 'keeping on going', Robert is enacting a form of resilience, yet also that of resistance, ensuring that he is neither erased nor left behind in the face of a punitive welfare system which he and others saw as intentionally built to break them down. Similarities can be drawn here to Hartman's (1997) concept of 'practice', which is used to describe how individuals living under oppressive and restrictive regimes may seek to navigate these conditions on a daily basis, through practices which may or may not be understood as political or constituting resistance.

The concepts of resistance and resilience (for example, getting by) have traditionally been seen as somewhat oppositional to one another (Katz 2004). Resistance has often been perceived as transformative and as striving for an alternative (Rakopoulous 2014a). Meanwhile, resilience has conventionally been understood as perpetuating the status quo and/or as lacking transformative potential (MacKinnon and Derickson 2012). DeVerteuil and Golubchikov (2016), however, argue for a move towards a critical resilience, whereby resilience is envisioned as having the potential to maintain previous and alternative practices. Scholars have drawn, for example, upon grassroots community cooking collectives and work co-operatives, which are seen not only as helping people to get by in the here and now, but also as enacting an alternative to austerity (Arampatzi 2017; Rakopoulos 2014a, 2014b). These arguments around the repositioning of resilience as a form of resistance are particularly pertinent to the experiences articulated by Robert, Nathan and many other participants in the study. By engaging in resilience practices such as those of self-care and keeping on going, participants such as Robert were able to ensure their ongoing survival and ultimately carve out a space for themselves in society, at a time when disabled people are becoming increasingly isolated and marginalised. These practices of self-care may therefore be seen as co-constituting those of both resilience and resistance.

Lorde (1988) demonstrates how resilience can constitute that of resistance, in noting how the struggle for survival is a political struggle. If a person is not permitted to live how they are living, or with the people who they are with, then survival becomes inherently radical, as a refusal to not exist (Bassel and Emejulu 2017). Individuals who fall outside the norms of hegemonic society thus have to work out how to survive in a system that denies their personhood. Bassel and Emejulu (2017), for example, use the term 'the politics of survival' to both capture and legitimise the wide range of resistances that minority women undertake in the everyday. In doing so, they seek to widen the label of 'activist' so as to incorporate the actions of as many women as possible. Chatterton and Pickerill (2010) and Bassel and Emejulu (2017) critique the conventional activist subject as masculine, often based upon someone who can take up arms and devote their lives to direct action. We might extend this critique by noting how the activist subject is also ableist, often based around notions of an able-bodied, mobile and agile subject. This paper, like Bassel and

Emejulu (2017), therefore seeks to give visibility and recognition to quieter and slower forms of resistance which disabled people may engage in, in the everyday.

In their study of women's resistance and survival under austerity, Bassel and Emejulu (2017) note how women are engaged in a radical 'politics of survival', which involved new emergent networks of solidarity and support. These networks were seen to have the potential to provide women with the knowledge necessary to withstand the punitive welfare system, and were driven by an ethic of care. Bassel and Emejulu (2017: 85) argue that here 'survival becomes a radical action in and of itself'. In my own research, participants similarly saw themselves as engaging in resistance when they advocated, supported and provided others with the necessary knowledge in order to navigate the welfare system. One participant, Carol, who is in her sixties, lives in the North East and has chronic health conditions along with poor mental health. She engages in disability activism and advocacy largely through online mediums, such as online support groups, one of which she established herself:

> Through my [online] support group which has been going quite a few years now, I've literally helped people get their money back, or helped them keep their money, by them understanding what they need to say when they're filling out the form, what information they need to include ... My aim is to keep as many disabled people alive as possible through this brutal process because many of them just cannot cope

Mutual aid provided through advocacy and online support groups may therefore be seen as a radical form of resistance and a politics of survival in the face of a dehumanising welfare system, as Alex further explains:

> I feel like I'm doing activism when I go out and support somebody through advocacy ... For us, the immediate situations of risk, are in those [welfare benefits and care] meetings ... We're being killed by being starved, we're being killed by being driven to suicide, we're being killed by not having the care packages we need. So, for us our frontline in that sense is those meetings, it's that advocacy ... War is being done on our people in those quiet, quiet brightly lit meeting rooms while nobody watches.

Alex is in her forties, she is a wheelchair user and lives in the North West of England. She notes here the importance of advocates in attending care and benefit assessments alongside disabled people, situations in which individuals are at risk of losing access to their basic human needs and means of survival. By supporting disabled people to 'keep on going' and to gain access to the support they were entitled to, advocacy was thought by both Alex and Carol to enable disabled people's survival and ongoing presence within society, against a backdrop of welfare cuts, which sought to exemplify disabled people's partial and fragmented citizenship.

Patricia Hill Collins (2000) notes how survival as a form of resistance derives from, and is grounded within, Black women's struggle, that is, through their efforts to provide for and ensure the survival of their children. Bassel and Emejulu (2017: 96) similarly argue that 'minority women are radical activists simply *because* they are survivors'. This 'politics of survival' therefore challenges conventional understandings around what constitutes activism, along with strands of social movement theory which fail to acknowledge these marginal and more everyday spaces and practices (Bassel and Emejulu 2017).

EVERYDAY ACTIVISM AND IN/VISIBILITY

Along with survival, resistance may also be seen as inherent in everyday acts of visibility and in occupying public space. Jessica, a participant in my doctoral study, told me that she saw her very existence as a form of resistance. Her words, 'My existence is resistance', are highlighted within the title of this chapter. Jessica is in her late thirties, lives in London and works for an international network advising on matters relating to independent living. She had been involved in various forms of disability campaigning from a young age, largely lobbying the government around issues of independent living and inclusive education. However, Jessica saw her most powerful form of activism as being her tenacity to keep accessing mainstream spaces in uncompromising ways, to be both seen and heard proudly in public: 'When I talk about activism in a lot of the spaces that I've been in, my pure existence is a form of challenge to the status quo because I've been accessing mainstream spaces in an uncompromising way.'

Jessica here is living the change that she wants to see (see Pottinger 2017 on prefigurative politics), that is, of the presence and inclusion of disabled people as equal citizens in our everyday society. Existence, being present, bodily positivity and 'keeping on going' may be seen as acts of resistance which individuals engage in, either in the private space of the home or, as Jessica notes, outside in public space. Jessica spoke a lot about the stigmatising nature of recent media representations of disabled people (that is, the rhetoric around 'scrounger', 'skiver' and 'welfare cheat' that has made disabled people increasingly fearful of public reaction), and how by 'keeping going' and being seen in public as a proud disabled woman she was able to both counter and challenge some of these narratives. Jessica's account therefore illustrates resistance not only through her determination to keep on going, but also through her tenacity to maintain both a visible and positive disabled identity and not to succumb to the demonising media rhetoric. Here we might draw upon the critical disability theorist McRuer's (2013) scholarship on 'compulsory able-bodiness'. He proposes the term 'compulsory able-bodiedness' to describe how able-bodiedness is governed within our society as both a norm and an ideal towards which we should all supposedly strive. However, he makes clear that the authority and hegemony of compulsory able-bodiedness is constantly at risk of being destabilised or disrupted (McRuer 2013). It is here that McRuer (2013) argues that disabled people may resist and challenge the status quo: by living openly and visibly as someone who is disabled, and without seeking to align themselves with everyday norms. Disabled people's existence (and bodily positivity) therefore become a key form of everyday resistance to the status quo (see Fish et al. 2018; Meleo-Erwin 2012). Jessica highlights the importance of disabled people being visibly present in society within the following quotation:

> I think having a disability in public space is essential because it's kind of what we're fighting for. The fact that disabled people aren't visible in public space and the fact that it's notable when they are, is an indication of where we still need to go, before we achieve an inclusive society ... I don't necessarily think you just need visible in terms of people campaigning, you need visible on a day-to-day basis. You're going to the supermarket, you see someone who has a disability or you are going into a classroom and you know that your best friend has dyslexia. They are all kinds of visibility. But it's not just about visibility, it's also about disabled people being able to be in society and be open about having impairments.

For around half of participants in my study, discriminatory representations of disability had in the past prevented them from claiming a positive, politicised disabled identity. Jessica told me how she saw recent media narratives around disability and welfare reforms as fundamentally challenging disabled people's citizenship and right to existence. Thus, 'keeping going', being actively seen in society and engaging in practices of self-care, were crucial strategies in challenging such narratives.

Linder et al. (2019), in their discussion of activism on American college campuses, similarly conceptualise Black, trans and disabled students as being activists through their mere presence in these dominant and exclusionary spaces (see Kitchin 1998 on being made to feel 'in' and 'out' of space). Here the students' activism stemmed from necessity rather than choice, with individuals simply trying to carve out spaces on campus for themselves to survive and thrive in (Linder and Rodriguez 2012). Therefore, their activism in large part involved 'simply' being present. As one of Linder et al.'s (2019) participants, Jason, noted: 'you may not identify as an activist, but your embodiment and your agency does that identification for you'. Activism can therefore at times be a pre-conscious action or behaviour and a form of self-preservation. One may not be aware, for example, that by virtue of being present in a certain space one is engaging in a form of resistance, that is, challenging the norms and customs which govern these spaces: for example, who belongs and who does not. Entering and being present in these spaces, however, can be integral to one's self-preservation and feelings of equal self-worth. Like the disabled people in my study, students' existence should be recognised for the labour that it is. In both a society and environment that is not designed for minority groups, showing up, taking space, being oneself, and asking for what one needs, are powerful forms of activism. Furthermore, not allowing oneself to be considered as 'less than' by others can be a key form of resistance, in contesting taken-for-granted assumptions, challenging prejudice and changing the shape of our society.

CONCLUSION

It is hoped that this chapter will serve as a form of resistance in itself, through giving both space and voice to the experiences of disabled people who are often silenced, sidelined and overlooked within our society. In this chapter I have shown how resistance may not constitute solely that of pre-determined forms (for example, protests, pickets, direct actions) but also be lived out through disabled people's everyday existence (and practices of self-care and mutual aid), along with their tenacity to keep accessing public space in uncompromising ways against a backdrop of stark hostility, discrimination, neglect and abuse, where disabled people's lives are frequently deemed as being of lesser value. Resistance must therefore be recognised as at times slow, gradual, and as continually in emergence, occurring across a number of different spaces beyond solely that of the public. Resistance also may not always be oppositional to a particular source of power, but be recognised as something immanent to everyday relationships.

Further, this chapter has challenged conventional assumptions about what it means to be a political actor and to engage in acts of resistance, seeing endurance and everyday existence as having the potential to be a form of resistance in itself, regardless of whether it leads to more visible and grandiose political actions. Thus, it has challenged the privileged and exclusionary identity of the 'activist' (Chatterton and Pickerill 2010), by drawing attention away from the extraordinary and moving it towards that of the banal and everyday. Resistance, therefore, may not be confined to a particular form, actor, space or temporality, but instead may be seen as more manifold, emergent and fluid.

Inevitably, some geographers may be concerned that by extending the boundaries and definition of resistance to incorporate smaller and quieter acts of everyday survival, we may run the risk of resistance entirely losing its meaning, or of diluting its significance, with resistance being identified in all acts which refuse to abide by the rules, norms or ideology of a dominant culture (Pile 1997). Moreover, I would argue alongside Abrahams (1992) that by drawing attention to the small political and resistant activities inherent in everyday life, we are instead not led to the naïve conclusion that the majority of people are apathetic, apolitical or dominated by institutional power. Further, the extension of the boundaries of resistance allows geographers to draw attention to, rather than silence or undermine, the everyday resistant actions of marginalised groups – for example, refugees, ethnic minorities and disabled people – who are often perceived as agentless and/or dominated by institutional power.

NOTES

1. The Independent Living Fund was a reserve provided by the UK government to enable disabled people with high care and support needs to live independently in the community rather than in residential care. The fund was closed by the UK government on 1 July 2015.
2. Nathan has asked me to use his real name in order to increase the visibility of his activism.
3. A UK organisation campaigning against the impact of government spending cuts on the lives of disabled people.
4. A non-partisan UK disability campaign.
5. A disability campaign group galvanising in opposition to the UK government's attacks on the human rights of disabled people.

REFERENCES

Abrahams, N. (1992) Towards reconceptualising political action. *Sociological Inquiry*, 62(3): 327–347.

Arampatzi, A. (2017) The spatiality of counter-austerity politics in Athens, Greece: Emergent 'urban solidarity spaces'. *Urban Studies*, 54(9): 2155–2171.

Askins, K. (2014) A quiet politics of being together: Miriam and Rose. *Area*, 46(4): 353–354.

Askins, K. (2015) Being together: everyday geographies and the quiet politics of belonging. *ACME: An International E-Journal for Critical Geographies*, 14(2): 470–478.

Bassel, L. and Emejulu, A. (2017) *Minority Women and Austerity: Survival and Resistance in France and Britain* (1st edn), Bristol University Press. https://doi.org/10.2307/j.ctt1t897zk.

Baumgardner, J. and Richards, A. (2000) *Manifesta: Young Women, Feminism, and the Future*, New York: Farrar, Strauss & Giroux.

Berghs, M., Chataika, T., El-Lahib, Y. and Dube, K. (eds) (2019) *The Routledge Handbook of Disability Activism*, London: Routledge.

Butler, J. (2016) Rethinking vulnerability and resistance. In: Butler, J., Gambetti, Z. and Sabsay, L. (eds), *Vulnerability in Resistance*, London: Duke University Press.

Campbell, J. and Oliver, M. (1996) *Disability Politics*, London: Routledge.

Chatterton, P. and Pickerill, J. (2010) Everyday activism and transitions towards post-capitalist worlds. *Transactions of the Institute of British Geographers*, 35: 476–490.

Chouinard, V. (2001) Legal peripheries: struggles over disabled Canadians' places in law, society and space. *The Canadian Geographer/Le Géographe Canadien*, 45(1): 187–192.

Clarke, J. and Newman, J. (2012) The alchemy of austerity. *Critical Social Policy*, 32(3): 299–319.

DeVerteuil, G. and Golubchikov, O. (2016) Can resilience be redeemed? Resilience as a metaphor for change, not against change. *City*, 20(1): 143–151.

DeVerteuil, G. and Wilton, R. (2009) Spaces of abeyance, care and suvival: the addiction treatment system as a site of 'regulatory richness'. *Political Geography*, 28(8): 463–472.

Emejulu, A. and Bassel, L. (2015) Minority women, austerity and activism. *Race and Class*, 57(2): 86–95.

Fish, J., King, A. and Almack, K. (2018) Queerying activism through the lens of the sociology of everyday life. *Sociological Review*, 66(6): 1194–1208.

Gitlin, T. (2003) *Letters to a Young Activist*, New York: Basic Books.

Goodson, I. (2001) The story of life history: origins of the life history method in sociology. *Identity: An International Journal of Theory and Research*, 1(2): 129–142.

Gray, D.E. (2009) *Doing Research in the Real World*, 2nd edn, London: SAGE.

Greer Murphy, A. (2017) Austerity in the United Kingdom: the intersections of spatial and gendered inequalities. *Area*, 49(1): 122–124.

Hartman, S.V. (1997) *Scenes of Subjection: Terror, Slavery, and Self-Making in Nineteenth-Century America*, New York: Oxford University Press.

Hedva, J. (2016) Sick woman theory. *Mask Magazine, 24: The Not Again Issue* (January 2016), available at www.maskmagazine.com/not-again/struggle/sick-woman-theory, accessed 5th February 2021.

Hill Collins, P. (2000) *Black Feminist Thought: Knowledge, Consciousness and the Politics of Empowerment*, New York: Routledge.

Horton, J. (2016) Anticipating service withdrawal: young people in spaces of neoliberalisation, austerity and economic crisis. *Transactions of the Institute of British Geographers*, 41(4): 349–362.

Horton, J. and Kraftl, P. (2009a) Small acts, kind words and 'not too much fuss': implicit activisms. *Emotion, Space and Society*, 2(1): 14–23.

Jordan, T. (2002) *Activism! Direct Action, Hacktivism and the Future of Society*, London: Reaktion Books.

Katz, C. (2004) *Growing Up Global: Economic Restructuring and Children's Everyday Lives*, Minneapolis, MN: University of Minnesota Press.

Kitchin, R. (1998) 'Out of place','knowing one's place': space, power and the exclusion of disabled people. *Disability and Society*, 13(3): 343–356.

Linder, C., Quaye, S.J., Stewart, T.J., Okello, W.K. and Roberts, R.E. (2019) 'The whole weight of the world on my shoulders': power, identity, and student activism. *Journal of College Student Development*, 60(5): 527–542.

Linder, C. and Rodriguez, K. (2012) Learning from the experiences of self-identified Women of Color activists. *Journal of College Student Development*, 53: 383–398.

Lorde, A. (1988) *A Burst of Light: Essays*, Firebrand Books: New York.

MacKinnon, D. and Derickson, K.D. (2012) From resilience to resourcefulness: a critique of resilience policy and activism. *Progress in Human Geography*, 37(2): 253–270.

McRuer, R. (2006) *Crip Theory: Cultural Signs of Queerness and Disability*, New York: New York University Press.

McRuer, R. (2013). Compulsory able-bodiedness and queer/disabled existence. In: Davis, L.J (ed.), *The Disability Studies Reader*, New York: Routledge.

Meleo-Erwin, Z. (2012) Disrupting normal: toward the 'ordinary and familiar' in fat politics. *Feminism and Psychology*, 22(3): 388–402.

Moffatt, S., Lawson, S., Patterson, R., Holding, E., Dennison, A., Sowden, S. and Brown, J. (2015) A qualitative study of,the impact of the UK 'bedroom tax'. *Journal of Public Health*, 38(2): 197–205.

Murray, C.A. and Field, F. (1990) *The Emerging British Underclass*, IEA Health and Welfare Unit: London.

Pain, R. (2014) Seismologies of emotion: fear and activism during domestic violence. *Social and Cultural Geography*, 15(2): 127–150.

Pearson, C. and Trevisan, F. (2015) Disability activism in the new media ecology: Campaigning strategies in the digital era. *Disability and Society*, 30(6): 924–940.

Peck, J. and Tickell, A. (2002) Neoliberalising space. *Antipode*, 34: 380–404.

Pile, S. (1997) Introduction: opposition, political identities and spaces of resistance. In: Pile, S. and Keith, M. (eds), *Geographies of Resistance*, London: Routledge.

Pottinger, L. (2017) Planting the seeds of a quiet activism. *Area*, 49(2): 215–222.

Prince, M.J. (2009) *Absent Citizens. Disability Politics and Policy in Canada*, Toronto: University of Toronto Press.

Rakopoulos, T. (2014a) The crisis seen from below, within, and against: from solidarity economy to food distribution cooperatives in Greece. *Dialect Anthropology*, 38: 189–207.

Rakopoulos, T. (2014b) Resonance of solidarity: meanings of a local concept in anti-austerity Greece. *Journal of Modern Greek Studies*, 37: 95–119.

Rose, N. (2001) The politics of life itself. *Theory, Culture and Society*, 18(6): 1–30.

Rose, M. (2002) The seductions of resistance: power, politics, and a performative style of systems. *Environment and Planning D: Society and Space*, 20(4): 383–400.

Ryan, F. (2019) *Crippled: Austerity and the Demonization of Disabled People*, Verso. https://www.versobooks.com/en-gb/products/729-crippled.

UNCRPD (2016) Inquiry concerning the United Kingdom of Great Britain and Northern Ireland carried out by the Committee under article 6 of the Optional Protocol to the Convention. United Nations Convention on the Rights of Persons with Disabilities.

Wilkinson, E. and Ortega-Alcázar, I. (2019) The right to be weary? Endurance and exhaustion in austere times. *Transactions of the Institute of British Geographers*, 44: 155–167.

Williams-Findlay, R. (2011) Lifting the lid on Disabled People Against Cuts. *Disability and Society*, 26(6): 773–778.

9. 'Bollocks to Brexit': the geographies of Brexit protest stickers, 2015–21

Hannah Awcock

INTRODUCTION

'Bollocks to Brexit' has become a well-known phrase in the United Kingdom (UK) since 2016. It was popularised by fluorescent yellow protest stickers, distributed by a group called the EU Flag Mafia in the aftermath of the European Union (EU) referendum on 23 June 2016. From there, it achieved widespread recognition and was even adopted by the Liberal Democrats as a campaign slogan in the run up to the EU elections in May 2019. This example raises several interesting questions: How could a simple sticker have so much impact? How has this, and other stickers relating to Brexit, shaped and reflected the fierce debates that have dominated British politics since 2016? How do stickers communicate their message and reflect broader trends in resistance?

Protest stickers are small pieces of self-adhesive paper or vinyl which express a political opinion or statement. They are a ubiquitous form of resistance within the urban landscape, adorning lamp posts, rubbish bins, bollards and walls in towns and cities all over the world. Ranging from hand-drawn to professionally printed, protest stickers are used to express opinions ranging from the far left to the far right (Awcock, 2021). Alongside Brexit, other recent examples include stickers that criticise Covid-19 lockdowns and vaccine programmes, and both transpositive and transphobic stickers. I have been photographing stickers since 2014, developing an archive of more than 6000 images from more than 50 locations. Stickers are cheap, easy and relatively low-risk, and as such they are an everyday form of resistance. It is important to acknowledge that putting up stickers is not low risk everywhere: the case of 'Sticker Lady', a street artist named Samantha Lo who was arrested for her use of stickers in Singapore in 2013, demonstrates that punishments can be harsh in some circumstances (Luger, 2016).

Stickers tend to reflect current events, and Brexit is no exception. Stickers encouraging passers-by to vote Leave or Remain started to appear on British streets in 2015. As the situation developed, so did the stickers, with calls to 'Stop Brexit' and assertions that 'Brexit means Brexit' appearing on the streets over the next few years. Even after the United Kingdom left the European Union on 31 January 2020, new designs continued to appear, with stickers calling to 'Rejoin the EU' available on the EU Flag Mafia website (https://www.euflagmafia.com/, n.d.).

Despite their pervasiveness, protest stickers have been largely overlooked by scholars of resistance, within geography and other disciplines (although Vigsø, 2010; Reershemius, 2019; Ritchie, 2019; and Conley, 2020 are exceptions to this). However, there is literature on related phenomena such as political street art (Awad and Wagoner, 2017), bumper stickers (Bloch, 2000a, 2000b) and yarn bombing (Mann, 2015). Like stickers, these objects and activities are not just a way of conveying a political message; they also enact politics themselves. As Taş (2017: 803) argues of political street art and graffiti: 'It not only represents but [also] performs resistance.'

There is a growing body of literature that critically reflects on how geographers define resistance and activism, and encourages others to consider more everyday, implicit, emergent and ambiguous acts when researching and writing about resistance (Horton and Kraftl, 2009; Chatterton and Pickerill, 2010; Luger, 2016; Hughes, 2020). Stickers are small, common but often overlooked, and frequently unclear in their authorship and/or intention, so align with these attempts to blur the boundaries of what constitutes resistance. They may not attract as much attention as a demonstration or a riot, but stickers are a significant and popular tool in repertoires of resistance that allows movements and activists to express themselves in, and shape, public space. Stickers constitute acts of resistance in two distinct ways. First, they are a relatively democratic method of participating in public debates. Stickers are an outlet for individuals and groups who would otherwise be unable to express publicly their views on Brexit, or any other contentious issue (Awcock, 2021). The second way that stickers constitute resistance is by subverting the functionality of objects in the urban landscape and turning them into political noticeboards. In so doing, protest stickers reveal possible alternatives in cities which are increasingly restricted (Mann, 2015; Mould, 2019). Protest stickers politicise the urban landscape, turning every surface into a potential canvas for a political message. This suggests the possibility of a city which every individual has a right to alter and influence. As such, all stickers in public space that were not put up by the local government, national government or landowner can be considered an act of resistance, albeit perhaps a small one. This is the case even if their message is not political, reinforces the status quo, or if they do not carry a message at all.

In this chapter I explore how a debate, issue, event or movement – in this case, Brexit – can be traced through protest stickers. My photographic archive includes 176 images representing 113 different designs of stickers that relate to Brexit, starting with the referendum campaign in 2015–16, through to Brexit Day on 31 January 2020 and its aftermath. All 176 images were taken in urban areas around the UK, except for two (one sticker was photographed in Vienna, and one in Berlin). Whilst protest stickers can be found in rural areas (Ritchie, 2019), they are more common in towns and cities. The objects to which the stickers were attached include lamp posts, road signs, phone boxes, bollards, bus shelters, walls, advertising boards, button boxes on pedestrian crossings, zebra crossing lights, rubbish bins, junction boxes, and even a section of the Berlin Wall. From the fluorescent yellow 'Bollocks to Brexit' sticker, to less common pro-Brexit stickers, Brexit has inspired multiple sticker designs that reflect all sides of the debate as it evolved over the course of half a decade. This chapter explores the ways in which these stickers function as visual and material objects, considering their design and production, and how their materiality impacts upon the ways they are interacted with once they have been put up in public space. I use this analysis to reflect on what a focus on protest stickers can contribute to broader geographies of resistance.

A CHRONOLOGY OF BREXIT THROUGH STICKERS

Protest stickers are quick, easy and cheap to make and distribute, which means that stickers responding to events can be produced rapidly. As Brexit progressed, the stickers relating to it also changed. As such, stickers can be used to trace events as they evolve, providing a sense of how individuals and groups react to developments. I do not pretend that protest stickers are an accurate barometer of public opinion: they tend to be used to express radical rather than moderate views, and a single enthusiastic stickerer can create the impression that there is widespread support for a particular point of view when that may not actually be the case. Brexit is a complex phenomenon that encompasses many issues, including migration, control, freedom, democracy and rights. It has been experienced in an infinite variety of ways by different people in different places, and the way that it was felt and experienced by an individual may have changed over time (Anderson et al., 2020). Despite the inevitable limits to what can be expressed on a sticker due to its size, the range and diversity of stickers relating to Brexit reflects this complexity and ambiguity. Protest stickers are just one of the many arenas in which the Brexit debate(s) played out, but they are one that highlights how resistance can function in everyday spaces, as this chapter will demonstrate.

Stickers relating to Brexit first began to appear in advance of the EU referendum on 23 June 2016. Most of these early stickers simply encouraged the viewer to vote one way or the other in the referendum. Slogans included: 'VOTE TO LEAVE THE EU', 'VOTE NO TO THE EU', 'I'M IN' and

'VOTE REMAIN TODAY' (see Figure 9.1).[1] Some included justifications for their position, such as one produced by the National Union of Rail, Maritime and Transport Workers (RMT) which read:

RMT
VOTE TO LEAVE THE EU
VOTE FOR JOBS AND SERVICES

Another, produced by the Alliance for Workers Liberty, an organisation that aims to educate socialists and the organised labour movement, read:

[Obscured]
VOTE TO REMAIN
FIGHT FOR A WORKERS' EUROPE

Note: Left to right: Egham, Surrey on 8 June 2016. and London on 15 July 2016.

Figure 9.1   Stickers referring to the EU referendum

In the wake of the referendum, the number of pro-Brexit stickers decreased. This echoes trends in social media posts relating to Brexit. Whilst there were many pro-Brexit posts on social media before the referendum, most posts that expressed an opinion about Brexit after the referendum were negative (Bouko and Garcia, 2019; Bouko et al., 2018). After the referendum, not all stickers contained a demand or instruction. Some simply expressed support and affection for the EU, often using popular song lyrics to play on the fact that 'EU' sounds like 'you', such as 'EU & ME ALWAYS', and 'ALL I WANT FOR

CHRISTMAS IS EU'. One design simply said 'i [heart] eu', superimposed over two clasped hands, one coloured with the flag of the European Union, the other with the flag of the United Kingdom. This is also the point at which the EU Flag Mafia began to distribute their yellow stickers. The original text read (see Figure 9.2):

BOLLOCKS TO BREXIT
IT'S NOT A DONE DEAL
#bollockstobrexit

As events relating to Brexit progressed, Brexit stickers also developed. Individuals or groups other than the EU Flag Mafia began to produce 'Bollocks to Brexit' stickers, including one that opted for the alternative spelling of 'Bollox to Brexit' in yellow text on a blue background, surrounded by the gold stars of the EU flag. Even pro-Brexit stickers played with the now well-known phrase, for example 'BOLLOCKS TO BRUSSELS' (with the 'O's replaced with a ring of stars like the EU flag) and:

BOLLOCKS TO REMAIN
BREXIT IS DEMOCRACY
BOLLOCKS TO THE EU
EUROPE IS NOT THE EU
https://thebrexitparty.org/

The EU Flag Mafia started to expand the variety of texts available, although the design style remained constant. Examples include:

BREXIT IS BONKERS
#WeareEUrope

and:

BOLLOCKS TO BREXIT
BOLLOCKS TO BORIS

In 2018 the Electoral Commission watchdog found that the Vote Leave and Leave.EU campaign groups had broken electoral law by not accurately declaring their spending during the referendum campaign, fining them £61,000 and

Note: Clockwise from top left: London, 21 September 2017; Alnwick, Northumberland, 4 August 2018; York, 12 February 2020; London, 4 June 2018.

Figure 9.2   A selection of Brexit stickers

£70,000, respectively (BBC News, 2018). Anti-Brexit stickers began to refer to this, arguing that voters had been deceived. Examples include:

> I [HEART] UK
> We were conned
> Only the rich can afford Brexit.
> SAVE BRITAIN – #StopBrexit

The EU Flag Mafia stickers also began to include this narrative:

> BREXIT IS A CRIME SCENE
> ELECTORAL LAW BREAKING, DARK MONEY
> 'LIES ON AN INDUSTRIAL SCALE'
> INTERFERENCE BY FOREIGN POWERS

and:

> VOTE LEAVE BROKE THE LAW
> #STOPBREXIT

Protest stickers were no longer objecting just to Brexit itself, but also to the way that it was achieved.

In April 2018, a group called People's Vote was launched in London to campaign for a second referendum on the final Brexit deal. The group produced its own stickers, which featured its logo and the words 'I demand a vote on the final Brexit deal' (see Figure 9.2). Other stickers echoed this call, for example one that read:

> PUT BREXIT TO THE PEOPLE
> TELL JEREMY CORBYN![2]

Others featured the hashtags #PeoplesVote and #FAIRVOTE. Stickers were also produced to promote the Put it to the People and Let Us Be Heard marches calling for a second referendum in London on 23 March and 19 October 2019. Stickers are often used to advertise protest events (Awcock, 2021), and once the event has occurred they serve as public reminders that it took place. The People's Vote campaign faltered after the victory of the Conservative Party in the General Election on 12 December 2019, but its stickers can still be found on the streets, although most are now so weathered that they are barely legible.

The scale of issues that stickers refer to range from the local to the international. Whilst a lot of stickers can be found in multiple locations across the UK and elsewhere, sometimes a sticker will relate specifically to the location it is found in. In the 2016 referendum, Scotland voted to remain in the EU. This threw fuel onto the smouldering fire of Scottish Independence, sparking calls for an independent Scotland to remain in or rejoin the EU. Although many of the Brexit stickers I have found in Scotland were the same as those in England, some did reflect Scotland's unique position, such as 'Scotland for a People's Vote' and 'BREXIT: R.I.P. U.K.' Two sticker designs imposed the ring of gold stars from the EU flag onto the Saltire. There is no text on either sticker, but the design implies Scottish support for the EU.

In 2019, stickers produced by another anti-Brexit campaign began to appear on the streets. The Hearts not Hate group aimed to highlight the benefits that EU membership provides. The stickers are red hearts that read 'we love ...' followed by an advantage of EU membership, and one or more of the following: www.heartsnothate.uk, #EUdoesthis, #stopthecoup, #sharethelove, and #loveEU. Examples of the benefits that the stickers mention are 'our friends & neighbours', 'climate change action', 'free movement', 'democracy', 'peace in Europe' and 'women's rights' (see Figure 9.2). The campaign was run by a group called North East for Europe, which campaigned against Brexit in general and a hard Brexit in particular.[3]

In this section, I have traced the progression of Brexit through 113 sticker designs found between 2015 and 2021. Not only do these designs serve as a reminder of the complicated and convoluted process of Brexit, but they also illustrate how activists and resistance movements respond to events and develop their arguments as the situation evolves. As such, stickers can provide valuable evidence of the ways in which resistance movements respond to changing circumstances and events. In the next two sections, I explore certain elements of the stickers in more detail: their method of production; their use of branding, symbolism, hashtags and humour; their materiality; and the various ways that they can be interacted with once up in public space.

DESIGNING AND PRODUCING PROTEST STICKERS

The variety of designs of protest stickers is dazzling. Brexit stickers are no exception, and out of the 113 designs collected during this research, there is a broad range of styles, colour schemes and images used. Despite this, there are some trends in the sample. Most stickers are mass-produced, but some – in this case, 11 of the designs – are hand-made. Whilst stickers can be mass-produced with a domestic printer, hand-making stickers requires even less equipment, although more elaborate designs are time-consuming. It is more common to find multiple examples of the same sticker (or different ones from the same 'series') in the same street or area when they have been mass-produced than when they are hand-made, presumably because it is much easier to produce stickers in large numbers when they are designed and made using technology. Vigsø (2010) argues that the primary purpose of what he calls 'extremist stickers' is to declare the presence of a particular perspective: to let others know that people who hold this belief or opinion exist. With the caveat that this is just one of several purposes for protest stickers, it is logical to conclude that the more stickers an activist can put up, the more effectively they will 'declare their presence' in a space. Arguably, this explains why mass-produced stickers are more common than hand-made ones.

Perhaps the most recognisable set of stickers are the 'Bollocks to Brexit' stickers, first produced by the EU Flag Mafia. The combination of a fluorescent yellow background, a blocky black font, and block capitals has become so recognisable that it is possible to identify a sticker as produced by the EU Flag Mafia even when it does not contain the 'Bollocks to Brexit' slogan. This is an example of what Beraldo (2020: 3) calls 'contentious branding': 'the process by which the ontological multiplicity of a social movement is differentiated into one recognizable entity, by means of a standardized semiotic repertoire'. Contentious brands can connect activists, social movements and resistance groups without requiring them to adopt shared strategies, interpretations or goals (Beraldo, 2020). 'Bollocks to Brexit' is an ideal example of this process, as a brand developed by an anti-Brexit protest group was adopted by, amongst others, an established political party. Arguably, the distinctive colour scheme and design of the stickers is as much a part of what made the brand recognisable as the slogan. This demonstrates how stickers can contribute to the development of a strong brand or collective identity for resistance movements.

Many stickers include symbols, and in the case of Brexit stickers, flags are common: 27 of the sticker designs include all or part of the European Union flag. The flag features a circle of 12 gold stars on a royal blue background. The EU flag has become a symbol in the Brexit debate, with anti-Brexit protesters covering themselves in flags at demonstrations. As a result, including the flag in the design of a sticker encourages the viewer to make the link to Brexit even if the word itself is not used. Examples of text on stickers like this include 'love will keep us together', and 'WE ARE ALL JUST PEOPLE'. One sticker does not use any words at all, it just features a gold heart inside the circle of gold stars. Other stickers do not use the flag directly, but instead draw on the blue and gold colour scheme to make the connection. Symbols are important to resistance movements, motivating people to take part and helping to construct a shared identity (Awad and Wagoner, 2020). They are particularly useful when designing protest stickers, as they can say a lot in a limited space. Using symbols is risky because there is no guarantee that the viewer will interpret them in the way that was intended, but the flag of the European Union has been used effectively in Brexit protest stickers. In this way, stickers not only shape the collective identity of resistance movements, but they also utilise and are shaped by them.

Nine designs make use of the British flag, either alone or in combination with the flag of the European Union. Eight of them are anti-Brexit. Benwell et al. (2021) explore how national flags can be used by citizens to reimagine the nation state. Citizens are not merely passive consumers of national symbols and narratives: they can (and do) manipulate them to propose alternatives. In many ways the Brexit debate was a manifestation of competing understandings of the British nation, and the stickers that include the Union Flag are a manifestation of that. Those that include the flag of the European Union alongside the Union Flag (for example, see the top left sticker in Figure 9.2) are using the flag as a national symbol to advocate for an alternative version of Britain to the one leaving the EU. Analysing the symbolism and branding utilised by protest stickers can shed light on the collective identities of resistance. The social identity approach acknowledges the importance of identity to moments of mass resistance such as riots and demonstrations (Stott and Drury, 2017), but by focusing on everyday forms of resistance such as protest stickers we can better understand how collective identities of resistance are (re)produced in between such dramatic moments of mass action.

Many of the stickers include one or more hashtags; 16 different hashtags feature in the sample. Online, hashtags serve as an indexing system, allowing social media users both to frame their own posts as being connected to a topic, and to find posts relating to that topic (Bonilla and Rosa, 2015). They enable social media users to communicate with a community of interest without necessarily knowing or following the other participants (Bruns and Burgess, 2011). As such, they can be an ideal tool to bring together individuals with similar political beliefs. On protest stickers, hashtags serve several purposes: they provide a method for viewers to find out more about the issue on social media, or even contribute to the debate themselves. They can also convey information; they rarely repeat text from elsewhere on the sticker, which would be a waste of valuable space. In this way, hashtags can categorise and frame stickers in the same way that they do social media posts. For example, one sticker reads:

I [heart] UK
WE WERE CONNED
STOP BREXIT
#FAIRVOTE

As well as pointing the reader towards a source of further information, the hashtag frames this sticker as being related to the campaign for a second, 'fair' referendum on Brexit. This is an example of overlap between physical and 'virtual' activism, as well as online and offline spaces of resistance. Stickers are just one of many resistance tactics which prove that the distinction between online and offline forms of activism is false. They help to 'underscore the slippery boundary between analogue and digital forms of activism' (Bonilla and Rosa, 2015: 11); acts of resistance can occupy both online and offline space simultaneously.

Some of the Brexit stickers are humorous and playful. These include those that play with song lyrics, such as 'Never going to give EU up', 'EU & ME ALWAYS' and 'ALL I WANT FOR CHRISTMAS IS EU'. Others use the shock value of obscenities to amuse the viewer, such as 'BOLLOCKS TO BREXIT' and 'BREXIT IS A SHIT IDEA'. One hand-made sticker even utilised caricature, featuring a drawing of a walrus with Boris Johnson's distinctive blond mop of hair. Despite its subjective and contextual nature, humour can be a powerful tool for resistance ('t Hart, 2007). In their analysis of the large number of neologisms that were created in the wake of Brexit, Lalić-Krstin and Silaški (2019) argue that the referendum result took many Remain supporters by surprise, and they turned to humour and ludicity to cope with the shock, as well as the fear and uncertainty of a future outside the EU. This could explain why there were more anti-Brexit neologisms created than pro-Brexit ones. This could also account for the use of humour in anti-Brexit stickers. In addition, humour can be beneficial to resistance movements in other ways, such as providing a morale boost, helping to unify a group and create a collective identity, and undermining those in authority ('t Hart, 2007). Like yarnbombs, humorous or shocking stickers can pull individuals out of their everyday routines, making them aware of urban spaces that they had ceased to notice, and thus creating a sense of possibility and potential (Mann, 2015). The use of techniques such as branding, symbols, hashtags and humour are common to many forms of resistance, not just stickers. However, the way that these methods are utilised through protest stickers is unique, as is the way that stickers manifest these techniques of resistance in public space.

INTERACTING WITH PROTEST STICKERS

Putting stickers up is not the only way in which they can be used to express resistance in public space. Stickers fade over time, their message gradually obscured by the efforts of wind, rain and the sun. Depending on the materials they are made of, this can take anything from a few weeks to several years. As a result of human intervention, however, many stickers do not get the opportunity to become weathered and faded. Stickers are peeled off, scratched away, written on, or covered up, often within hours of being put up (see Figure 9.3). Frequently, it is not possible to understand the motives of the person who interacted with the sticker; they may be an employee of the local authority or landowner tasked with cleaning the streets, or they might have been a bored commuter absentmindedly picking at a sticker while they wait for the bus. Occasionally, however, the way that a sticker is interacted with can hint at, if not actually reveal, the intention behind it. The sticker in the bottom right of Figure 9.3 has been altered: instead of reading 'SAY BOLLOCKS TO BREXIT' it was changed to 'SAY yes TO BREXIT', a substantially different message. In this way, the material condition of a sticker can provide clues as to how observers responded to it. It may be impossible to know for certain why a sticker was altered, but the fact that stickers are altered is worthy of note.

These interactions are the most literal example of how protest stickers enable a broad range of people to participate in public debates, converting everyday public spaces into spaces of resistance. They also highlight the way that public space is constantly being (re)produced, emphasising 'the generally unfinished nature of urban public space as relational, processual and ephemeral' (Landau-Donnelly, 2021: 37).

Feigenbaum (2014) has called for researchers to pay more attention to the role of material objects in activist communication. Stickers are one such object, and the various ways that stickers are interacted with highlight the importance of their material qualities. Whether they are made from matte or glossy paper impacts upon how easy it is to write on them. A ballpoint pen is unlikely to leave a visible mark on a glossy vinyl sticker, and although a permanent marker pen is not exactly specialist equipment, most people do not carry them around regularly. The type of adhesive used (and how long the sticker has been in place) affects how easy they are to peel off. Anyone who has tried to remove a stubborn price sticker will know how long it can take; removing multiple stickers from a street can become very time-consuming. It might be easier or faster to scratch them off with a key or similar object, but that obscures the message – sometimes only partially – rather than removing it entirely. In short, the material qualities of stickers affect the opportunities available for interacting with them, and as such impact upon how public debates unfold through stickers.

CONCLUSION

Protest stickers can significantly contribute to our understanding of the geographies of resistance. They are pervasive in many places, and are utilised by both individual activists and more organised groups from across the political spectrum, to inscribe political slogans and statements onto the urban fabric. Their everyday, 'small' nature is precisely what makes them so interesting, providing compelling evidence for expanding definitions of resistance. In this, I echo scholars such as Horton and Kraftl (2009), Chatterton and Pickerill (2010), Luger (2016) and Hughes (2020: 1156) in their calls to take seriously 'the ambiguous, unremarkable, (un)intentional subjects, materials and practices' of resistance. Stickers do not typically cause major disruption or attract significant media attention. The intention behind them, and the impacts of them, are often not clear. However, I argue that stickers constitute resistance, because they are a relatively democratic method of participating in public debates and they subvert the functionality of objects in the urban landscape. In this way, even stickers with an ambiguous or apolitical message can be classified as resistance. As I have demonstrated in this chapter, analysing stickers can shed light on significant elements of resistance, including collective

Note: Clockwise from top left: someone has tried to remove this sticker in Hull, 3 February 2019; this sticker in Swansea has been scratched with a key or something similar, 23 June 2018; the message of this sticker in Hull has been altered with a ballpoint pen, 5 July 2019; this sticker in Brighton was covered up with something else, but the weather has revealed it again, 5 January 2020.

Figure 9.3   *Stickers that have been interacted with*

identity, symbolism, material culture and access to public space. Stickers also encourage us to expand what is considered a space of resistance. They blur distinctions between spaces, merging online and offline activism and turning everyday street furniture such as lamp posts and junction boxes into spaces for radical debate. Every space has the potential to be a space of resistance; all it takes is something as 'simple' as a self-adhesive piece of paper.

NOTES

1. I have tried to reproduce the text of stickers as closely as possible. If a sticker contains block capitals, then I have also reproduced this as it is an important element of the overall feel of the sticker. When the sticker uses line breaks, I have included them. Sometimes, not all the text on a sticker is legible. I have used '*obscured*' to indicate this.
2. This sticker is also referring to another Brexit-related issue. Although the Labour Party supported Remain during the referendum campaign, the party's leader at the time, Jeremy Corbyn, was criticised for failing to take a firm stance on Brexit during the campaign.
3. Supporters of a 'hard' Brexit wanted a clean break from the EU economically, with the UK outside of the single market and customs union. The alternative was a 'soft' Brexit, in which the UK would have retained close economic ties with the EU.

REFERENCES

Anderson, B., Wilson, H.F., Forman, P.J., Heslop, J., Ormerod, E., and Maestri, G. (2020) 'Brexit: Modes of Uncertainty and Future in an Impasse.' *Transactions of the Institute of British Geographers*, 45, no. 2, 256–269.

Awad, S., and Wagoner, B. (eds) (2017) *Street Art of Resistance*. Cham: Palgrave Macmillan.

Awad, S.H., and Wagoner, B. (2020) 'Protest Symbols.' *Current Opinion in Psychology*, 35, 98–102.

Awcock, H. (2021) 'Stickin' it to the Man: The Geographies of Protest Stickers.' *Area*, 53, no. 3, 522–530.

BBC News (2018) 'Brexit: Vote Leave broke Electoral Law, says Electoral Commission.' Last modified 17 July 2018, accessed 28 June 2021 at https://www.bbc.co.uk/news/uk-politics-44856992.

Benwell, M.C., Núñez, A., and Amigo, C. (2021) 'Stitching Together the Nation's Fabric during the Chile Uprisings: Towards an Alter-Geopolitics of Flags and Everyday Nationalism.' *Geoforum*, 122, 22–31.

Beraldo, D. (2020) 'Movements as Multiplicities and Contentious Branding: Lessons from the Digital Exploration of #Occupy and #Anonymous.' *Information, Communication and Society*, 25, no. 8, 1098–1114.

Bloch, L. (2000a) 'Setting the Public Sphere in Motion: The Rhetoric of Political Bumper Stickers in Israel.' *Political Communication*, 17, 433–456.

Bloch, L. (2000b) 'Mobile Discourse: Political Bumper Stickers as a Communicative Event in Israel.' *Journal of Communication*, 50, 48–76.

Bonilla, Y., and Rosa, J. (2015) '#Ferguson: Digital Protest, Hashtag Ethnography, and the Racial Politics of Social Media in the United States.' *American Ethnologist*, 42, no. 1, 4–17.

Bouko, C., and Garcia, D. (2019) 'Citizens' Reactions to Brexit on Twitter: A Content and Discourse Analysis.' In: Kopf, S. and Miglbauer, M. (eds), *Discourses of Brexit*. Abingdon: Routledge, pp. 171–190.

Bouko, C., de Wilde, J., Decock S., de Clercq, O., Manchia, V., and Garcia, D. (2018) 'Reactions to Brexit in Images: A Multimodal Content Analysis of Shared Visual Content on Twitter.' *Visual Communication*, 20, no. 1, 4–33.

Bruns, A., and Burgess, J. (2011) 'The Use of Twitter Hashtags in the Formation of Ad Hoc Publics.' Paper presented at The Future of Journalism 2011, Cardiff University, Cardiff, UK, 8–9 September. Accessed 10 July 2016 at http://eprints.qut.edu.au/46330/.

Chatterton, P., and Pickerill, J. (2010) 'Everyday Activism and Transitions towards Post-capitalist Worlds.' *Transactions of the Institute of British Geographers*, 35, no. 4, 475–490.

Conley, J. (2020) 'Voting, Votive, Devotion: "I Voted" Stickers and Ritualization at Susan B. Anthony's Grave.' *Journal of Feminist Studies in Religion*, 36, no. 2, 43–62.

Feigenbaum, A. (2014) 'Resistant Matters: Tents, Tear Gas and the "Other Media" of Occupy.' *Communication and Critical/Cultural Studies*, 11, no. 1, 15–24.

Horton, J., and Kraftl, P. (2009) 'Small Acts, Kind Words and "Not Too Much Fuss": Implicit Activisms.' *Emotion, Space and Society*, 2, no. 1, 14–23.

Hughes, S.M. (2020) 'On Resistance in Human Geography.' *Progress in Human Geography*, 44, no. 6, 1141–1160.

Lalić-Krstin, G., and Silaški, N. (2019) '"Don't go Brexin' my Heart": The Ludic Aspects of Brexit-induced Neologisms.' In: Koller, V., Kopf, S., and Miglbauer, M. (eds), *Discourses of Brexit*. London: Routledge, pp. 222–236.

Landau-Donnelly, F. (2021) 'Contentious Walls: Inscribing Conflicts into Vancouver's Chinatown Murals.' *CAP – Public Art Journal*, 3, no. 2, 28–41.

Luger, J. (2016) 'Singaporean "Spaces of Hope?" Activist Geographies in the City-State.' *City*, 20, no. 1, 186–203.

Mann, J. (2015) 'Towards a Politics of Whimsy: Yarn Bombing and the City.' *Area*, 47, 65–72.

Mould, O. (2019) 'The Spark, the Spread and Ethics: Towards an Object-orientated View of Subversive Creativity.' *Environment and Planning D: Society and Space*, 37, no. 3, 468–483.

Reershemius, G. (2019) 'Lamppost Networks: Stickers as a Genre in Urban Semiotic Landscapes,' *Social Semiotics*, 29, no. 5, 622–644.

Ritchie, E. (2019) 'Yes after No: The Indyref Landscape, 2014–16.' *Journal of British Identities*, 2, 1–30.

Stott, C., and Drury, J. (2017) 'Contemporary Understanding of Riots: Classical Crowd Psychology, Ideology and the Social Identity Approach.' *Public Understanding of Science*, 26, no. 1, 2–14.

'T Hart, M. (2007) 'Humour and Social Protest: An Introduction.' *International Review of Social History*, 52, no. S15, 1–20.

Taş, H. (2017) 'Street Arts of Resistance in Tahrir and Gezi.' *Middle Eastern Studies*, 53, no. 5, 802–819.

Vigsø, O. (2010) 'Extremist Stickers: Epideitic Rhetoric, Political Marketing, and Tribal Demarcation.' *Journal of Visual Literacy*, 29, no. 1, 28–46.

10. Struggles around housing: La Plaza De La Hoja in Colombia

Karen Schouw Iversen

INTRODUCTION

Located in the middle of Colombia's capital of city of Bogotá, the Plaza de la Hoja housing project stands out from the surrounding city landscape. A series of functionalist, neo-brutalist concrete buildings, its exteriors have been compared to a prison (see Pabón, 2015). Divided into 12 towers, varying in height and interconnected through walkways that form a narrow rectangle, Plaza de la Hoja encircles a courtyard and a small parking area. Along the side of one of the towers, visible from the bustling Carrera 30, a vertical garden has been planted, fitting with the project's name, which translates into the 'square of the leaf'. A spacious concrete square, doubling as a skate park, stretches out in front of the housing complex. Spreading across it, a large mural displays a giant leaf, in turn consisting of smaller leaves, painted in blue and yellow, depicting plants from disparate parts of Colombia, upon which the word *vida*, or life, has been painted in large white letters (Figure 10.1).

Figure 10.1   *Plaza de la Hoja (left) and the mural (right), February 2018*

Housing 457 families, Plaza de la Hoja is one of nine housing compounds built in Bogotá as part of former president Juan Manuel Santos's flagship Free

Housing Programme (*Programa de Vivienda Gratuita*). The latter constitutes part of a wider transitional justice process in Colombia, aiming to address the social consequences of the country's civil conflict (Summers, 2012). Dating back to the 1960s, Colombia's conflict has left over 8 million people internally displaced (UARIV, 2021), many of whom have migrated from the countryside to major cities where they frequently settle in marginalised and peripheral areas, facing disproportionate levels of violence and lack of access to public services (Centro Nacional de Memoria Histórica, 2013: 74–75; Zeiderman, 2016). Responding to the challenges facing those victimised by this conflict, the Colombian government has entitled internally displaced persons and other groups afflicted by the conflict to humanitarian assistance and a comprehensive set of rights restitution measures, including the payment of damages,[1] land restitution, and preferential access to subsidised housing (Forero-Niño, 2012; Summers, 2012).

The Free Housing Programme is one of the policies introduced as part of these rights restitution measures. During its first phase, 100 000 two-bedroom housing units were constructed (El Congreso de Colombia, 2012; Ministerio de Vivienda, 2015). These were allocated by the Department of Social Prosperity (DPS) to households which had applied to be part of the programme, according to criteria privileging displaced families which had previously been promised housing subsidies that had not materialised, as well as families deemed to be particularly vulnerable (El Presidente de la República de Colombia, 2012). Ownership of the flats was transferred to the households for free, with the condition that the families could not sell or rent out the flats during the first ten years after receiving the housing, and that they continue to pay bills and service charges (Sliwa and Wiig, 2016).

This chapter zooms in on the most visible project built as part of the Free Housing Programme: Plaza de la Hoja. Drawing on a Foucauldian understanding of power and resistance, it analyses the housing complex as a spatial technology of control, while simultaneously exploring the emergent resistance that the project has enabled.

Two aspects of Foucault's writings inform this chapter. Firstly, Foucault rejected grand narratives of power, instead detailing its operation in concrete contexts. In doing so, he examined the forms of knowledge and governmental technologies – the 'mundane programmes, calculations, techniques, apparatuses, documents and procedures' (Rose and Miller, 2010: 273) – through which power operates, crucially exploring power's manifestation in specific spatial configurations (Elden and Crampton, 2016; Sharp et al., 2000). In this chapter, I analyse Plaza de la Hoja as a governmental technology that illuminates power relations existing between the internally displaced and the state in Colombia.

Secondly, Foucault (1982) emphasised that power cannot exist without resistance. Moving away from an understanding of power as repressive and prohibitive, Foucault (1991: 194) instead argued that 'power produces; it produces reality'. In doing so, he highlighted that power facilitates as much as it constrains, and that it also has positive dimensions, opening up the possibility that there can also be a 'power to resist' (Sharp et al., 2000: 2). Additionally, Foucault (1982: 786) saw power as relational, noting that 'it brings into play relations between individuals (or between groups)'. For him, this means that power presupposes the freedom of the individual, so that 'there is no relationship of power without the means of escape or possible flight' (Foucault, 1982: 794). In other words, power relations always inherently involve at least the possibility of resistance. In this chapter, I explore how Plaza de la Hoja, as a spatial technology of power, has brought such possibilities.

In doing so, I draw on Massey's (1999, 2005) writings on space. Foucault's understanding of power and resistance sits well with her conceptualisation of space as an 'always unfinished and open' process (Massey, 2005: 221). She argues for the need to see space as fundamentally dynamic, treating it as relational and 'constituted through interactions', as well as containing multiplicity and 'the possibility of the existence of more than one voice' (Massey, 1999: 3). In this sense, space is 'never finished; never closed' (Massey, 1999: 3). While geographers have examined the relationships that exist between space and power in detail (Allen, 2003; Elden and Crampton, 2016; Harvey, 1990; Meusburger et al., 2015; Philo, 2001), Massey's (1999, 2005, 2009) work reminds us of the need to also examine the multiplicity and heterogeneity of the power relations that constitute and are constituted by space. This includes the need to empirically explore resistance that occurs in concrete spaces.

This chapter aims to contribute to our understanding of critical geographies of resistance through an empirical exploration of these geographies as they pan out in Plaza de la Hoja. As discussed by Sharp et al. (2000: 26), the 'abstract forces of domination and resistance become tangible relations of power-creating subjects, identities and knowledges, but only when enunciated in particular places at particular times'. To render concrete these 'abstract forces', this chapter employs data from fieldwork conducted in Bogotá between October 2017 and August 2018 – including frequent visits to Plaza de la Hoja, and 14 interviews undertaken with its residents – to explore how power and resistance are 'entangled' (Sharp et al., 2000: 20) in the Plaza de la Hoja project.

The chapter proceeds as follows. In the next section I analyse Plaza de la Hoja as a spatial technology of control that renders the continued socio-economic marginalisation of the internally displaced politically invisible. The housing project creates the illusion that the state has cared for this group, while they continue to face persistent discrimination, barriers to enter the labour market, and disproportionate levels of crime and violence, thus reinforcing power relations that place the displaced in a marginal position within Colombian society. Nevertheless, I argue that Plaza de la Hoja has also brought new opportunities for resistance that its residents have utilised. Finally, I explore these opportunities, detailing how its residents have taken advantage of Plaza de la Hoja's layout and central location to organise collectively and to connect their struggles to other social processes that are ongoing in the city.

PLAZA DE LA HOJA: A TECHNOLOGY OF INVISIBILITY

From a Foucauldian perspective, Plaza de la Hoja – and the Free Housing Programme more broadly – can be analysed as a governmental technology that reinforces, perpetuates and reveals power relations that exist between the internally displaced and the state in Colombia. In this section, I detail how the housing project functions as what anthropologist João Biehl (2005: 259) calls a 'technology of invisibility' that sustains the marginal positioning of the internally displaced within Colombian society.

Writing about an asylum in Porto Alegre in Brazil, Biehl (2013: 4) reflects on the spaces in which the people unwanted by society – 'the mentally ill and homeless, AIDS patients, the unproductive young, and old bodies' – are abandoned by the state. Here, spatial configurations produce invisibility, and this invisibility, in turn, enables abandonment, involving 'an indispensable tool of containment (a structured non-intervention) within the calculations of life processes' (Biehl, 2005: 264). Biehl (2005: 259) terms the procedures, techniques and spatial configurations permitting such abandonment 'technologies of invisibility'.

Plaza de la Hoja can be understood as such a 'technology of invisibility' (ibid.) because the project allows the government to celebrate its advances in protecting the rights of the displaced, at the same time as the housing complex has not redressed the continued socio-economic marginalisation facing this group of people, thus rendering their marginalisation politically invisible.

These dynamics are evident from interviews detailing daily life in Plaza de la Hoja. The flats themselves are poorly constructed. The project was handed over in a condition referred to in Spanish as *obra negra*,[2] meaning that, while the rough construction of the flats was complete, they had simple, unpainted concrete walls, ceilings and floors. As Maritza,[3] a street vendor who I interviewed, related, 'they didn't hand over the flats the way they were supposed to. No, because they were designed one way, and handed over in another, in *obra negra*' (interview, 9 May 2018). She said that the flats, 'had problems with damp. There are people for whom, still, if it rains, and with the winter[4] time we are in, water comes into their flats' (interview, 9 May 2018). Similarly, Edwin, an indigenous Pijao man, told me that 'unfortunately when they handed this over, it was badly constructed' (interview, 19 February 2018).

The residents in Plaza de la Hoja also lacked communal and recreational spaces, and the flats were small. 'We don't have a parking lot in this project, we don't have a park, we don't have somewhere our elderly, children, or infants, can have a recreational space', Edwin related (interview, 19 February 2018). Similarly, William, another resident, noted that 'for the children and youth there's a lack of a recreational space' (interview, 18 April 2014). In addition, the flats – which all have two bedrooms, a small open plan living room and kitchen, and a bathroom – were not big enough for the size of most families living there. As Edwin told me: 'the flats should have been occupied by two, three, maximum five people. But it is a lie, in many of the flats, there are 10, 12, 15, even 20 people' (interview, 19 February 2018).

Beyond providing residents with shelter, receiving housing in Plaza de la Hoja has done little to restore the socio-economic rights that the internally displaced have lost through their displacement, something which is a stated aim of the government's rights restitution policies (see El Congreso de la República de Colombia, 2011). Specifically, the project has failed to address the precarious employment and exploitative labour market conditions facing residents, as well as high degrees of criminal violence and continued social discrimination.

Plaza de la Hoja's residents reported facing structural barriers to accessing the labour market. The case of Juan Camilo illustrates this. A divorced man in his late fifties, Juan Camilo was unemployed, earning just enough to eat through selling coffee on the street. For him, receiving the flat meant little while he was still unable to work. 'What I need is to work. I am not asking for anything, I am only asking for an opportunity, for them to give me the green light for something, so I can work' (interview, 25 February 2018).

He could not afford to pay for water and electricity and they had already cut off his gas. He was worried that the state would take the flat back if he could not pay his bills; a threat all too real, as Presidential Decree 1077 of 2015 clearly states that paying bills is a prerequisite for living there (El Presidente de la República de Colombia, 2015). 'Where am I going to end up, in the streets?' he asked (interview, 25 February 2018).

While he had received a flat, Juan Camilo still felt socio-economically marginalised. He had accrued high amounts of debt; everything he owned he had bought on credit, including his fridge. 'I have this [flat], which the state gave me,' he noted, 'but I don't have employment, I don't have furniture, I don't have a family, I don't have anything' (interview, 25 February 2018). He continued, 'I feel displaced by the government, I feel displaced by the community, by the society, and by the [state] entities that are against us' (interview, 25 February 2018).

Similar stories of unemployment or precarious employment were abundant in my interviews with the residents in Plaza de la Hoja. Camila, a young, single mother of three, related how she struggled to survive after the father of her children left her. 'They gave us this flat, right? But things have been difficult, woman, it has been very hard without support from a man' (interview, 21 April 2018). She struggled finding stable employment, barely surviving. 'I've had to go and do the washing up in restaurants, for 15 000 pesos,[5] sometimes they give me 25 000'[6] (interview, 21 April 2018). Camila could not afford to pay her bills. 'The little I have I use for eating' (interview, 21 April 2018). Receiving the flat had therefore not redressed her marginalisation. 'They gave us this house, this flat – and may God forgive me – for nothing' (interview, 21 April 2018).

Similarly, Edwin related how, while in the countryside he could sustain his family through rearing chicken, pigs and cows, he was unable to find employment in the city because of his background in agriculture. 'The majority of the community doesn't have employment. They have to beg for food because there hasn't been an institutional offer' (interview, 19 February 2018). He went on to note that 'you have to fulfil a string of requisites, when we don't know the city well, and we don't have experiences in the city, and that is where we practically face a wall that we have to overcome to be able to live in dignity' (interview, 19 February 2018).

In addition to facing obstacles in the labour market, the residents in the Free Housing Programme projects also faced high crime rates in the surrounding area, as well as continued discrimination and stigma in the city. The case of Alba hints at this. An indigenous woman, Alba was in her fifties. She was displaced to Bogotá in the early 2000s after her husband, a demobilised member of a guerrilla group, was assassinated, and Alba's daughter was kidnapped, along with her daughter's son, who they have not seen since. For Alba, coming to Plaza de la Hoja had done little in terms of repairing the damage done through the conflict. 'They killed my husband, and I was left adrift. And yes, I have this house, I am the owner of this house, but they haven't repaired me, and I don't have a job, nobody will give me a job' (interview, 27 February 2018). She felt abandoned by the government. 'It's a lie that these people care about you. They never care about you. They make you tell them everything, that you tell them everything you know, but in the end, they abandon you' (interview, 27 February 2018).

Alba's disappointment with the government's response was not limited to her inability to find a job in the city, but was instead also related to the continued social disenfranchisement her family faced. 'My son is 16 years old, and he has been using drugs since he was 9', she recounted (interview, 27 February 2018). Her adult daughter, who was sleeping in the room next door, was recovering from an illness related to substance use. Another of Alba's sons was serving time in prison, accused of stealing a phone. 'I have a son who is in prison, unjustly!' (interview, 27 February 2018). In Plaza de la Hoja, Alba felt rejected both by her neighbours and by the population of Bogotá. 'They treat me like a thief, they treat me like a drug dealer, they say I sell drugs' (interview, 27 February 2018).

As suggested by Alba's story, the Free Housing Programme projects are disproportionately afflicted by crime. In Bogotá many of the projects are located in areas plagued by both criminal and political violence, with reported incidences of homicides emerging in some of them (*El Tiempo*, 2017). Despite its more central location, Plaza de la Hoja is no exception. Juliana, for instance, related how there was initially a lot of drug-dealing in the housing project, 'but now they have learnt that they cannot do it here, they have found other places to do it' (interview, 14 April 2018). Edwin recalled how they had to erect a fence because so many of the flats were broken into. 'There were break-ins in some flats at the beginning because we didn't know the people, and there was a minimum of five flats per week that were broken into' (interview, 19 February 2018). Similarly, Maritza said that she felt unsafe in the surrounding area. 'If you go out you get robbed, attacked, everything. If you just pass under this bridge at night, you'll get robbed or attacked' (interview, 9 May 2018).

While residents are disproportionately afflicted by crime, Plaza de la Hoja has also failed to mitigate the social stigma that those internally displaced often face in the city. Like Alba, many of the residents who I spoke to reported experiencing persistent discrimination from their neighbours outside the housing project. Patricia, a woman in her forties, told me that she could not send her son to the local school because the teachers had treated him differently for being displaced. 'The teachers, how do I say this ... they treat displaced people like the worst, yeah?' (interview, 17 February 2018). Similarly, Edwin recounted persistent rejection by the surrounding community. 'We have felt, even now, a discrimination on part of the upper-class society. The residents here see us as ... "mosquitos" we call it here – this stigma that we don't have the capacity to be part of this society' (interview, 19 February 2018).

Zooming in on Plaza de la Hoja, then, illuminates the key role of space in sustaining power relations predicated on marginality. Understood as a 'technology of invisibility' (Biehl, 2005: 259), Plaza de la Hoja reinforces, perpetuates and makes invisible the continued socio-economic disenfranchisement of the internally displaced in Colombia. Its flats are small, poorly constructed, and residents lack access to recreational spaces. They face obstacles in the labour market, are disproportionately afflicted by crime and violence, and face stigma and discrimination from other, non-displaced, residents in Bogotá.

Simultaneously, Plaza de la Hoja makes it seem as though the state has solved the issue of displacement, having, after all, provided the internally displaced with flats in a high-profile project in the centre of the city. As Edwin put it, 'the government wants us to appear like we're a community that has been well attended to by the national government' (interview, 19 February 2018). For him, the government tried to 'put makeup on us, make it look like we're the best, that we're in a good location and have everything, when many of us here don't even have anything to eat' (interview, 19 February 2018). The hyper-visible presence of the internally displaced in the city, represented by the Plaza de la Hoja housing project, renders invisible the fact that Juan Camilo cannot afford furniture, that Edwin faces discrimination, and that Alba's daughter is lying sick in her bedroom.

These dynamics are not unique to Plaza de la Hoja, but are also evident throughout the Free Housing Programme more broadly. Its implementation has allowed the Colombian government to celebrate its advances in terms of the housing it offers to the displaced. The project has been lauded as a success by both the media and the government (Arcieri, 2015; Barajas, 2018). Upon handing over the 100 000th housing unit to Osiris Cárdenas, a single mother in Montes de María, Santos exclaimed that 'the children of Osiris are studying and now they can live in a decent house. This is something we want for all of Colombia' (cited in Arcieri, 2015, translated from Spanish).

Thus, the Free Housing Programme sweeps under the rug the continued marginalisation of many of those who have been granted flats. The limited evidence available suggests that the projects frequently lack adequate access to public services, particularly public transport; that residents still face barriers in the labour market; and that many are built in peripheral areas that suffer from broader social problems (Gilbert, 2014; Ruiz, 2018). Reports of violence breaking out in the projects have emerged (Correa et al., 2014; *El Tiempo*, 2017), and the Ministry of Housing has already taken back flats that it has granted, alleging that they have been used for 'illicit activities' (Ministerio de Vivienda, 2020).

Evidence from both the Free Housing Programme and empirical data describing daily life in Plaza de la Hoja suggests that the housing project reproduces power relations that position the internally displaced in a marginal position. Nevertheless, we should not forget Foucault's (1982) insistence that power cannot exist without the possibility of resistance, nor Massey's (1999, 2005) contention that space is fundamentally open and always in the process of being negotiated. In the next section I draw on these insights in detailing emergent forms of resistance in Plaza de la Hoja, highlighting how this has partly been enabled by its spatial layout.

PLAZA DE LA HOJA REVISITED: NEW OPPORTUNITIES FOR RESISTANCE

While constituting a technology of invisibility (Biehl, 2005), Plaza de la Hoja has also provided its residents with new opportunities for resistance, highlighting the possibility for 'reversal' at the heart of power (Foucault, 1982: 794), as well as the fundamental openness of space (Massey, 2005).

The opportunities for resistance brought by Plaza de la Hoja cannot be fully comprehended without first acknowledging the rich legacy of activism that exists amongst the internally displaced in Colombia. Since the mid-1990s, this group has mobilised collectively to demand access to the rights restitution measures promised to them by the Colombian state (Osorio Pérez, 2007; Olarte and Wall, 2012; Zeiderman, 2013).

A crucial tactic in this mobilisation has been the occupation of public spaces, such as parks, squares and government offices (Olarte and Wall, 2012). When the Free Housing Programme was announced, several sites provided for the project by the local government in Bogotá were occupied by displaced activists to make sure that the government did not back down on its promises (see Canal Capital Bogota, 2013; Caracol Radio, 2013). The Plaza de la Hoja housing project itself stands on a site which was occupied to express a demand for housing in May 2013, when over 500 people took over the square (Caracol Radio, 2013). To demand inclusion into the project, the internally displaced have also occupied other strategic public spaces, including government buildings (Motoa Franco, 2015) and Bogotá's main airport (*El País*, 2015).

For Carolina Olarte and Illan rua Wall (2012), the occupation of symbolically important public spaces has allowed the internally displaced in Colombia to contest the invisibility confronting them. By articulating their demands in a highly visible manner, they 'refuse the place assigned to them in the political order' (Olarte and Wall, 2012: 333). In this section I explore how the residents in Plaza de la Hoja have utilised this space to challenge their political invisibility. They do so by engaging in forms of activism in which they challenge their marginalisation, and demand more from the state than the meagre shelter they have been accorded, as well as by strategically using the spatial layout and central location of Plaza de la Hoja to build connections with, and participate in, wider struggles happening in the city.

The residents who I spoke to in Plaza de la Hoja continued the legacy of resistance and activism of the internally displaced more broadly in Colombia, engaging in a diverse set of activities that challenged their political invisibility and the social conditions facing them in the housing project.

Patricia, for instance, became involved in community work after she came to Plaza de la Hoja. She was not content to accept the marginalisation facing the residents, but instead worked to actively challenge it. In particular, she was concerned about the dismal employment prospects facing the residents. 'That is a fight that I am fighting for my daughters, because I have seen that they have no employment opportunities' (interview, 17 February 2018). She was also concerned about reparations: she related how she had participated in a protest demanding the payment of damages, despite already having received this herself, because 'there are a lot of people here who haven't received the payment of damages, and I am fighting for them' (interview, 17 February 2018).

Patricia was far from the only person becoming involved in community work in Plaza de la Hoja. Her close neighbour, Jennifer, was similarly engaged in activities to improve the conditions in the housing project, focused on local youth and women. 'I am particularly worried for the kids who use drugs … and I started working with women, because when I arrived here, I noticed a lot of the women were very submissive towards their husbands' (interview, 14 December 2017). When I spoke to her, Jennifer took part in an informal group run by the women in Plaza de la Hoja, meant as a space for them to socialise and engage in entrepreneurial activities where they could generate a steady income. The group had turned one of the unused terraces in the housing project into a communal area. In this way, they were able to negotiate the lack of communal spaces in Plaza de la Hoja, establishing somewhere for them to meet.

Other residents joined or founded organisations working more explicitly for the rights of the internally displaced after arriving in Plaza de la Hoja. William, for instance, related how he had helped form an organisation which was primarily involved in claiming rights through official procedures such as petitions.[7] Similarly, Juan Camilo was a member of an organisation working for the internally displaced, as well as a workers' organisation. As a space, then, Plaza de la Hoja has brought together a group of people previously dispersed throughout the city and allowed them to organise collectively. In Plaza de la Hoja, William, Juan Camilo, and others like them, have been able to meet others facing similar predicaments and have used this opportunity to form organisations that actively challenge their marginalisation and political invisibility.

The residents' efforts to challenge their marginalisation and political invisibility have been further enabled by Plaza de la Hoja's spatial layout and central location, which has allowed them to engage in highly visible tactics in the form of occupations and public protests. Plaza de la Hoja is situated at the intersection between two principal motorways: Carrera 30, which connects the northeast of Bogotá with the southwest of the city, and Calle 19, which connects the centre of the city with the western parts of Bogotá. On multiple occasions, the residents in Plaza de la Hoja have blockaded these to draw attention to their plight, according to three functionaries who I interviewed at the Ministry of Housing. The functionaries hyperbolically claimed that the residents in Plaza de la Hoja would protest at the slightest opportunity. 'They don't use the procedure of sending a petition, presenting it, and waiting for a response, but at once they use direct action' (interview, 2 November 2017). They continued, 'they will block a street ... anything that occurs to them that is against the law!' (interview, 2 November 2017). In this way, the residents have used the strategic location of Plaza de la Hoja to challenge their marginality, continuing a pre-existing legacy amongst the displaced in Colombia of using public space to draw attention to their marginalisation, thus contesting their political invisibility (Olarte and Wall, 2012).

In addition, the spacious square stretching out in front of Plaza de la Hoja, combined with its central location, has allowed the residents to connect their struggles to wider protest movements in Bogotá. When I conducted fieldwork in the area, residents in Plaza de la Hoja maintained close ties with activists at the nearby National University – a five-minute bus ride away – who held frequent workshops at the housing project.

Importantly, the project has itself also become a site for demonstrations in the city, which often start in Plaza de la Hoja and end in Plaza de Bolívar, Bogotá's main square. In November 2017, for instance, there was a march from Plaza de la Hoja to Plaza de Bolívar, demanding that the Santos administration comply with the peace agreement reached with the FARC, Colombia's largest guerrilla group, in 2016 (ONIC, 2017). During subsequent President Iván Duque's inauguration, protestors gathered outside Plaza de la Hoja in a demonstration 'for life and peace' that commemorated the high number of activists assassinated in the country since the signing of the peace agreement (*El Tiempo*, 2018; *pulzo.com*, 2018). Amid the national strikes that saw widespread protests against President Duque across Colombia from November 2019, protestors also gathered outside Plaza de la Hoja (*El Tiempo*, 2019), and in a second wave of national strikes starting in April 2021, Plaza de la Hoja was again a key place where protestors congregated (*El Tiempo*, 2021). This is facilitated by Plaza de la Hoja's central location in the city, but also by its unique architecture, as the large concrete square stretching in front of it is a perfect meeting place for protestors.

CONCLUSION

Plaza de la Hoja can be understood as 'technology of invisibility' (Biehl, 2005) that serves to render the socio-economic marginalisation of the internally displaced in the city politically invisible. Housing 457 families in a hyper-visible brutalist concrete building in the middle of Bogotá, the project sweeps under the carpet the poor living conditions, discrimination and continued socio-economic barriers that still face these families. In this way, the Free

Housing Programme allows the state to celebrate its advances in protecting the rights of the internally displaced, while most face persistent marginalisation, reminding us of the role of space in reinforcing and revealing dominant power relations (Harvey, 1990; Philo, 2001; Allen, 2003; Meusburger et al., 2015; Elden and Crampton, 2016).

At the same time, the Plaza de la Hoja project has also provided new opportunities for resistance and collective organisation. In its concrete towers, displaced people from all over Colombia have been brought together and have used this proximity to strategise and organise collectively in ways that challenge their political invisibility. Its residents have not passively accepted their marginalisation, but have instead engaged in community work and activism that seeks to transform the local environment in Plaza de la Hoja and to challenge their positioning. The central location of Plaza de la Hoja, combined with the large square in front of it, has also meant that the housing project has become a key space in which activists in the city congregate to challenge processes of violence, connecting the struggles already happening in Plaza de la Hoja to wider struggles happening in Bogotá more broadly. A site where the internally displaced have been rendered invisible and forgotten, through a government policy appearing to care for them while their socio-economic marginalisation continues, Plaza de la Hoja has repeatedly turned into the very site where that invisibility has been contested through public demonstrations; reminding us of the importance of Foucault's (1982) insistence that power always inherently involves the possibility of resistance, as well as the continued relevance of Massey's (2005) call to never treat space as closed or finished.

NOTES

1. In Spanish: *indemnización*. This refers to economic compensation for victimising acts which occurred during the conflict, including for forced displacement.
2. Literally 'black construction', a construction term used to refer to the erection of the basic external structure of a building.
3. All names mentioned are pseudonyms to protect the identity of the participants.
4. 'Winter' here means the rainy season.
5. Just over £3.
6. Just over £5.
7. This is a procedure set out in the Colombian Constitution whereby citizens can send petitions to state entities and receive a response to their queries.

REFERENCES

Allen, J. (2003) *Lost Geographies of Power*. RGS-IBG book series. Malden, MA: Blackwell Publishers.

Arcieri, V. (2015) Santos al entregar la casa 100.000: 'Vamos a seguir con nuestra política social de vivienda y educación gratis'. *El Heraldo*, 26 November. Bolivar.

Available at: https://www.elheraldo.co/bolivar/santos-al-entregar-la-casa-100000-vamos-seguir-con-nuestra-politica-social-de-vivienda-y (accessed 10 October 2020).
Barajas, Y.R. (2018) La vivienda gratuita es un éxito y se debe mantener: MinVivienda. *Vanguardia*, 2 June. Available at: https://www.vanguardia.com/economia/nacional/la-vivienda-gratuita-es-un-exito-y-se-debe-mantener-minvivienda-LEVL434834 (accessed 10 October 2020).
Biehl, J. (2005) Technologies of invisibility: politics of life and social inequality. In: Inda, J.X. (ed.), *Anthropologies of Modernity: Foucault, Governmentality, and Life Politics*. Malden, MA: Blackwell Publishing, pp. 248–271.
Biehl, J. (2013) *Vita: Life in a Zone of Social Abandonment*. Berkeley, CA: University of California Press.
Canal Capital Bogota (2013) *Desplazados se tomaron lote 'Las Margaritas' en Kennedy – YouTube*. Available at: https://www.youtube.com/watch?v=0Y35O_FtV6Y&ab_channel=CanalCapitalBogota (accessed 11 October 2020).
Caracol Radio (2013) Distrito y víctimas llegaron a un acuerdo para levantar la toma en predio de La Hoja. 4 May. Available at: https://caracol.com.co/radio/2013/05/04/bogota/1367681820_892914.html (accessed 10 October 2020).
Centro Nacional de Memoria Histórica (2013) *¡Basta Ya! Colombia, Memorias de Guerra y Dignidad: Informe General*, ed. Comisión Nacional de Reparación y Reconciliación (Colombia). Segunda edición corregida. Bogotá: Centro Nacional de Memoria Histórica.
Correa, P., Cuevas, A., Silva, S., et al. (2014) La otra cara de las viviendas gratis. *El Espectador*, 4 October. Available at: http://www.elespectador.com/noticias/nacional/otra-cara-de-viviendas-gratis-articulo-520618 (accessed 28 April 2017).
El Congreso de Colombia (2012) Law 1537. Available at: http://www.suin-juriscol.gov.co/viewDocument.asp?id=1683011 (accessed 20 August 2018).
El Congreso de la República de Colombia (2011) Ley 1448 de 2011. Available at: https://www.unidadvictimas.gov.co/es/ley-1448-de-2011/13653 (accessed 14 July 2018).
Elden, S. and Crampton, J.W. (2016) Introduction: space, knowledge and power: Foucault and geography. In: Elden, S. and Crampton, J.W. (eds), *Space, Knowledge and Power: Foucault and Geography*. Abingdon: Taylor & Francis, pp. 1–16.
El País (2015) Desplazados se tomaron el puente aéreo de Bogotá. 10 September. Available at: http://www.elpais.com.co/colombia/desplazados-se-tomaron-el-puente-aereo-de-bogota.html (accessed 29 April 2017).
El Presidente de la República de Colombia (2012) Decree 1921. Available at: https://www.funcionpublica.gov.co/eva/gestornormativo/norma.php?i=49407 (accessed 6 October 2020).
El Presidente de la República de Colombia (2015) Decreto Único Reglamentario 1077 de 2015. Available at: http://www.alcaldiabogota.gov.co/sisjur/normas/Norma1.jsp?i=62512 (accessed 20 August 2018).
El Tiempo (2017) Balacera en Usme dejó dos muertos. 5 September. Available at: https://www.eltiempo.com/bogota/balacera-en-usme-deja-dos-muertos-127210 (accessed 26 June 2019).
El Tiempo (2018) 'Que la paz no nos cueste la vida', lema de protesta pacífica. 7 August. Available at: https://www.eltiempo.com/politica/partidos-politicos/que-la-paz-no-nos-cueste-la-vida-lema-de-protesta-pacifica-253062 (accessed 12 October 2020).

El Tiempo (2019) Manifestantes en Bogotá se reúnen en la Plaza de la Hoja. 25 November. Available at: https://www.eltiempo.com/colombia/otras-ciudades/en-vivo-manifestaciones-del-25-de-noviembre-por-el-paro-nacional-en-colombia-436982 (accessed 12 October 2020).

El Tiempo (2021) Paro Nacional: así amanece Bogotá tras jornada de movilizaciones. 27 April. Available at: https://www.eltiempo.com/bogota/paro-nacional-en-vivo-movilizaciones-marchas-en-bogota-28-de-abril-584188 (accessed 23 June 2021).

Forero-Niño, L. (2012) Colombia's historic victims and land restitution law. *Law and Business Review of the Americas* 18(1): 97–103.

Foucault, M. (1982) The subject and power. *Critical Inquiry* 8(4): 777–795.

Foucault, M. (1991) *Discipline and Punish: The Birth of the Prison*. Reprint. Penguin Social Sciences. London: Penguin Books.

Gilbert, A.G. (2014) Free housing for the poor: An effective way to address poverty? *Habitat International* 41: 253–261.

Harvey, D. (1990) Between space and time: reflections on the geographical imagination 1. *Annals of the Association of American Geographers* 80(3): 418–434.

Massey, D. (1999) Philosophy and politics of spatiality: some considerations. The Hettner-Lecture in Human Geography. *Geographische Zeitschrift* 87(1): 1–12.

Massey, D.B. (2005) *For Space*. London. SAGE Publications.

Massey, D. (2009) Concepts of space and power in theory and in political practice. *Documents d'Anàlisi Geogràfica* 55: 15–26.

Meusburger, P., Gregory, D., Suarsana, L., et al. (eds) (2015) *Geographies of Knowledge and Power*. New York: Springer Berlin Heidelberg.

Ministerio de Vivienda (2015) Portal Minvivienda 457 familias de escasos recursos hoy cuentan con una vivienda digna en la Urbanizacion Plaza de la Hoja en Bogota. Available at: http://www.minvivienda.gov.co/sala-de-prensa/noticias/2015/enero/457-familias-de-escasos-recursos-hoy-cuentan-con-una-vivienda-digna-en-la-urbanizacion-plaza-de-la-hoja-en-bogota (accessed 7 October 2020).

Ministerio de Vivienda (2020) Portal Minvivienda El Minvivienda revoco subsidio de vivienda gratis por uso para actividades ilicitas en la urbanizacion El Tejar. Available at: http://www.minvivienda.gov.co/sala-de-prensa/noticias/2020/septiembre/el-minvivienda-revoco-subsidio-de-vivienda-gratis-por-uso-para-actividades-ilicitas-en-la-urbanizacion-el-tejar (accessed 10 October 2020).

Motoa Franco, F. (2015) Toma de desplazados en Bogotá destapó peligroso depósito de llantas. *El Tiempo*, 22 September. Available at: http://www.eltiempo.com/bogota/toma-de-desplazados-en-bogota-destapo-peligroso-deposito-de-llantas/16382954 (accessed 29 April 2017).

Olarte, C.O. and Wall, I.R. (2012) The occupation of public space in Bogotá: internal displacement and the city. *Social and Legal Studies* 21(3): 321–339.

ONIC (2017) Únete al Cecerolazo como la ONIC. Available at: https://www.onic.org.co/comunicados-de-otros-sectores/2203-unete-al-cecerolazo-como-la-onic (accessed 12 October 2020).

Osorio Pérez, F.E. (2007) *Territorialidades en suspenso: desplazamiento forzado, identidades y resistencias*. Bogotá, Colombia: Consultoría para los Derechos Humanos y el Desplazamiento.

Pabón, G. (2015) Develamos el interior de la 'Plaza de La Hoja': hogar de 457 familias. *Civico*, 22 October. Available at: https://www.civico.com/bogota/noticias/develamos-el-interior-de-la-plaza-de-la-hoja-el-hogar-de-457-familias-desplazadas (accessed 5 June 2019).

Philo, C. (2001) Accumulating populations: bodies, institutions and space. *International Journal of Population Geography* 7(6): 473–490. DOI: 10.1002/ijpg.243.

pulzo.com (2018) La otra cara de la posesión: con marchas, le recuerdan a Duque los líderes sociales. 7 August. Available at: https://www.pulzo.com/nacion/marchas-por-vida-paz-durante-posesion-ivan-duque-PP535989 (accessed 12 October 2020).

Rose, N. and Miller, P. (2010) Political power beyond the State: problematics of government. *British Journal of Sociology* 61: 271–303.

Ruiz, L.K.C. (2018) El programa de las 100 mil viviendas gratis y su impacto en la dinámica social, cultural y ambiental de los beneficiarios de los proyectos del municipio de San José de Cúcuta, periodo 2013–2015. *Respuestas* 23(Extra 1). Universidad Francisco de Paula Santander: 81–85.

Sharp, J.P., Routledge, P., Philo, C., et al. (2000) Entanglements of power: geographies of domination/resistance. In: Sharp, J.P., Routledge, P., Philo, C., et al. (eds), *Entanglements of Power: Geographies of Domination/Resistance*. Critical geographies. London, UK and New York, USA: Routledge, pp. 1–42.

Sliwa, M. and Wiig, H. (2016) Should I stay or should I go: the role of Colombian free urban housing projects in IDP return to the countryside. *Habitat International* 56: 11–19.

Summers, N. (2012) Colombia's victims' law: transitional justice in a time of violent conflict? *Harvard Human Rights Journal* 25: 18.

UARIV (2021) Víctimas por Hecho Victimizante. Available at: https://www.unidadvictimas.gov.co/es/registro-unico-de-victimas-ruv/37394 (accessed 29 March 2021).

Zeiderman, A. (2013) Living dangerously: biopolitics and urban citizenship in Bogotá, Colombia. *American Ethnologist* 40(1): 71–87.

Zeiderman, A. (2016) *Endangered City: The Politics of Security and Risk in Bogotá*. Global Insecurities series. Durham, NC: Duke University Press.

11. 'What size is the room?': using the law to resist the UK's bedroom tax
Mel Nowicki

INTRODUCING THE BEDROOM TAX

Since 2008, the United Kingdom (UK) has been largely governed under principles of austerity, a now-normative condition first established in the aftermath of the global financial crash. Central to the austerity regime has been the decimation of welfare, including legislation that has penalised people in receipt of benefits in a range of ways, including through their homes. This chapter explores the role of the law in both curtailing people's rights to home, and providing grounds for resistance. I argue that the domestic is not solely a site constrained by legal frameworks, but also a space through which resistance can be enacted. And whilst these acts might not in all cases look like popular imaginings of resistance – for example, large-scale public protests and other forms of direct action – they are nonetheless fundamental in eroding the influence of austerity. More than this, in the case of the bedroom tax, these piecemeal forms of resistance have to date been the most successful in enabling people to reclaim their legal rights to home. This chapter examines the ways in which social tenants and empathetic stakeholders have utilised spaces of law to resist the imposition of the UK's 'bedroom tax', and is based on research I conducted in 2014–17 exploring the impact of the policy. Methods consisted of (anonymised) interviews with affected social tenants, housing associations, charities and related stakeholders, and observation of online support groups.

The bedroom tax (officially the 'removal of the spare room subsidy') is one of a suite of measures introduced by former Prime Minister David Cameron's Conservative–Liberal Democrat Coalition government in the 2012 Welfare Reform Act, the crowning jewel of austerity politics. It constituted a drastic overhaul of the British welfare system, and included measures such as stringent Work Capability Assessments for those in receipt of Employment Support Allowance,[1] and mandatory contributions to council tax regardless of household income (Nowicki 2018). The bedroom tax comprised the core housing element of the Act, signalling a significant shift in welfare governance and reconstituting definitions of value and space in the social housing context. The policy affects social tenants in receipt of housing benefit,[2] reducing the amount of rent eligible for housing benefit for those deemed to have one or more 'spare bedroom'. The rules allow one bedroom for a single adult (over 16) or adult couple, and one bedroom per two children (one room per child is permissible if they are different sexes and over the age of ten).[3]

An initial impact assessment in 2013 by the Department for Work and Pensions estimated that around 660 000 working-age social tenants would be affected by the policy; this has since risen by 50 000 (Department for Work and Pensions 2012; Jayanetti 2021a). The government framed the decision to implement the bedroom tax as one based around fairness and tenure equality, stating that the policy was introduced in order to bring social rents 'in line with the private rented sector' (Department for Work and Pensions 2014). The 'removal of the spare room subsidy' tapped into a growing rhetoric regarding social housing tenants as taking up valuable space that they do not need, at a cost to the taxpayer. This further entrenched narratives of people in receipt of state support as 'scroungers': lazy non-contributors to society (Tyler 2013). The bedroom tax's introduction was the product of a long lineage of discrediting those in receipt of welfare that stretches back to the 1970s, and gained particular traction during Margaret Thatcher's premiership (1979–90). The shift from Keynesian to neoliberal ideology during this period augmented social housing from being a product of post-World War II egalitarianism, to a dysfunctional system that enabled people to 'get away with' having low housing costs. This rhetoric became especially pertinent in areas of the country where housing costs are high, such as inner London (Hamnett 2012). This already present sentiment was exacerbated all the more in the wake of the 2008 financial crash and resulting recession, where scapegoating the working class became a common method of distracting people from the real reasons behind their own increasing precarity; namely, cuts to crucial welfare services, cuts to wages and growing costs of living in real terms (Nowicki 2018; McKenzie 2015).

However, arguably the public mood regarding social housing at the time was somewhat misread in regard to the 'removal of the spare room subsidy'. Shortly after it was announced, the policy's official title became largely obscured, and it is now widely known as the 'bedroom tax'. This was much to David Cameron's consternation, who stated: 'I don't accept the bedroom tax is a tax – it's an issue about benefit' (Brown 2013a). The Labour Party's Lord Best, who is often attributed with coining the term, defended the policy's unofficial renaming, arguing that 'if you have to pay a sum of money and you can't escape from doing so, and that sum of money goes to the government – it looks to me all very much like having a tax' (Brown 2013b). The policy's popular renaming helped to cement negative public feeling towards it in a way that other measures introduced in the Welfare Act had not. The use of the word 'bedroom' conjures up imagery of an aspect of home most associated with intimacy and the private. The bedroom connotes many intensely personal activities in human life: the bedroom is where we sleep, where we have sex, where we retreat in order to be alone, where we ready ourselves for the day, where we recover when we are unwell. The term 'bedroom tax' has also been compared to and evoked memories of the much maligned Conservative taxation of the late 1980s and early 1990s, the 'poll tax'[4] (Stephenson 2013). The bedroom tax therefore gained traction as a controversial and invasive policy before it had even been implemented and its impact fully realised. This certainly helped to legitimise early acts of resistance, particularly in relation to its legal curtailment of rights to domestic space.

The policy also proved particularly controversial due to its disproportionate impact on disabled people. According to research conducted by Moffatt et al. (2015), around a third of all social tenants affected by the policy are living with a disability. In part for these reasons, the bedroom tax instigated public empathy and collective action against the policy in a way not seen with other elements of welfare reform. The bedroom tax was framed by those seeking to resist it as the insertion of discriminatory legislation into the home, and as this chapter will attest, it was through these legislative spaces that social tenants and housing associations began to fight back. After outlining growing interest in the legal sphere in geographical scholarship, the remainder of the chapter highlights three instances of legally framed resistance to the bedroom tax: tenants taking the government to court, the establishment of social media legal advice groups, and housing associations and charities taking advantage of legal and policy loopholes. Through these three examples, the chapter concludes by calling for an expansion of what we understand as resistance, where resistance takes place, and who is able to resist.

LEGAL GEOGRAPHIES, INTIMATE LIFE AND EMERGENT RESISTANCE

In recent years, legal geography has emerged as growing sub-discipline. Spearheaded by the Canadian geographer Nicholas Blomley, the co-constitution of space and law has become consolidated as a significant area of inquiry within the subject, with the legal and the geographical being more clearly understood as intrinsically connected to one another (Blomley 1994). As David Delaney (2015: 99) notes, 'in our world, there is nothing in the world of spaces, places, landscapes, and environments that is not affected by the workings of law'. Most recently, the role of law in shaping space, and vice versa, has been explored through a feminist lens by Katherine Brickell and Dana Cuomo, among others. Brickell and Cuomo identify what they term 'feminist geolegality' as the intersection between feminist geopolitics and legal geographies (Brickell and Cuomo 2019). They argue for an understanding of the geopolitical and the legal which acknowledges that traditional understandings of geopolitics (warfare, terrorism, and so on) and 'banal' intimate violences as inseparable. As Sjoberg and Gentry (2015: 358) highlight, 'Looking at where women are and where gender is shows that war, terrorism and insecurity are as often in the bedroom as on the battlefield, and as often in the family home as in houses of government'. Extending discussion of the entanglements of law, geopolitics and feminism, Brickell and Cuomo call for further interrogation of the ways in which the legal becomes inscribed onto bodies, homes, and other so-called everyday spaces. In doing so, they reveal the complexities of the legal arena as a site of control, but also as a means of resistance by which women and other marginalised groups struggle for transformation (Brickell and Cuomo 2019).

This is certainly true of the bedroom tax, the intimacies of which are writ large in its name. The bedroom tax serves as an example of national legislative decision-making about who is deserving of what kind of home. This is particularly pertinent considering that the bedroom tax disproportionately impacts disabled people who are in need of extra space for a wide range of reasons, from storing medical equipment, to having to sleep in separate rooms from partners due to their condition. As scholars in the field of disability geographies have noted, disabled people are commonly figured as tragic characters, 'failing to meet normal standards of form, mobility and ability' (Parr and Butler 1999: 3). The disabled body is constructed via a spatial logic that separates people both corporeally and psychologically on the basis of their disability (Imrie and Edwards 2007). This is built into the bedroom tax, which renders the disabled body invisible at the same time as de-valuing it through disproportionately punitive legislation. And yet, in keeping with legal geographers' understanding of law and space as co-constituted, the law has served as a means of resistance, as well as subjugation, for those impacted by the bedroom tax. As the following sections explore in greater detail, it is the very confines of the legal sphere as a mechanism of separation and categorisation (Brickell and Cuomo 2019) that have been utilised by both social tenants and empathetic housing association employees as a means of challenging the bedroom tax. Such forms of legal resistance can be considered within the remit of what Sarah Hughes refers to as emergent resistance: forms of resistance that do not necessarily fit with pre-determined typologies (Hughes 2020). Tracing resistance in its becoming, Hughes (2020: 1143) argues: 'prevents a foreclosure of emergent forces into predetermined forms (e.g. of activist, intentional subject, protest, tactic or dispute), and thereby keeps open the category of resistance to other subjects, materials, spaces and temporalities which do not always cohere to an (expected) resistant form'.

The examples in this chapter speak to such emergent resistance through a consideration of the ways in which social tenants and empathetic stakeholders (housing associations, housing and welfare charities) have challenged the bedroom tax, identifying and navigating legal spaces through which to resist its imposition in largely mundane settings not usually equated with resistance movements: online social media groups and housing association offices. The chapter's first case study, of social tenants taking the government to court, is a far more spectacular and perhaps expected form of resistance. However, what remains external to expected resistant forms are the people enacting it: disabled, working-class social tenants, a group of people for whom the courtroom is often associated as a punitive, rather than emancipatory, space. In sum, as the remainder of this chapter explores, the relationship between the law, the body and the domestic is not one that is solely constraining and destructive, but also a site through which we might better understand the ways in which varying forms of resistance emerge.

LEGALLY CHALLENGING THE GOVERNMENT

Challenging the bedroom tax using legal routes has proved to be a prevalent, and at times successful, means of resisting its implementation. In doing so, social tenants affected by the bedroom tax further legitimise their challenge to government by using governance structures themselves as a means of resistance. This use of legal frameworks in resisting the bedroom tax can be found at every level of the national court system. Since its implementation, the policy has been contested in both First-Tier and Upper Tribunals[5] on a wide range of grounds: from discrimination against disabled people, in particular those who need overnight care, specialist equipment storage, or separate rooms from partners; to discrimination against single parents who do not have primary custody of their children; to appeals on the grounds of rooms being too small or of an inappropriate shape to be considered a bedroom. Legal challenges to the bedroom tax have since risen through the courts, taking place in both the Court of Appeal and the Supreme Court, the highest in the UK legal system. Cases such as that of the Carmichaels, widely reported at the time, brought to public attention components of the bedroom tax that discriminate against the specific needs of many disabled people. Jacqueline Carmichael, who has spina bifida, was subject to the bedroom tax despite having to sleep in a separate room from her husband (who is also her full-time carer) due to her condition. They took their case to court,[6] and at a tribunal hearing in 2014 a judge ruled that the Carmichaels were entitled to two bedrooms, and that the bedroom tax should not have been imposed (Royal Courts of Justice 2014).

Later that year, a group of disabled adults, including the Carmichaels, took their concerns further, making a case against the bedroom tax in the Court of

Appeal[7] on the grounds that the policy was a curtailment of their human rights. The Court ruled against their case, stating that 'although the under-occupancy rules were discriminatory, for disabled adults the discrimination was justified and therefore lawful' (Leigh Day 2014). However, in January 2016, the Court of Appeal went on to rule in favour of two other parties penalised by the bedroom tax, on the grounds that in their cases the policy was unlawful.[8] The policy was challenged by the grandparents of a teenager who needs overnight care, and by a victim of domestic violence whose 'spare' room consists of a panic room to protect her from a violent ex-partner (BBC 2016). A further victory was won in November 2016, when the same group whose case had been rejected by the Court of Appeal won in the Supreme Court.[9] Collectively, these rulings mean that social tenants whose partners need to sleep in separate rooms due to medical conditions, who act as overnight carers for disabled family members, or social tenants who have panic rooms installed, are now able to challenge the legality of their penalisation using the Supreme Court rulings as case-based evidence. This was strengthened further by another Supreme Court case in 2019[10] where the Court ruled that a man, known as RR, should not be penalised by the bedroom tax as it was a curtailment of his human rights. Alongside this, it was ruled that it is not legal for local authorities to apply the bedroom tax in cases where it would lead to a breach of the Human Rights Act (Leigh Day 2019). These successes have again set precedent for other households in similar circumstances to challenge the bedroom tax through the use of case law as evidence of discrimination. Although a case law approach is unable to provide a universal challenge to the bedroom tax, it has nonetheless broken ground for its dismantling through providing a means of protection for a range of groups.

The success of these legal challenges highlights the ways in which law can be used to expose and redress spatial injustice (Delaney 2016). These challenges to the bedroom tax focused on the ways in which the legislation discriminates against disabled people, and those protecting themselves from domestic violence, asking the courts to redraw understandings of the 'spare bedroom' in many instances as a necessary space for the assurance of wellbeing and safety. They brought to the fore the ways in which governments often discriminate against disabled bodies, and particularly how policies such as the bedroom tax discount the spatial and architectural needs of those who are marginalised by a political discourse that understands home and housing through the lens of able-bodied needs only (Imrie and Edwards 2007). To return to Brickell and Cuomo's (2019) emphasis on the intricate relationship between the body, law and resistance, these examples highlight the ways in which tenants repurposed the categories of spare bedroom etched into the bedroom tax. In this way, they were able to utilise the legal sphere to highlight the discrimination that the bedroom tax imposed upon their bodies and domestic needs.

VIRTUAL LEGAL SPACES: THE ROLE OF SOCIAL MEDIA IN LEGALLY CHALLENGING THE BEDROOM TAX

Reworking the law from a barrier to an aid has been utilised to challenge the bedroom tax in other ways than through the high-profile cases discussed above. A key method of resistance also lies in the use of social media, in particular Facebook groups, that provide support and information for those affected by the bedroom tax. In these groups, members receive and share advice based on their experiences, with the goal of appealing the policy through the tribunal system. Although perhaps not immediately identifiable as such, due to their association with the everyday (often wrongly placed in opposition to the spectacular and political), these seemingly mundane virtual spaces constitute an important method of reframing the legal system as a means of protecting homes under threat from welfare reform.

Social tenants affected by the bedroom tax use these groups to post queries relating to the size and shapes of their rooms, looking for advice on whether they are able to launch an appeal on the basis that what their local authority has deemed a 'spare bedroom' is in fact too small to be legally classed as such. Other members post previous disputes that claimants have won on similar grounds in order to help people to build their cases. Pinned posts in the groups highlight areas of potential appeal by positing questions such as 'What size is the room?', 'Can you easily fit a bed and basic bedroom furniture in there?', and 'Would the bed be too near, or obstructing, the radiator?'. The groups also often include links to templates for appeal letters in order to help those fighting bedroom tax decisions to navigate the legal process. Using amalgamated knowledge, group members encourage one another to take action and fight to reverse local authority decisions. Here, social media also functions to de-mystify the court room; a space usually understood as a site of resistance only for those who have high levels of economic and social capital. Social media in this instance reconstructs the courtroom as an attainable site through which resistance to the bedroom tax can be sought, and rights to social housing re-established. Here, the very mechanisms that have been used to categorise and define who is and is not deserving of multiple bedrooms are repurposed, providing routes through which to reclaim what does, and crucially what does not, count as a spare bedroom.

The phenomenon of social media as a key contemporary site of resistance and dissent has garnered academic interest particularly since the 2011 Arab Spring and the global Occupy movement of the same year, which were the first high-profile instances of social media's role in global political activism (Gerbaudo 2012). Indeed, social media is often in part attributed to the overthrowing of dictators across Egypt, Tunisia, Morocco and Libya during the Arab Spring period (Tudoroiu 2014). Since 2011, the optimistic stance that social media is a positive tool for change has been complicated by rises in far-right political extremism, the 2016 election of Donald Trump in the United States, and rampant Covid-19 pandemic conspiracies facilitated by Facebook and other platforms. However, social media nonetheless continues to provide an integral means of resistance for people who are socially and spatially excluded and marginalised. This at times contradictory relationship highlights the ways in which modes of resistance are entangled in power relations. In the case of Facebook, its status as one of the world's most influential companies means that it can exert huge influence on national politics, whilst at the same time providing an integral means of communication for grassroots resistance movements. This makes it an especially important and fascinating platform for geographers interested in examining the relationship between power and resistance.

Social media in the context of the bedroom tax has provided a means of connecting people who are often excluded from both traditional spaces of public protest, and from the legal sphere: sites often demarcated by socio-political barriers such as gender, race, dis/ability and economic and educational attainment. Members of the bedroom tax support groups encourage others to take an active role in establishing legal challenges through publicising and celebrating group members' appeal wins, and reiterating the far-reaching impact of individual successes. This emphasis on both a long-term solution to the bedroom tax on an individual scale, and the contribution of individual wins in dismantling the legislation more widely, encapsulates a form of piecemeal resistance that supports larger outcomes. The continual challenging and dismantling of the law that underpins the bedroom tax has the potential to eventually erode its legal legitimacy altogether.

Social media support groups provide mechanisms to connect and construct networks of community-based activism. They are also an important means of circumventing socio-economic geographical barriers to the legal sphere. Social tenants who may not otherwise have been able to become involved in organised resistance, due to disability or low incomes restricting their mobility, are enabled and empowered by the construction of a virtual network. Mobilities scholarship has identified sociality and community identity as being produced through networks of people and ideas that cannot necessarily be ascribed to living in close geographical proximity (see Cresswell 2010). This, too, can be said of immobility (or reduced mobility) and exclusion from traditional spaces of resistance such as the street or public square. For those who are unable, or decide not to, engage in more publicly performative forms of resistance, communities that are unbound by spatial fixity become key sites through which to challenge punitive laws and reclaim rights to home. Such social media groups also work to de-mythologise and reframe the legal spaces of the city from spaces of intimidation to spaces of emancipation. First-Tier or Upper Tribunal appeals are dealt with on a case-by-case basis, and are much smaller in scale than the Supreme Court hearings in terms of their potential for immediate and widespread change. They are nonetheless crucial spaces through which social tenants challenging the bedroom tax can potentially regain autonomy over their own homes, and pave the way for others to do the same. The Facebook groups do not evoke the spectacle of resistance that Supreme Court victories do. They do, however, entrench resistance into the everyday experience of living with the bedroom tax by normalising social tenants' understanding that they have both the legal right and resources to challenge it. By utilising an everyday space such as a social media site to encourage resistance and reworking (Katz 2004) of the law, group members consequently open up the legal space of the courtroom as an emergent site of revolt.

FINDING OTHER MEANS: DISCRETIONARY HOUSING PAYMENT AND LEGAL LOOPHOLES

It is not just tenants themselves who have used legislation as a means of resisting the bedroom tax. Housing associations and housing and welfare charities have also provided support for people through the use of alternative financial streams and legal loopholes found in the bedroom tax. Discretionary Housing Payment (DHP), a pot of funding allocated to local authorities to provide housing support, as well as other forms of welfare support such as tax credits and Employment Support Allowance (ESA), were used where possible to cover the shortfalls created by the bedroom tax. The role of these stakeholders as key challengers of the bedroom tax further highlights the potentially powerful effects of multiple, piecemeal methods of resistance.

Indeed, throughout the research project, I found that housing associations themselves also faced precarious outcomes as a consequence of the bedroom tax, namely through a loss of income from residents. There were therefore high levels of motivation to find ways of working around the legislation. Employees of housing associations and charities who I interviewed often talked of the varying ways in which they tried to offset the worst effects of the bedroom tax. The welfare officer for a small housing association, managing properties predominately in an east London borough with high levels of deprivation, told me that their organisation had (as of 2014) not evicted anyone as a consequence of the bedroom tax, and that this was largely due to the existence of DHP. Indeed, all housing associations I spoke with cited DHP, a funding source that had been more commonly used to support private rather than social tenants, as the most common and effective means of reducing the impact of the bedroom tax in the short-to-medium term.

A welfare adviser for a UK debt charity confirmed that DHP provided a vital source of relief for clients affected by the bedroom tax. They helped clients to apply to their local authority for DHP funding, as well as looking into whether they were eligible for further tax credits or higher levels of ESA in order to make up some of the income lost through the bedroom tax. Housing associations and charities relied on using some government schemes to mitigate the effects of others, combating the loss of income in one area by attempting to extract more money from another. Similarly to the example of the Facebook support groups, this is an approach that utilises legal and policy knowledge to subvert and challenge the bedroom tax.

This was also evident in the emergence of a legal loophole in the bedroom tax legislation which housing associations and charities utilised to help clients claim back lost income. 4(1)(a) of Schedule 3 of the Housing Benefit and Council Tax Benefit (Consequential Provisions) Regulations 2006 effectively exempted tenants who have been continuously in receipt of housing benefit at the same address since 1 January 1996 (Wilson 2016). This again enabled those working in housing support to employ legal frameworks as a means of reducing the impact of the bedroom tax. Indeed, one housing association welfare officer informed me that at least 30 of the households affected within the housing association that he worked for had been exempted from the bedroom tax as a consequence of the loophole. Until its closure by the Department for Work and Pensions in 2014, they had found the loophole a highly successful method of using legal routes to counteract the bedroom tax.

However, whilst such support and commitment to mitigating the harms caused by the bedroom tax and enabling people to remain in their homes is commendable, these methods are ultimately short-term and responsive, rather than transformative, in their approach. Reliance on DHP as a mitigation strategy is particularly precarious, as DHP funding allocations from central government continue to be cut. Although DHP funding was increased from £139.5 million to £180 million in 2020/21 as a consequence of the coronavirus pandemic, it has since been cut back to £140 million for the 2021/22 financial year; a reduction of 22 per cent, and lower than previous years' budgets (Jayanetti 2021b). This is in spite of fears that rent arrears are only set to spiral in the aftermath of eviction moratoriums and other protective measures ending in 2021 (although these measures did not include a bedroom tax moratorium). In sum, the utilisation of alternative legislation as a method of resistance can only go so far when that too is being dismantled by those in government.

CONCLUSION

This chapter has highlighted the various ways in which legal frameworks have been used to resist the bedroom tax. From ambitious legal challenges taken to the Supreme Court, to the establishment of Facebook groups advising affected social tenants on how to contest implementation on a range of legal grounds, the very legal systems that have been used to categorise and constrain social housing tenants have been reconstituted as a means of resistance. Empathetic stakeholders, too, have used alternative legislation and legal loopholes to mitigate the impacts of the bedroom tax. Together, these methods highlight the complex relationship between law and space, whereby legal frameworks can contribute to the protection as much as to the dismantling of spatial injustice (Delaney 2016). Alongside this, the chapter has contributed to resistance scholarship in its challenging of the expected subjects and spaces of resistance to government policies. Through these piecemeal and emergent forms of resistance, individuals have both protected themselves from reductions in housing benefit, and paved the way for others to do so. As Delaney (2016: 268) notes, legal geography is an important facet in understanding 'how unjust geographies are made and potentially un-made'.

And yet, the bedroom tax remains. Indeed, recent estimates indicate that the number of people affected by the legislation has risen by 50 000 as a consequence of soaring numbers of benefit claims due to rising unemployment and illness during the Covid-19 pandemic (Jayanetti 2021a). Yet, despite its growing prevalence, the bedroom tax, once a headline staple and cause for multiple large-scale marches on Parliament, has receded in public memory; what the journalist Frances Ryan refers to as a form of 'political amnesia' (Ryan 2019). Perhaps, then, in a climate where political outrage has long moved on, the continuation of these piecemeal legal resistances have become ever more crucial in this battle of attrition: dismantling the bedroom tax, one legislative piece at a time.

NOTES

1. Work Capability Assessments (WCAs) are designed to determine whether a claimant is eligible for employment support allowance or should be seeking work. They have been hugely controversial since their implementation, with regular instances where claimants have been found fit for work despite having severe diagnosed health conditions (see the Spartacus Network's 2015 testimony for some detailed examples of these). The discriminatory nature of WCAs against disabled people was also illuminated when in 2013 a three-judge panel ruled that WCAs substantially disadvantage claimants with mental health disabilities (*Secretary of State for Work and Pensions v MM & Anor* [2013] EWCA Civ 1565).
2. In the UK, tenants renting from both social landlords (generally local authorities or housing associations) and private landlords are eligible for state support with rent, although the rules vary between social and private housing.
3. There are several other instances where the rules allow a separate bedroom:

- Any other child (other than a foster child or child whose main home is elsewhere).
- Children who can't share because of a disability or medical condition.
- A carer (or team of carers) providing overnight care.
- An approved foster carer who is between placements, but only for up to 52 weeks from the end of the last placement.
- A newly approved foster carer for up to 52 weeks from the date of approval if no child is placed with them during that time.
- Rooms used by students and members of the armed or reserve forces who are away but intend to return home. (Department for Work and Pensions 2014).

4. Much like the bedroom tax, the poll tax is a well-known instance of Conservative policy that many argued explicitly targeted the poor and working classes through the disproportionate taxation of larger, usually working-class, households (Esam and Oppenheim 1989).
5. First-Tier and Upper Tribunals form part of the 2007 overhaul of the tribunal system in the UK. First-Tier Tribunals are divided into seven chambers, structured around subject areas. There are four Upper Tribunals, where decisions made in First-Tier Tribunals can be appealed.
6. Case title: *(Secretary of State for Work and Pensions v Carmichael and Sefton BC)*.
7. Case titles: *R (on the application of Carmichael and Rourke) (formerly known as MA and others)* and *R (on the application of Daly and others) (formerly known as MA and others) (Appellants) v Secretary of State for Work and Pensions (Respondent)*.
8. Case numbers: C1/2014/2539 and C1/2015/0502.
9. Case title: *R (Carmichael) v Secretary of State for Work and Pensions* [2016] UKSC 58 (*'Carmichael SC'*).
10. Case title: *RR v Secretary of State for Work and Pensions*.

REFERENCES

BBC. 2016. 'Bedroom tax': government loses Court of Appeal cases. Accessed at: http://www.bbc.co.uk/news/uk-35418488.

Blomley, N. 1994. *Law, Space and Power.* New York: Guilford Press.

Brickell, K & Cuomo, D. 2019. Feminist geolegality, *Progress in Human Geography*, 43(1): 104–122.

Brown, C. 2013a. Cameron: bedroom tax is not a tax, *Inside Housing.* Accessed at: http://www.insidehousing.co.uk/tenancies/cameron-bedroom-tax-is-not-a-tax/6525647.article.

Brown, C. 2013b. Peer defends 'bedroom tax' term, *Inside Housing.* Accessed at: http://www.insidehousing.co.uk/peer-defends-bedroom-tax-term/6526030.article.

Cresswell, T. 2010. Mobilities I, *Progress in Human Geography* 35(4): 550–558.

Delaney, D. 2015. Legal geography I: constitutivities, complexities and contingencies, *Progress in Human Geography*, 39(1): 96–102.

Delaney, D. 2016. Legal geography II: Discerning injustice, *Progress in Human Geography*, 40(2): 267–274.

Department for Work and Pensions. 2012. Housing benefit: under occupation of social housing. *Impact Assessment*.

Department for Work and Pensions. 2014. *Housing Benefit Claimant Factsheet Removal of Spare Room Subsidy*.

Esam, C. and Oppenheim, P. 1989. *A Charge on the Community: The Poll Tax, Benefits and the Poor*. Child Poverty Action Group.

Gerbaudo, P. 2012. *Tweets and the Streets: Social Media and Contemporary Activism*. London: Pluto.

Hamnett, C. 2012. Moving the poor out of central London? The implications of the coalition government 2010 cuts to housing benefits, *Environment and Planning A*, 42(12): 2809–2819.

Hughes, S. 2020. On resistance in human geography, *Progress in Human Geography*, 44(6): 1141–1160.

Imrie, R. and Edwards, C. 2007. The geographies of disability: reflections of the development of a sub-discipline, *Geography Compass*, 1(3): 623–640.

Jayanetti, C. 2021a. 50,000 more homes hit by Britain's bedroom tax, as scientists warn of Covid-19 risk, *Open Democracy*. Accessed at: https://www.opendemocracy.net/en/opendemocracyuk/50000-more-homes-hit-bedroom-tax-scientists-warn-covid-19-risk/

Jayanetti, C. 2021b. Cut of £40m in help for tenants will 'drive up homelessness', *The Guardian*. Accessed at: https://www.theguardian.com/money/2021/jun/06/cut-of-40m-in-help-for-tenants-will-drive-up-homelessness.

Katz, C. 2004. *Growing Up Global: Economic Restructuring and Children's Everyday Lives*. Minneapolis, MN: University of Minnesota Press.

Leigh Day. 2014. Bedroom tax housing benefit appeal victory. Accessed at: https://www.leighday.co.uk/News/2014/April-2014/Bedroom-Tax,-housing-benefit-appeal-victory.

Leigh Day. 2019. Man wins Supreme Court bedroom tax case. Accessed at: https://www.leighday.co.uk/latest-updates/news/2019-news/man-wins-supreme-court-bedroom-tax-case/.

McKenzie, L. 2015. *Getting By: Estates, Class and Culture in Austerity Britain*. Bristol: Bristol Policy Press.

Moffatt, S., Lawson, S., Patterson, R., Holding, E., Dennison, A., Sowden, S and Brown, J. 2015. A qualitative study of the impact of the UK 'bedroom tax', *Journal of Public Health*, 38(2): 197–205.

Nowicki, M. 2018. A Britain that everyone is proud to call home? The bedroom tax, political rhetoric and home unmaking in U.K. housing policy, *Social and Cultural Geography*, 19(5): 644–667.

Parr, H. and Butler, R. 1999. New geographies of illness, impairment and disability, in Butler, R. and Parr, H. (eds), *Mind and Body Spaces: Geographies of Illness, Impairment and Disability*. London: Routledge, pp. 1–24.

Royal Courts of Justice. 2014. *Case No: C1/2013/2452 & C1/2013/2453*. Accessed at: https://www.judiciary.uk/wp-content/uploads/JCO/Documents/Judgments/ma-and-ors-v-soswp-judgment.pdf.

Ryan, F. 2019. The bedroom tax is still ruining lives. Its victims need to know they matter. *The Guardian*. Accessed at: https://www.theguardian.com/commentisfree/2019/oct/31/bedroom-tax-victims-forgotten-welfare-reform.

Sjoberg, L. and Gentry, C.E. 2015. Introduction: gender and everyday/intimate terrorism, *Critical Studies on Terrorism*, 8(3): 358–361.

Stephenson, N. 2013. Is the bedroom tax the new poll tax? *Huffington Post*. http://www.huffingtonpost.co.uk/nick-stephenson/bedroom-tax-new-poll-tax_b_3745509.html.

Tudoroiu, T. 2014. Social media and revolutionary waves: the case of the Arab Spring, *New Political Science*, 36(3): 346–365.
Tyler, I. 2013. *Revolting Subjects: Social Abjection and Resistance in Neoliberal Britain*. London: Zed Books.
Wilson, W. 2016. Under-occupying social housing: housing benefit entitlement. House of Commons Library Briefing Paper Number 06272.

12. Bearing witness at a Home Office reporting centre

Amanda Schmid-Scott

INTRODUCTION

> 'There is this witnessing role to what we're doing. [The Home Office] know we're there. I'm not saying they would behave otherwise, but we're there witnessing it'
> (Sarah, signing support volunteer).

My encounter with Home Office[1] reporting began during my PhD fieldwork in the spring of 2017. I joined as one of approximately 15 volunteers with a signing support group who regularly attend Patchway Police Station – the designated Home Office reporting centre for the region, located 7 miles north of Bristol – to support asylum seekers during their regular (often weekly or bi-weekly) reporting appointments. Reporting to the Home Office, typically referred to as 'signing' or 'signing on', is a mandatory requirement for asylum-seekers awaiting a decision on their application to remain in the United Kingdom (UK).[2] Despite the Home Office purporting it as an administrative procedure, one of several problematic aspects of reporting is that the Home Office utilises these sites for targeting potential deportees, meaning that each time an individual attends their reporting appointment, they face possible detainment and removal.[3]

The presence of signing support volunteers is intended to offer emotional and practical support to asylum-seekers, or 'signers', during their appointments. Yet beyond the basic levels of emotional and administrative support they are able to offer, the volunteers often spoke of their presence as 'witness bearers' to what occurred at the reporting site, which for them held significant value. Indeed, as Sarah's words at the beginning of this chapter indicate, volunteers often expressed some degree of ambivalence with regard to what they were able to achieve in terms of altering what occurred within these sites of reporting. However, gradually over time, I became especially interested in the potency of bearing witness and its significance as an act of resistance. I was curious as to whether the mere presence of the volunteers held the potential to impact upon the Home Office officers and how they operated within these sites. To what extent could witnessing serve to avert situations of suffering and injustice? Was witnessing, as Currans (2017) ponders, an act of great profundity, or was it complacent? Could it be understood as a mode of resistance in itself?

In this chapter, I explore the significance of bearing witness as a mode of resistance within the context of Home Office reporting. Beyond the overt, physical or material mode commonly associated with the term, there was a distinctly performative and symbolic quality to the volunteers' role within the reporting space which, I argue, subtly and momentarily reconfigured the power dynamics within the space. Hollander and Einwohner (2004) define symbolic resistance as accomplished through more subtle yet intentional behaviours, citing Pickering's (2000) study of the women in Northern Ireland who remained defiantly silent during police raids. The witness-bearing which signing support volunteers engaged in on a regular basis, I suggest, engenders a performative, yet distinctly oppositional response to the violence of border control and management practices (Schmid-Scott 2021). I first begin by exploring how signing support volunteers, most of whom are white, British-born, retired women, from an above-average socio-economic background, are able to occupy the reporting centre. I draw from Koopman's work on accompaniment, to examine the role that their positionality plays in how the women employ their 'privileged outsider body' (Koopman 2011: 278) to inhabit the space alongside the signers, who are perceptibly more vulnerable. By routinely venturing into this precarious site, these women leverage their privileged positionality, and gain access to and knowledge of the otherwise discreet nature of its practices.

Following this, I focus on witness-bearing as enabling a counter-gaze within the context of the reporting site and the Home Office officials who govern the space. I suggest that the volunteers' counter-gaze represents a momentary disruption to the one-way, hegemonic gaze of the officials and, by extension, the state. I then explore how bearing witness, as an act of embodied presence, serves to hold the Home Office officers to account. I argue that, beyond the administrative and emotionally supportive elements of their role, what can be understood as acts of 'resilience' (Katz 2004: 244) which enable the signers to better withstand the pernicious practices structuring their encounters with border control regimes, bearing witness offers an alternative form of political engagement, which despite its indeterminate political outcomes is an important act of resistance, in unsettling the reporting space's usual manner of operation. This chapter therefore contributes to an expanding body of work which highlights the quietly disruptive actions or moments, often at the level of the everyday, which are not necessarily transformative or even effective in resisting power, yet which remain purposefully oppositional (Hughes 2020; Katz 2001, 2004; Pottinger 2017).

The claims made are based on qualitative research conducted over 11 months in 2017 and 2018, including participant observation at a Home Office reporting centre in Patchway, and in-depth interviews with signing support volunteers. Home Office reporting is an under-researched phenomenon within academic debates regarding the lived experience of asylum in the UK, and to date has received little attention across both policy and media discourses. This is somewhat surprising given that reporting is a mandatory requirement for asylum-seekers awaiting a decision on their asylum application, and constitutes a significant component of the lived experience of asylum-seeking in the UK. I suggest that these reporting spaces provide a unique site for examining the modes of resistance which individuals are able to forge within these sites, which is especially significant given that reporting is framed by the Home Office as an administrative process. While I have explored the ways in which asylum-seekers resist these processes elsewhere (Schmid-Scott 2021), in this chapter I specifically focus on how signing support volunteers respond to the seemingly mundane, yet violent operations of these sites. By focusing on their role as witness bearers to the practices constituting Home Office reporting, I demonstrate the potency of this act as a mode of resistance to the violence of border control regimes.

HOME OFFICE REPORTING AND THE HOSTILE ENVIRONMENT

I interviewed Sarah, a volunteer with the signing support group in Bristol, in late 2017. During that period, the impact of Immigration Acts 2014 and 2016 were beginning to take effect. In Theresa May's now infamous press interview with the *Daily Telegraph* in 2012, she promised to make the UK a 'really hostile environment for illegal migration'.[4] While the policies concerning immigration and welfare towards migrants had been growing increasingly restrictive, they thoroughly intensified in the period following May's appointment as Home Secretary in 2010. May oversaw the introduction of the Immigration Acts 2014 and 2016, which essentially restricted access to basic life necessities for unauthorised migrants living in the UK, including restricting access to housing, employment, healthcare and bank accounts, as well as restricting appeal rights (Yeo 2020: 29). While Home Office reporting is intended as a means of keeping track of people while their asylum claim is pending, in recent years its role has evolved to pursue 'other Immigration Enforcement priorities', for example seeking to enforce National Health Sevice (NHS) charges for medical treatment (Bolt 2017: 14). Further compounding the challenges that regular reporting entails for asylum-seekers, several Home Office buildings and local police stations across the country have closed in recent years, in order to consolidate resources and cut costs (Burridge 2019), significantly increasing the difficulties that individuals face in travelling to and from their appointments (Schmid-Scott 2021).

I started my fieldwork conducting focus groups with asylum-seekers based in Bristol and Salford, before committing to volunteering with the signing support group based in Bristol. The practice and nature of Home Office reporting, functioning as an accompaniment to these other restrictive and harmful policies, emerged as a theme early on in my research, and as a particularly pernicious feature of the UK's asylum system. While the reporting centre at Patchway, in terms of its basic physical setting, is a typical administrative environment, it is also a space wrought with much tension and ambiguity. This is due to the fact that the Home Office utilises these sites to expedite the removal process for 'failed' asylum claimants. This means that during their reporting appointment, individuals can be subjected to – often intimidating – questioning by Border Enforcement officers, and may also be arrested and detained. In such cases, signers are escorted to a holding cell within the reporting centre and await transportation to an immigration removal centre.

Signing support groups are local groups which operate in several locations throughout the UK, providing support to migrants including asylum-seekers during their Home Office reporting appointments. While each group varies in size, formality and how it is organised, the signing support group in Bristol operates through a rota system whereby volunteers, in groups of two or three, attend at regular time slots in shifts throughout the week. The primary role of volunteers is to offer practical support to individuals, usually in the form of helping to fill out any forms they may be required to complete, directing them to various local migrant advice and support services, or contacting their solicitor in the case of a detainment. The role also encompasses an emotionally supportive element, which usually involves chatting to people as they wait in the queue to report. However, as I explore through this chapter, in speaking about their role at the reporting centre, volunteers would often reflect on the significance of witness-bearing, which clearly provided a sense of purpose to their role and went beyond their ability to alter Home Office behaviour and practice.

THEORISING REPORTING

Exploring the role of witness-bearing in the context of Home Office reporting first requires some analysis of the purpose and effect of reporting within the broader context of the UK's asylum policy, in order to make sense of the intentions for resistance within these sites. While there exists limited ethnographic scrutiny of reporting practices in the UK, there is some recent notable scholarship discussing its role within a wider critical discussion of Britain's immigration control regime. Hasselberg (2016) argues that, alongside immigration detention and the chronic uncertainty that people experience whilst awaiting deportation, reporting functions as an additional means for the state to enact surveillance and control techniques over foreign nationals. As a technique of the state, Hasselberg discusses reporting as serving as a 'public display' (ibid.: 89) of a person's condition of unworthiness to reside in the UK, and to convey a message that the state is still in control over the geographical and social borders that citizens want to maintain (Leerkes and Broeders 2010: 843, cited in Hasselberg 2016).

I agree that whilst there is clearly a symbolic role which reporting performs in reinstating the state's desire to appear 'in control' of immigration, I suggest that rather than this representing a public display – for, as I have argued (Schmid-Scott 2021), reporting is an often unknown phenomenon within the wider process of claiming asylum, and garners little attention across popular media (see also Burridge 2019) – it constitutes a discreet, banal form of violence which is part of a broad political agenda for making life unliveable for 'unwanted' migrants. Prior research has emphasised how the techniques of insecurity and mobility produce a 'politics of discomfort' (Darling 2011), which serves to control and constrain migrants during their asylum claim process. Using discomfort as a means to gradually wear down the physical and mental reserves of those subjected to reporting, as discussed by Fisher et al. (2019), where reporting is a form of 'ritualised movement' (ibid.: 643) for the purpose of control, suggests an understanding of these sites as enabling more surreptitious ways for both controlling and removing migrants. These accounts demonstrate the 'ricochet' effects of asylum policy, whereby the political realm which determines these processes becomes experienced in the intimate encounters of the everyday (Conlon and Hiemstra 2017: 5). Hence, migration control operates not only through more overt displays of violence, such as detainment and enforced removals, but also through the exclusionary mechanisms of bureaucratic practices and systems (Lindberg 2021), illustrating how different forms and sites of violence are in fact closely related (Pain 2015). Reporting constitutes a largely concealed, banal enactment of violence over migrants, where state violence is put to work upon bodies in the intimate realm through everyday indignities of surveillance and control, which is sustained by the continual and imminent threat of detainment and deportation (Schmid-Scott 2021). Such attempts to control, manage and punish migrants who become subject to these harmful yet largely concealed measures are motivated by the political agenda for creating and maintaining the hostile environment, as discussed above. Whilst, in the UK, this narrative – premised on a culture of racism and hostility towards 'unwanted' migrants – has generated some public criticism, there is clearly some degree of public support for the enforcement of stricter border control measures, of which reporting, albeit lesser known, forms a part.

Given how these racialised fissures are becoming increasingly normalised (Zetter and Pearl 2000), displays of welcoming support and resistance play a distinctly important role in offering a vital form of solidarity to asylum-seekers (Burridge 2019). Indeed, alongside the clear value that signers placed in the volunteers being able to contact their solicitor in the event of a detainment, signers would also speak about the comfort it brought them simply knowing of the volunteers' presence with them in the space. In this chapter, my analysis of the signing support group and the volunteers' role as witness bearers is situated amidst an engagement with reporting as an impenitent yet largely inconspicuous display of the state's desire to compound the violent effects of asylum policy, and therefore suggests that support groups offer a vital form of solidarity and resistance.

BEARING WITNESS AS RESISTANCE

There is an important and growing body of theoretical work exploring witnessing as a significant political act (Agamben 1999; Felman and Laub 1992; Givoni 2011; Kurasawa 2009). Scholarship has often focused on the political potential of bearing witness as a particular kind of 'speech act' (Givoni 2011: 147), appropriated within notions of testimony which emphasise its ethical character as an act compelled by duty. Agamben (1999) speaks of a compulsion to tell when confronted with suffering. It is this compulsion, suggests Holocaust survivor, writer and chemist Primo Levi, that is the impetus for survival. Levi's infamous words: 'I am at peace with myself because I bore witness' (Levi 1997: 219; cited in Agamben 1999: 17), reveal a certain unease about his own survival that is in some way quelled or justified through the very act of witnessing. Kurasawa (2009) identifies witnessing as one of the defining socio-cultural practices of our epoch, a mode of response to political crises and human rights abuses which has become increasingly favoured (ibid.: 106). This depiction captures one aspect of how we as human beings might articulate a particular kind of response to suffering. Rather than segregating suffering to 'the realm of the inhuman and the incomprehensible' (ibid.: 100), which arguably serves to remove it from public engagement and scrutiny, and in defiance to the human tendency to turn away from suffering (Levinas 1981), or to occupy a state of denial (Cohen 2001), bearing witness constitutes an embodied refusal to look away, which requires 'bodily presence and affective investment' (Currans 2017: 92). Bearing witness can thus be understood as an enhanced act of bodily presence, in defiance against the onlooker's inclination to turn away from an encounter with suffering. In this sense, as McGranahan (2020: 107) writes, 'to witness is to attest to something, to confirm a truth, to give context to a claim'. Beyond the purely physical, for which the body becomes the sole vessel of resistance and thus is materially oppositional, witnessing can be understood as a performative gesture of oppositional consciousness towards suffering and instances of injustice. It is a way of being present and staying with (Naef 2006).

Relating to the significance of the politicised nature of witnessing and its disruptive potential, in her study of Israeli checkpoints in the occupied Palestinian territories, Braverman examines the role of the 'counter-gaze' in understanding how the women of the Jewish Israeli organisation Machsom Watch (MW) ('Checkpoint Watch') attempt to disrupt the 'binary constellation of power [versus] powerless' (Braverman 2009: 211) between Israeli soldiers and Palestinian residents. While the checkpoint itself is configured as a 'dichotomised space', a 'constant contestation between the powerful and powerless', producing 'docile and governable bodies' (ibid.: 212), Braverman contends that the MW women attempt to break the unidirectional checkpoint gaze through their own counter-gaze, in what is therefore a politicised act. The MW women's counter-gaze represents an act of presence which constitutes a third party within a scene usually comprised only of soldiers and Palestinians. Braverman therefore considers the women's counter-gaze as transforming the political, social and ethical consciousness of its actors, and by exposing the otherwise secretive and 'clandestine aspect of its existence' (ibid.: 211). This notion of the counter-gaze as a disruption to the power dynamics operating within the Israeli checkpoint is productive for exploring the role of signing support volunteers at the reporting centre. Attending to the subtle, uncertain yet interruptive moments which are not often aligned with conventional conceptualisations of resistance (Hughes 2020), Braverman's account of the women's gaze represents an act which serves a purpose beyond its transformative ability.

In geography, conventional conceptualisations of resistance have tended to focus on an overt, organised opposition to power (Hughes 2020), and where an attentiveness to the spectacle of violence has created an expectation for an equally spectacular response to it (Piedalue 2022). Indeed, such claims to resistance are often rather optimistic in how they envisage an effective challenge to power and violence operating, in particular, for understanding which forms of resistance may be possible within the context of border control and management regimes. In these accounts, power is imagined as fixed and linear, emanating from one circumscribed realm 'out there'; which, as Maiguashca (2013: 123) notes, frames power in terms of its coherent singularity 'to be captured and redistributed'. In so doing, these approaches project a notion of resistance as oppositional, dichotomous and entirely external to its alternate force, foregrounding the structurally organised positions that facilitate transformational change (see Duncan 1990; Duncan and Duncan 1988; Peters 1998). They also fail to account for the 'quietly political' (Askins 2015: 475), or seemingly unremarkable contestations and resistances which do not cohere to an expectant resistant form (Hughes 2016, 2020). Hughes argues that regarding resistance as constituting certain 'coordinates' of intentionality, linearity and opposition against a sovereign power ultimately renders other modes of politics invisible (Highes 2020: 2–3; Hughes 2016; Amoore 2005). As Katz (2004) suggests, it is possible to distinguish different expressions of resistance, between forms of resistance which involve oppositional consciousness and achieve emancipatory change, forms of reworking that 're-calibrate' the organisation, but not the polarisation of power relations, and forms of resilience that enable people to survive without changing the circumstances that make such survival so hard. These alternative ways of understanding resistance also reflect Gill's (2016: 168) call to engage with 'post-heroic' forms of activism, which challenge the machismo that besets notions of the 'militant' activist figure, invoked to describe mostly male individuals 'dedicated to revolutionary change' (Chatterton and Pickerall 2010: 476). These accounts highlight the extent to which women, commonly associated with the everyday mundanity of the domestic sphere, thus become disavowed from the 'romance of resistance' (Sparke 2008: 423). While feminist scholars more recently have been attuned to incorporating more modest, quotidian acts of kindness, connection and creativity within notions of activism (Hughes 2020; Pottinger 2017), little attention has been paid to the significance of witness-bearing as a form of oppositional resistance within the context of border management processes.

In this chapter, I consider how reflecting on the role of the signing support volunteers as witness bearers can bring to light a particular expression of resistance which is premised on an acknowledgement that the UK's border control regime is violent. As Kurasawa (2009) notes, part of what witnessing achieves is the basic recognition that situational or structural violence exists. Distinguishing this act from the administrative and emotionally supportive elements of the volunteers' role, which can be defined through Katz's (2001) understanding of resilience, which enables signers to better withstand the violence of these border practices, witness-bearing provides an important form of oppositional politics which represents a momentary challenge to how this border control process usually operates, despite its indeterminate political outcomes.

LEVERAGING PRIVILEGE

There were some significant access negotiations with regard to my fieldwork which were relevant in shaping my understanding of the positionality of the signing support volunteers and the resultant power dynamics within the reporting space. During the beginning stages of my fieldwork, I became aware of how my gender, relatively young age and nationality could be perceived as 'harmless' in being able to conduct research in the reporting centre, and in seeking to negotiate interviews with Home Office staff. In other words, these were aspects of my identity which provided some purchase on how I was being perceived by those in power, most likely connected to not being considered a threat, or possibly even a 'professional' researcher (Lindberg and Borelli 2019: 27). Reflecting on these aspects of my identity, and how they were potentially interpreted by Home Office staff, also intersected with the identities and positionalities of the other signing support volunteers. In her description of the Israeli MW women activists at the Palestinian checkpoint, Braverman (2009) perceived them as 'out of place' in what is a highly militarised and insecure space, most often occupied by young male military officers. The women, she states, are from an above-average socio-economic background and therefore suspend their privileged spatial confinement 'in order to attain first-hand knowledge of the checkpoint space' (ibid.: 212). Similarly, during my fieldwork it also occurred to me how incongruous the presence of the signing support volunteers often appeared within the reporting centre itself. A significant majority of the signing support volunteers are white British women, aged in their sixties and seventies, and from an educated, middle-class background. None of the volunteers had previously been required to frequent the inside of a police station with any regularity; less still had they been in situations where they were required to regularly liaise with guards wearing flak jackets and carrying batons. While it is true that the signing support volunteers choose to enter a space not usually assigned to them, I suggest that rather than this representing a suspension of their privilege, instead the volunteers leverage their privileged status, in being able to enter the space without fear of harassment, unlike the signers. Reflecting on Koopman's powerful work on accompaniment, in which she explores the role of protective accompaniers in Colombia used as 'unarmed bodyguards' in conflict situations, she describes the act of placing bodies that are less at risk next to bodies that are under threat (Koopman 2011: 278). In considering why accompaniment is an effective peace-building tool used in the midst of conflict, Koopman notes that accompaniers are 'not just any body ... but a privileged outside body that is less likely to be killed' (ibid.). This notion of privileged positionality also relates to Judith Butler's observation that certain bodies are at a heightened risk of exposure to violence without protection, enacted through distinct policies which fall systematically on certain genders, social classes, and racial and ethnic groups (Butler 2003; Hillyard and Tombs 2007). Hence, in an age of increasing state-enforced violence and insecurity, accompaniment provides an alternative way for vulnerable groups to be protected from violent state actors.

By routinely visiting the reporting centre, the volunteers enter what is not only a highly policed (in Patchway's case, a literal police station), but also a mentally and physically stressful environment, which was in contrast to their customary privileged spatial boundaries. This recognition of their 'privileged outside body' whose lives 'count' more (Koopman 2011: 280), undoubtedly facilitated their initial access and continued presence within the reporting space itself. While they occupy privileged positions within society, they claim the space as a witness space in a way that those subjected to border control tactics are not able to (Currans 2017). This venturing, I suggest, can itself be understood as a political act, by throwing into question the hegemonic bureaucratic system which attempts, analogous to the Palestinian checkpoint, to 'monopolise access to and knowledge of' (Braverman 2009: 212) reporting spaces and their activities. Meanwhile, for signers who are differentially exposed to its threat, they enter the space with fear (Schmid-Scott 2021).

While this form of resistance works from a position of privilege, this is not to say that, beyond their role as signing support volunteers, these women were politically disengaged. Over the course of my fieldwork, many of the volunteers discussed their involvement in various forms of pro-migrant and feminist struggle, and several told me about frontline activist work which they had engaged in earlier on in their lives. It was clear during conversations and in interviews with volunteers that they regarded their role at the reporting centre as an important enactment and continuation of these distinctly oppositional politics. Yet, volunteers were also mindful of the limitations that their role afforded, in terms of being able to recalibrate power relations within the space. I asked Gaie, a signing support volunteer in her sixties, whether she felt able to challenge the Home Office officials within the reporting centre. She told me:

> We have to appear to be neutral in the sense that ... we don't have the power, obviously the Home Office has all the power, and we don't want to jeopardise being here ... I always try to be polite [to the Home Office], I say hello and goodbye ... that's roughly as far as it goes.

While there was an innate awareness amongst the volunteers of their own limitations in being able to directly challenge or overturn power relations within the space, given that access was dependent on collegial relations between them and Home Office officials, this awareness was rooted in an understanding that they were required to exhibit a degree of neutrality and politeness during their interactions. In this sense, the volunteers utilised these characteristics as deliberate tactics, in order to maintain access to the space. These tactics, which were also supported by their racial and class privilege, rather than directly challenging the power relations, held the potential to subtly shift the power dynamics, which I will further explore below.

THE COUNTER-GAZE: BEARING WITNESS AND SPEAKING OUT

The reporting centre enforces various forms of surveillance over signers each time they attend their reporting appointments. As soon as they walk into the building and enter the waiting area, they are subjected to visual and audio surveillance through a visible 360 degree camera and a large microphone which protrudes awkwardly from the ceiling. The actual reporting appointment takes place inside a small, enclosed office with a door operated automatically by the officer conducting the reporting process. The reporting office itself is officially out of bounds to signing support volunteers, and those reporting enter either alone or with any family member also required to report. However when someone is detained, this is visible to the other signers as well as to the volunteers, as Border Enforcement guards will escort the person from the small office and walk past the waiting area – where the signers are waiting – to a different room for further questioning, and then through automatic locked double doors on to the holding cells, also clearly visible from the waiting area. Unsurprisingly, witnessing others being detained at the reporting centre was particularly harrowing for those waiting to report.

Foucault's work on visibility deals with the hierarchy of power created through being watched, and builds on Lacan's notion of the gaze, in describing the anxious state that emerges when one becomes conscious of being watched (Foucault 2019/1975) As Foucault argued, the panopticon as depicted by Jeremy Bentham had the effect of 'induc[ing] in the inmate a state of conscious and permanent visibility, that assures the function of power' (ibid.: 201). In a similar way, the experience of unyielding surveillance, even beyond the walls of the reporting centre, was commonly shared by signers, and several articulated a continual sense of anxiety that they may be arrested and detained at any time, experienced even from within their own homes (Schmid-Scott 2021).

In essence, alongside immigration detention and electronic tagging, reporting serves as an additional technique for the control and surveillance of migrants subjected to this practice. Yet, over time, I came to understand the significance of the volunteers' presence and its subtle impact on the power dynamics within the space. In being witness bearers to the degrading techniques of control and surveillance that the signers repeatedly undergo, the volunteers subvert the hegemonic one-directional gaze of the officers towards the signers. Through introducing a counter-gaze, the volunteers temporarily reconfigure the power dynamics within the reporting space, towards less binary and more nuanced relationships between the various actors that operate within the space (Braverman 2009).

This first became apparent to me several months into my time as a volunteer. On a cold January morning in 2017, Sajeed (not his real name), a middle-aged man from south Asia, was detained at the reporting centre. As Sajeed was led away to the holding cells, Sarah noticed in his file that he was regularly seeing a mental health counsellor, which meant that he had a mental health condition. According to Rule 35 of the Detention Centre Rules, a person with a mental health condition should only be detained in 'very exceptional circumstances', the rule being designed as a safeguard for victims of torture or those whose health would be at risk from continued detention.[5] After several minutes, a Home Office Border Enforcement officer emerged from the locked double doors to where the holding cells are located. Sarah approached her and said, 'The man you've just detained has a mental health counsellor which means he has a mental health condition, which really means he shouldn't be detained'. The Border Enforcement officer looked slightly affronted by this rather direct though politely delivered challenge, and replied: 'Well, I can tell you in a private conversation, but I won't in front of all these people', signalling the queue of people waiting to report. Sarah and the officer disappeared around the corner and minutes later Sarah reappeared, sharing in a hushed voice that the officer had said they were only going to detain him for one night, and then he would be released, but that this was 'off record'. We had not heard of this type of practice before, which seemed completely illogical. Sarah wondered if his detainment was being deployed as some kind of warning to others: an attempt to exert control through instilling fear (Pain 2014). Or perhaps she had been lied to, as the officer could have presumed that the volunteers might cause a disruption were Sajeed to be detained in the circumstances they had been informed of. When I later telephoned the Home Office to follow up on what had happened to Sajeed, I was told that he was still being held in immigration detention, despite his mental health counsellor submitting evidence that he had a mental health condition. His solicitor prepared an appeal.

While this interaction demonstrates the limited scope for what is possible to challenge with regard to how the Home Office operates – even when volunteers do on occasion traverse the boundary of mere witnessing by intervening and speaking out – it also points to the discomfort that officers feel when they are under the gaze of the volunteers. Indeed, the very system upon which border control practices are built depends on a culture of secrecy and obscurity, which is rooted in the desire to avoid having to give account of one's actions (Schmid-Scott 2021; see also Arendt 1951; Gill 2016; Stivers 2015). Yet, by introducing their counter-gaze, and in this case by challenging the officers detaining Sajeed, the volunteers disturb the usual discreetness with which these spaces operate, and temporarily hold the officers themselves within their own space of surveillance. Although the reporting space and process, like the Israeli checkpoint, is designed to surveil 'outwards' towards the 'other'

(Braverman 2009: 212), the volunteers' gaze destabilises that one-way mode of visibility, reconfiguring a complex and conflicted relationship between Home Office officers, signers and volunteers, and thereby demonstrating the evolving and fluid nature of power within the space.

HOLDING TO ACCOUNT

In seeking to articulate the significance of their role in the reporting centre, volunteers frequently turned to the symbolic aspect of their presence, rather than to any tangible or physical confrontation that they were able to display. Sophy, a volunteer in her seventies, said when I asked her to reflect on her role as a signing volunteer: 'I think it is valuable that we are a presence. It's sort of symbolic clearly, because it's so limited. We can't stop what the Home Office is doing, even though it's so outrageous and not even according to their own rules' (interview, August 2017).

Gaie also articulated how she perceived their role at the reporting centre:

> I guess the main reason we're there is for the signers, but it may also feed into [the Home Office's] conscience that we can monitor real excess. We may not be able to change it but I think being there may have a small effect ... I think it's a rebuttal of the awful press and the media, I don't know how many asylum seekers read the dreadful press, and hear it, so I guess it's sort of a rebuttal of those ideas and feelings (interview, December 2017).

Here, Gaie makes a distinction between what she regards as the main purpose of their role – constituting the emotionally and administratively supportive aspects, which relate to Katz's strategies of resilience and endurance (Katz 2004; MacLeavy et al. 2021) – and the sheer act of being present itself, which serves to hold the officers to account. Similarly to Sarah, both Gaie and Sophy's comments reflect the value of making the Home Office accountable, which is enabled through their own presence at the reporting centre, despite acknowledging the limitations in being able to alter what occurs there.

As a volunteer with the signing support group, I myself was perpetually troubled by the apparent ineffectiveness of our work: not only in altering Home Office practice, but also in failing to challenge the more conspicuous acts of vindictiveness and incompetence that the Home Office officers demonstrated on a regular basis (Schmid-Scott 2021). Yet, by repeatedly positioning themselves within the reporting space as witness bearers, volunteers assume a role of oppositional consciousness. While I found that most of the volunteers were rather ambivalent about whether their presence altered Home Office behaviour – indeed, as Gaie later reflected, 'it's almost impossible to know' – their embodied presence ensures that the officers' behaviour is held to account.

Furthermore, as the volunteers' comments indicate, their embodied presence holds value in serving to challenge the hostility of border management practices, offering a visible symbol of acceptance and care which, as Gaie describes, is also a 'rebuttal' to the culture of hostility and unwelcome. One way to understand this dimension of their presence is to consider it as 'remaking society at the local level' through the repeated will to engage (Askins 2015: 476). Indeed, as Askins writes, such sustained encounters can challenge dominant discourses of difference and exclusion, performed through embodied activities of care.

CONCLUSION

In this chapter, I have explored the significance of bearing witness within the context of Home Office reporting, as constituting a mode of resistance which holds potency, through both its ability to disrupt the hegemonic gaze of the Home Office officers over signers, as well as its capacity to rupture the usual discreetness with which the reporting process occurs. By contextualising Home Office reporting within the broader pernicious landscape of the UK's immigration policy, and the methods of control and surveillance which constitute its everyday functioning, I show how bearing witness performs a distinctly important task, whereby the volunteers' embodied presence both attests to the violence of this bordering practice, whilst also subtly and momentarily shifting the power relations with the space. The recognition of the privileged body in contrast to the precarious body is indicative of how the signing support volunteers were able to leverage their own positionality in order to venture safely into the site on a regular basis, and bear witness to the usual hiddenness of its operation. The presence of volunteers therefore produces an additional gaze, alongside that of the Home Office officers, challenging and reconfiguring the hegemonic gaze of the officers and, by extension, of the state.

Overall, despite the obvious and numerous barriers to challenging the Home Office, the act of bearing witness to these everyday practices established a mode of response which held value, not necessarily in its transformative potential, but in the act of being present itself. Through choosing to be present and alongside those individuals repeatedly subjected to one of the more pernicious, yet distinctly hidden, features of the UK's immigration policy, their witnessing constitutes a mode of response which actively choses to see, and to know. Bearing witness can thus be constituted by its capacity to be confronted with reality itself.

NOTES

1. The Home Office is a ministerial department of the United Kingdom government, responsible for immigration, security, law and order.
2. During the Covid-19 pandemic, and following pressure from dozens of migrants' rights organisations who threatened bringing legal action against the Home Office, the Home Office shifted the requirement to report from in-person to reporting by telephone. The Home Office then announced it would shift the requirement to reporting by telephone as a standard requirement and from April 2022, this was largely implemented instead of attending a Home Office reporting centre. Home Office guidance currently states that a person on a reporting regime will be considered for a variety of methods to report, including in person or 'a combination of telephone reporting, digital bail or electronic monitoring' (Home Office 2023). While the decision to shift to telephone reporting shows progress from the Home Office, reporting in person still occurs for many people on immigration bail, and individuals are not permitted to request telephone reporting themselves. Also significantly, the mental, physical and financial impact of reporting for years on end has already taken its toll on thousands of migrants, and who continue to be subjected to these demeaning surveillance strategies.
3. Failing to submit fresh evidence on your asylum claim, or failing to attend regular reporting appointments, are grounds for detainment, which can result in signers becoming a target for detainment. However, as Yeo (2020: xxviii) states, detainments can often occur at random, for 'any decision to detain is inherently arbitrary'. Rather than 'identifying high-risk migrants, planning their removal, putting their documents in place ... and then detaining and removing them', migrants of any given nationality are often 'rounded up solely because of their nationality for group removals on chartered flights', with around 2000 people expelled in this manner every year (ibid.: 236).
4. The *Daily Telegraph* Theresa May interview in 2012: 'We're going to give illegal migrants a really hostile reception', available: https://www.telegraph.co.uk/news/0/theresa-may-interview-going-give-illegal-migrants-really-hostile/.
5. The Detention Centre Rules (2001) 238/Rule 35.

REFERENCES

Agamben, G. (1999) *Remnants of Auschwitz: The Witness and the Archive*. New York: Zone Books.

Amoore, L. (2005) Introduction: global resistance – global politics. In Amoore, L. (ed.), *The Global Resistance Reader*. Abingdon: Routledge, pp. 1–13.

Arendt, H. (1951) *The Origins of Totalitarianism*. San Diego, CA: Harcourt Brace.

Askins, K. (2015) Being together: everyday geographies and the quiet politics of belonging. *ACME: An International E-Journal for Critical Geographies*, 14, pp. 470–478.

Bolt, D. (2017) *An inspection of the Home Office's Reporting and Offender Management processes, December 2016–March 2017*. Independent Chief Inspector of Borders and Immigration. London, UK.

Braverman, I. (2009) Checkpoint gazes. In Isin, E. and Nielsen, G. (eds), *Acts of Citizenship*. London: Zed Books, pp. 211–214.

Burridge, A. (2019) Asylum reporting as a site of anxiety, detention and solidarity. In Jones, R. (ed.), *Geographies of Justice and Social Transformation*. Athens, GA: University of Georgia Press, pp. 193–220.

Butler, J. (2003) *Precarious Life: The Powers of Mourning and Violence*. London and New York: Verso.

Chatterton, P. and Pickerill, J. (2010) Everyday activism and transitions towards post-capitalist worlds. *Transactions of the Institute of British Geographers*, 35(4), pp. 475–490.

Cohen, S. (2001) *States of Denial: Knowing about Atrocities and Suffering*. Cambridge: Polity Press.

Conlon, D. and Hiemstra, N. (eds) (2017) *Intimate Economies of Immigration Detention: Critical Perspectives*. Abingdon: Routledge.

Currans, E. (2017) *Marching Dykes, Liberated Sluts, and Concerned Mothers: Women Transforming Public Space*. Urbana, Chicago and Springfield, IL: University of Illinois Press.

Darling, J. (2011) Domopolitics, governmentality and the regulation of asylum accommodation. *Political Geography*, 30(5), pp. 263–271.

Duncan, J. (1990) *The City as Text: The Politics of Landscape Interpretation in the Kandyan Kingdom*. Cambridge: Cambridge University Press.

Duncan, J. and Duncan, N. (1988) (Re)reading the landscape. *Environment and Planning D: Society and Space*, 6, pp. 117–126.

Felman, S. and Laub, D. (1992) *Testimony: Crises of Witnessing in Literature, Psychoanalysis and History*. New York and London: Routledge.

Fisher, D.X.O, Burridge, A. and Gill, N. (2019) The political mobilities of reporting: tethering, slickness and asylum control, *Mobilities*, 14(5), pp. 632–647.

Foucault, M. (2019/1975) *Discipline and Punish: The Birth of the Prison*. Transl. by Alan Sheridan. London: Penguin Books.

Gill, N. (2016) *Nothing Personal? Geographies of Governing and Activism in the British Asylum System*. Chichester: John Wiley & Sons.

Givoni, M. (2011) Witnessing/testimony. *Mafte'akh*, 2e, pp. 147–169.

Hasselberg, I. (2016) *Enduring Uncertainty: Deportation, Punishment and Everyday Life*. New York and Oxford: Berghahn Books.

Hillyard, P. and Tombs, S. (2007) From 'crime' to social harm? *Crime, Law and Social Change*, 48, pp. 9–25.

Hollander, J.A. and Einwohner, R.L. (2004) Conceptualising resistance. *Sociological Forum*, 19(4), pp. 533–554.

Home Office (2023) *Reporting and offender management Version 6.0, General Instructions Immigration Removals, Enforcement and Detention*.

Hughes, S. (2016) Beyond intentionality: exploring creativity and resistance within a UK Immigration Removal Centre. *Citizenship Studies*, 20(3–4), pp. 427–443.

Hughes, S.M. (2020) On resistance in human geography. *Progress in Human Geography*, 44(6), pp. 1141–1160.

Katz, C. (2001) On the grounds of globalisation: a topography of feminist political engagement. *Signs: Journal of Women in Culture and Society*, 26(4): 1213–1234.

Katz, C. (2004) *Growing up Global: Economic Restructuring and Children's Everyday Lives*. Minneapolis, MN: University of Minnesota Press.

Koopman, S. (2011) Alter-geopolitics: other securities are happening. *Geoforum*, 42(3), pp. 274–284.

Kurasawa, F. (2009) A message in a bottle: bearing witness as a mode of transitional practice. *Theory, Culture and Society*, 26(1), pp. 92–111.

Levinas, E. (1981) *Otherwise Than Being or Beyond Essence*. New York: Springer.

Lindberg, A. (2021) Minimum rights policies targeting people seeking protection in Denmark and Sweden. In Abdelhady, D., Gren, N. and Joormann, M. (eds), *Refugees and the Violence of European Welfare Bureaucracies*. Manchester: Manchester University Press, pp. 85–102.

Lindberg, A. and Borrelli, L. (2019) Let the right one in? On European migration authorities' resistance to research. *Social Anthropology/Anthropologie Sociale, Special Issue*, 27(S1), pp. 17–32.

MacLeavy, J., Fannin, M. and Larner, W. (2021) Feminism and futurity: geographies of resistance, resilience and reworking. *Progress in Human Geography*, 45(6) 1558–1579.

Maiguashca, B. (2013) Exploring the conditions of possibility for political agency: rethinking politicisation from a feminist perspective. In Maiguashca, B. and Marchetti, R. (eds), *Contemporary Political Agency: Theory and Practice*. Abingdon, UK and New York, USA: Routledge, pp. 118–136.

McGranahan, C. (2020) Ethnographic witnessing: or hope is the first anthropological emotion. *Journal of Legal Anthropology*, 4(2), pp. 101–110.

Naef, R. (2006) Bearing witness: a moral way of engaging in the nurse–person relationship. *Nursing Philosophy*, 7, pp. 146–156.

Pain, R. (2014) Everyday terrorism: connecting domestic violence and global terrorism. *Progress in Human Geography*, 38(4), pp. 531–550.

Pain, R. (2015) Intimate War, *Political Geography*, 44, pp. 64–73.

Peters, E. (1998) Subversive spaces: First Nations women and the city. *Environment and Planning D: Society and Space*, 16(6), pp. 665–685.

Pickering, S. (2000) Women, the home and resistance Northern Ireland. *Women and Criminal Justice*, 11, pp. 49–82.

Piedalue, A. (2022) Slow nonviolence: Muslim women resisting the everyday violence of dispossession and marginalization. *Environment and Planning C: Politics and Space*, 40(2), pp. 373–390.

Pottinger, L. (2017) Planting the seeds of a quiet activism. *Area*, 49(2), pp. 215–222.

Schmid-Scott, A. (2021) Bureaucracy, violence, resistance: an account of Home Office reporting in Britain. Doctoral thesis, University of Exeter, Geography Department.

Sparke, M. (2008) Political geography – political geographies of globalization III: resistance. *Progress in Human Geography*, 32(3), pp. 423–440.

Stivers, C. (2015) Rule by nobody: bureaucratic neutrality as secular theodicy. *Administrative Theory and Praxis*, 37, pp. 242–251.

Yeo, C. (2020) *Welcome to Britain: Fixing our Broken Immigration System*. London: Biteback Publishing.

Zetter, R. and Pearl, M. (2000) The minority within the minority: refugee community-based organisations in the UK and the impact of restrictionism on asylum-seekers. *Journal of Ethnic and Migration Studies*, 26(4), pp. 675–697.

13. 'Unleashing the beast': emergent resistance in White charity
Kahina Meziant

INTRODUCTION

> "For me that's what blues and this Sri raga are, that's unleashing the beast and it's about letting out the pain, so the joy can fill the space"
> (Interview with Mark, 4 June 2020).

This chapter examines how cumulative, transgressive practices emerge as resistance in the United Kingdom (UK) voluntary and community sector (VCS) through an empirical account, focusing on community music practices between racialised migrant[1] 'students' and non-migrant music tutors. To make sense of these relationships, I identify a set of normative or institutionalised socio-spatial practices in UK asylum politics, such as im/mobilisation, 'White governmentality', as well as transgressions of these practices. I show how subtle transgressive acts contribute to the emergence of resistance by examining how various actors involved in the lived realities of migrants through the charity sector respond to multiple cultural and institutional forces. I pay special attention to how quiet transgressions and sonic practices (and properties) can rework power structures in organisations.

To make the case for 'quiet' forms of resistance, Deleuze and Guattari define politics as being 'attuned to wholes, bodies ... concerned with processual masses that are perpetually becoming' (Merriman, 2018, p. 8). This implies that political practices are always unfinished, in the process of becoming, and without known outcome. The focus of this chapter is on how resistance as a form of "political response" (Katz, 2001, p. 1219) manifests for various actors subjected to varying constraints and racialised political regimes in which outspoken resistance is often synonymous with increased repression (Scott, 1985) or, for organisations, limits opportunities to access funding. As such, the chapter demonstrates how looking at seemingly non-political transgressive practices through the lens of emergence helps to broaden imaginaries of resistance and ultimately strengthen acts of resistance.

The responses of the VCS to migration and asylum vary greatly across the UK. A closer look at a specific context and location, on the other hand, provides a vantage point for understanding the myriad ways in which resistance emerges, even when this does not appear to be so. This chapter draws on extensive participatory (or engaged) institutional ethnography (Billo and Mountz, 2016) conducted over two years with a charity I am calling 'Segue', based in the North East of England, that focuses on community music-making. Segue tackles some of the everyday challenges faced by people in the asylum system from a cultural and creative perspective. The group meets once a week in a venue provided by a local cultural hub[2] to hold free music lessons and opportunity for socialisation.

Im/mobilisation, Resistance, Whiteness

The UK's hostile political climate on the matter of immigration has been characterised by the im/mobilisation of people seeking asylum. Mobilisation manifests, for instance, through the dispersal scheme, a policy that distributes newly arrived people across the UK (Darling, 2016; Phillips, 2006). This practice splits family bonds, and disregards individuals' desire to establish somewhere on their own terms. Dispersal accommodation is managed by private companies contracted by the Home Office that have no formal knowledge of the experiences of forced migration. Accounts of people in the asylum system forced out of their accommodation, for various reasons, are numerous (see Phillips, 2006). As for immobilisation, it shows in the limited formal rights, services, infrastructures and access to work (Clayton and Vickers, 2019) granted to people in the system and migrants in general. The restrictions limiting access to the labour market that they are subjected to hinder social and spatial mobility, resulting for many in enhanced feelings of being 'cast away' and 'contained' within their accommodation or neighbourhood (Mayblin et al., 2020).

At Segue, the constraints arising from this im/mobilisation are addressed by creating a 'safe space' where coming together does not induce a financial burden,[3] yet brings about a weekly opportunity to establish new relationships, engage in an activity that is not ordinarily accessible for free, and explore a part of the city and artistic space that would be out of reach for most participants. In light of such a policy context, Segue in its very nature constitutes a form of resistance. However, the charity cannot be considered outwardly resistant. It does not position itself on a political spectrum and avoids explicit associations with political agendas in general, focusing entirely on music-making and 'developing a sense of community', as the charity's mission outlines. It also does not take part in asylum rights campaigns and does not advocate policy changes in the area of migration, or even position itself in relation to this. As such, it does not align with the trajectory of accounts that frame resistance as a set of practices determined a priori that are linear and that are expressed openly (Hughes, 2020). However, in this account I draw attention to socio-spatial practices that I interpret as transgressive (not in nature, but through their context), which ultimately constellate resistance for different actors (members of the charity, organisation, music tutors, researcher) in rather subtle ways, and the effects that such an exercise can have on future configurations of the organisation. I provide here an account in support of the argument for a broader understanding of resistance within geography in order to consider these cumulative, 'mundane' and less antagonistic practices as those through which histories of resistance and liberation are written.

Although they cannot be conflated, work on Whiteness and White governmentality, for example by Hesse (1996), Nayak (2012), Tolia-Kelly (2016, 2006) and Saldanha (2007), provide tools for identifying the processes of racialisation through structural and normative practices that are at once social and material. These, I argue, speak to the experiences of migrants in the context of charity work. This is foundational to understand how the transgressions of socio-cultural and spatial norms operate in relation to different kinds of forces. The unintentionality of these practices to be transgressive, as well as their cumulative and material nature, provide ground for the emergence of a political response upon which resistance can come to rest (Katz, 2001).

I continue by introducing my research approach, emphasising the opportunities for ethnographic work that is engaged and active in order to capture emergence. I demonstrate this with a descriptive account, written from an auto-ethnographic standpoint, of an exceptional[4] session that I co-organised as part of my volunteer work at Segue. This session, which took place in a local pub in January 2020, illustrates how emergence coalesced, through the spatial, the material, and the sonic and auditory qualities of the space and event. I analyse the account through a socio-spatial lens, examining the nature of the intimate relationship between power structures and resistance that crystallises in the space of the pub, and suggests that looking at these as ever-emerging political responses helps us to see how shifts can occur for the benefit of people in the system (Griffin, 2023; Hughes, 2020, 2018).

LOCATING THE EVENT

White Governmentality and the Asylum System

In this chapter, the term 'Whiteness' refers to a Foucauldian system of governmentality (Hesse, 1996; Nayak, 2012; Rose and Miller, 1992) in the sense of a "matrix within which are articulated all those dreams, schemes, strategies, and manoeuvres of authorities that seek to shape the beliefs and conduct of others in desired directions by acting upon their will, circumstances, or environment" (Rose and Miller, 1992, p. 273). Hesse (1996, p. 97) describes how the 'disciplinary logic of "Whiteness"' evolved since the decline of the British Empire (and the inception of Britain as a nation) to show how disseminating Whiteness as a structure was made possible not only through discourse (and imaginary), but also pragmatically. In light of such historical accounts,[5] the Whiteness of the VCS is also documented and critiqued (Ainsworth, 2018; Charity So White, 2019; Nayak, 2012).

However, intimate accounts of everyday strategies of and against White governance in the context of asylum are lacking. Charities across the country provide a variety of 'services' to assist those seeking asylum in the process of 'integrating into British society' after often traumatic experiences of displacement, persecution, and ongoing political and economic insecurity. The motivation comes out of a desire to support 'social cohesion', 'conviviality', harmony, and is animated by a humanitarian or anti-racist impulse (Bonnett, 1990; Ellul-Knight, 2019). While some charities explicitly 'fill the gaps' in the absence of welfare support (for example, due to being destitute[6]) (Mayblin and James, 2019, pp. 382–383), others, such as Segue, focus on social and cultural aspects of newcomers' life in the city.

Despite the best intentions, tensions and discriminatory behaviour occur in the sector, though not always explicitly. For example, Charity So White is a campaign that sparked a Twitter conversation in 2019 after the discovery of racist and prejudicial training content produced and used by Citizens Advice for a course on working with so-called 'BAME[7] communities' (Charity So White, 2019). The campaign's leadership team addresses institutional racism in the charity sector, primarily through advocacy, with the goal of shifting power structures. According to Nayak (2012), Whiteness in the VCS manifests itself through governance structures, decision-making, and consultation mechanisms. At Segue, this is echoed by music tutor Mark[8] in the following quote: 'at that time, it did have, like, on the Board of Trustees all, you know, middle-class White British citizens, and well, ones with, with good jobs and they were all doing that kind of thing' (Interview with Mark, music tutor, 4 June 2020).

Referring to the composition of Segue's Board of Trustees some years ago, Mark's uneasiness regarding their racial and socio-economic status reflects his general opinion on charity policy. When I first joined Segue, he explained how registering as a charity impacted upon the ethos of the project. Since its inception in 2008, he had witnessed several iterations and always advocated for grassroots organising and a collective ownership approach. Although Mark is aware of the problems that bureaucracy and rigid structures imply for members, the apparent need for funding, coupled with the insecurity that people in the system experience, seem to tie in Segue to a regulated non-profit model that stifles more radical aspirations. Maintaining an informal status was and remains unsustainable largely due to operational and financial reasons.

Segue's music sessions are structured into three 'moments' (choir/percussion, guitar, and violin classes) run by three tutors and two substitute teachers, who are all White and sit on the Board of Trustees. A recently appointed project coordinator oversees decision-making alongside the governing board members and identifies as White, British. While we cannot equate Britishness with Whiteness, nor can we reduce Whiteness to a phenotypical argument, the way Whiteness is reflected in Segue's administration could be seen to reflect the (racialised) government's position on asylum (for example, paid staff must be legally permitted to work in the UK), as well as the country's approach to welfare as a humanitarian responsibility channelled through the VCS (Tyler et al., 2014). As a result, those who are not challenged by it can justify their charitable impulse toward those oppressed by the asylum regime. As Ella's (one of the three tutors) comment below illustrates, the power relation contrasting 'service provider' with 'service user' persists and goes unchallenged:

> [I]t may be that just a lot of the people who come to Segue don't want to take part in the organisation of it, that's fine, I wouldn't want to say to somebody you know, you must be the Secretary because you are a migrant and you have to be one, but again, it's maybe not being so proactive about finding that out. (Interview with Ella, music tutor, 30 April 2020)

Although Ella is right, that it is not fair to assume that their ethnicity should determine whether people should take on an administrative or teaching role, she also points at the lack of proactivity in finding out, thus demonstrating a willingness to critically examine her own and the group's action. Indeed, by establishing structures, consultation and decision-making mechanisms that do not account for the temporalities (Clayton and Vickers, 2019) and concerns of migrants, VCS organisations sometimes fail to create a space that fosters self-expression and agentic propositions. Importantly, they build and maintain structures that depoliticise asylum (Darling, 2014), which (unwittingly) leaves unchallenged the taken-for-grantedness of occurring processes of racialisation. Additionally, often, people in the asylum system who I met through my research do not see how inequality operates and how the expression of their agency is managed in the charity. This explains why the order of things is not often explicitly challenged. White people in charge of administering the charity seem to be conscious of the expression of their own Whiteness as limiting in this particular context (Hesse, 1996). During my interview with her, Ella demonstrated a keen awareness of issues surrounding race in the group, and eagerness to work through them, although she seemed unsure how to:

> [T]his is something that I think all of the Segue organisation people at the minute are aware of, and we know that Segue would work best if the people who Segue is mainly for were organising and taking the lead, because like I was saying earlier, I don't know how it is to be a migrant, I don't know how it is to be an asylum seeker, so I don't know kind of what's most appropriate and what's most needed really. (Interview with Ella, 30 April 2020)

In a Foucauldian understanding of power, resistance is always-already embedded into power; otherwise, the relationship would be one of domination (Hoy, 2004). Thus, one of the prerequisites for shifting these power relations is a readiness to engage in critical conversations with power. It is through this dialogue that the possibility of resistance becomes apparent (Hughes, 2016). Indeed, Ella and Mark are aware of these dynamics and welcomed the opportunity to reflect on these questions as part of my interviews. The core tension lay in how to unsettle the multiple ways in which they were directly or indirectly contributing to reinscribing racialising structures, and what that meant for them:

> Mark: ... looking at me being a White middle class male and representing and being the voice of this thing [Segue] and ... essentially having that power, it doesn't sit right. I understand that it's an issue ... of exactly what you are talking about, these sort of 'ease' sides of the asylum process. And I can see how you could totally come at it from an angle like that and tear it apart. I'm sure everyone's coming at it with the best intentions, but that's the way that the system ends up being you know. [B]ut yeah, I should certainly, [but] I guess I don't think of it on that macro kind of [level], I'm just thinking about what am I going to do in today's session. (Interview with Mark, 4 June 2020)

Mark's recognition that one could come at it and 'tear it apart', and that 'the system' is responsible for this power imbalance, made me reconsider White governmentality as a set of principles that not only seeks to shape the conduct of Black and Brown people, but also one that obstructs the possibilities for thinking and organising otherwise.

Praxis as Liberation

By observing and actively participating in Segue for about two years (May 2018 to September 2020), I have gained an appreciation for the subtle expressions of division between migrants and non-migrants, as well as the intricate unfolding of resistance within the charity. Being embedded in the space for this period of time enabled me to witness and feel my way into the dynamics that form the charity in ways that other shorter, less in-depth auto-ethnographic approaches would not have allowed me to. I use the term 'auto-ethnographic' here to signal my observations of the organisation's power geometries and the way such a perspective mobilises the researcher beyond their intellect (Adams et al., 2014; Brown-Vincent, 2019). It understands that 'knowing is feeling is knowing' (McKittrick, 2020, p. 60). In that sense, I anchor my work in de- and anti-colonial feminist theory that emphasises the power of relational and collaborative approaches that make visible and aim to unsettle dominant knowledge production frameworks in academic research (Brown and Knopp, 2008; Chowdhury et al., 2016; Kindon et al., 2007; McKittrick, 2020; Nagar and Shirazi, 2019). In light of that, I envision my research project in the organisation as an 'engaged ethnography' that is participatory and action-oriented. Rather than assuming the role of a neutral agent painting an 'objective' picture of a 'reality' that has yet to be discovered, this account stems from a complex, partial and situated body, within and outside of Segue (Haraway, 1988).

Here, I speak with a distinct 'privilege' owed not only to my academic position, but also from my lived experience of migration as a result of war and the search for safety.

However, as Luntz in Mullings (1999, p. 341) rightfully points out, it is important in such a context that the researcher does not assume 'shared positionalities based upon ethnicity'. My praxis is driven by a commitment to expose and transform the workings of Whiteness in the charity sector. It means that I have designed my research project around and alongside connections made in the local VCS while putting myself at their service. A longitudinal, embedded and engaged ethnography seems particularly useful to capture emergent resistance, although I recognise that the information which I receive in my role as a researcher "will always be partial" (Mullings, 1999, p. 349). Ella's reflection on my role in the organisation aptly illustrates this insider/outsider position:

> Well you are a Segue member who comes and sings and chats to people and kind of takes part, so I think that's how maybe you are seen by a lot of people, and obviously I know that you are researching things to do with migration and charities and citizenship, so in that way you are kind of an observer, and you have also been, or are very part of the organisation, so in that way you are kind of, very useful and very important because you have lots of experience and knowledge that I think other people in the organisation don't have around kind of, migration and citizenship and the asylum process. (Interview with Ella, 30 April 2020)

The empirical account that I am now turning to consists of what can be described as an action–reflection (Cahill, 2007; Freire, 2017) process enabled by my active participation in the group. This account may appear straightforward/linear to the reader, but it was more messy, unintentional and riddled with doubts than it appears. This was due, in part, to my awkward position as a Segue volunteer/member/researcher, but also to the inherent unpredictability and serendipitous nature of inductive qualitative research (Brown and Knopp, 2008). I believe that the emergent nature of the research process itself is what enabled me to capture and get a sense of how emergence comes about in the context of resisting White governmentality.

AUTO-ETHNOGRAPHIC ACCOUNT OF A PUB VISIT WITH RACIALISED MIGRANTS

On 13 January 2020, Segue gathers in a local pub, less than half a mile away from the usual location. Our agreement with the usual venue's landlords calls for a five-week winter break to allow for general upgrades to the space as well as potential private hiring. Because interrupting gatherings for an extended amount of time has historically been shown to contribute to a reduction in participation, leaving many individuals feeling isolated, we seized this chance to explore new locations and interact with some of the numerous cultural landmarks nearby. I decided to act as a 'connector' and organise the first music session in a pub renowned in the local community for its folk scene. The pub owner was delighted with my request and even provided us complementary tea and coffee. This gesture was welcome, as it is typical for the group to socialise around a drink and some snacks in between music classes. Besides, some members previously expressed discomfort with alcohol being offered in the room where the sessions are held, so offering alcohol-free options indicated a form of respect.

Public houses are quintessentially British socialisation spaces, historically aptly defined by Brian Harrison as "a 'masculine republic' on every street" (Harrison, 1973, in Kneale, 2021, p. 5). In addition to gender, race is another site of normative behaviour for pubs, with Black and Brown people attending less frequently than White people (this will be discussed further below). However, it is not coincidental that I picked this pub among all those in the area. The Queen's Head[9] stands out from other pubs by presenting as an openly political place with a generally left-leaning philosophy that is sympathetic to the realities of migrants and marginalised genders. It regularly hosts fundraising events for non-profits such as Freedom from Torture and 'all-female' concerts. We were offered a room which is located on the right side after passing through a narrow entrance corridor. Another area, opposite ours, acts as the main pub space where regular customers would normally sit when coming for a drink, and houses the bar. It did not seem awkward to anyone that alcohol was served on one side of the pub, whilst on the other side we sipped on tea and coffee.

We arrive at the pub in three groups of 4–5 people at around six o'clock. I notice that the atmosphere is different to the usual sessions. Many of us are unsure of how to behave in this new space, and what will happen. Besides, the space is small, and the layout invites the group to turn towards the centre of the room where chairs and a table are positioned to invite people to sit not as an audience, but as active creators of the scene. There is a sense of possibility. Mark takes out Boomwhackers,[10] which rapidly take on a central material significance in an ice-breaking exercise. Each 'tube' has a distinct musical pitch and provides the person holding it with a distinct sense of sonic agency. He suggests that we each grab one and introduce ourselves in turn by singing our names and describing something we like or dislike, followed by a sequence of Boomwhackers strikes that the rest of the group repeats afterwards to encourage deeper listening and attunement. We laugh, and the atmosphere feels warm.

The evening progresses, punctuated by tea and coffee breaks and chats. We move on to perform songs from our repertoire, including one of the most popular Ukrainian folk songs, *Ніч яка місячна*,[11] accompanied by the violin-taught group, a few guitars and a piano. We have sung this song countless times, and every time it brings a smile to our faces, as we all wonder how we manage to sing in Ukrainian. I notice that our voices draw the attention of customers sitting on the other side of the wall. Occasionally, the doors separated by a narrow corridor connecting both rooms open, letting the group be partly visible and audible to the 'regular' customers in the other room.

A small group gathers around Mark, who in his usual way kickstarts the collective writing of the lyrics of a song that begins to emerge. The acoustics of the room, as is often the case in pubs, is such that no distinct sound emerges above the others, no dominant voice "colonize[s] [the] space" (Kanngieser, 2012, p. 8), and even the sounds of instruments seem to blend into a comforting ambient soundscape. Massood and Layla, two regular members, actively participate in the production of the song, while Silvia, occasional choir lead, takes out a piece of paper and begins scribbling the words that come out from those sitting around the table. 'How do you say "peace" in Farsi?' asks Mark, 'صلح' answers Layla, as Silvia struggles to keep up with the spelling of words in a variety of languages.

Reza, another active member, joins the group in the centre and begins playing a few chords on his guitar, which become the song's riff. Azam, his brother, comes next: he sits at the piano, and before we know it, the violins and even the Boomwhackers have entered the (metaphorical) stage, each bringing their own gift to the scene without any direction other than what the emergent song demands for. The chorus of the music being written evolves and alters as vibrations touch each and every ear, every body, as we all sing. At some point, it appears that a consensus is reached; the riff sets the tone, we have lyrics, and anyone holding an instrument or tapping their foot on the hardwood floor conspires to create a new set of dynamics, upsetting the traditional service user–service provider dichotomy. Two of the regular folk artists make an appearance. Their usual folk music session begins in 30 minutes, in the room in which we are set up. One is surprised, possibly uneasy, while the other appears fascinated by what is happening. They were not expecting to see us: a bunch of predominantly Black and Brown people who do not frequently (if at all) visit this pub. One of them pulls out his guitar and begins playing along with the rest of the group, while the other simply stares, perplexed by the situation. The atmosphere shifts once more as we repeat the chorus, as if it were an incantation (Figure 13.1).

Debriefing

The general mood and responses were good. Members who are experiencing the asylum system and expressed a desire to visit that area of town felt at ease in the pub and did not hesitate to use the piano or take up space in the room. Those who are shyer in general did not grow less shy, but they appeared more engaged as there was less structure in the evening's progress to rely on, and less room than usual within which they could make themselves less visible. Members of the public participated in the session, either partially or entirely, with their own instruments if they brought them, or simply by singing. Now that I have recounted the scene, I move on to explain what I identified as socio-spatial and sonic transgressions, and how I attended to them as way of expanding what constitutes resistance in emergence.

Emergent Resistance

Although the lyrics of the song suggest a type of resistance that is overt and oppositional, I would like to draw attention to the more subtle ways in which resistance constellated, collectively, unintendedly and sonically. Following Foucault, Hughes argues that "[t]racing the trajectory of resistance cannot be separated from power and yet crucially, the shape of such resistant forms remains [predominantly] delineated *a priori*" (Hughes, 2020, p. 1142). Not presenting itself as an activist organisation, and explicitly positioning itself as apolitical, does not preclude the emergence of resistance in the organisation. An attention to the sonic practice of collective music-making in a place where migrants are not used to being seen lends itself well to identifying emergence.

As argued by Kanngieser, space and sound 'co-create' one another, and "[cultural geographies show that] the social, the oral and the aural are intertwined (Wood et al., 2007) and ... the dialogic processes of utterances may enact different collective and public spaces" (Kanngieser, 2012, p. 2). In other

Police	Partob in
Eager to	the East
Arrest	America wants
Criminals	to Control
Everywhere	the Earth
People	And they
Eating	call it
Animals it's a	Peace
Climate	Paix
Emergency	صلح (Solh)
Puppets in	Friede
England	Vrede
Are	Hasiti
Catching	Paz
Elephants in	Salem
the room	Baris

Figure 13.1   Song written on the night, 13 January 2020

words, sound allows space to come into being through its interaction with social and sonoric agents in a way that cannot be predetermined. Inside the pub, this refashioning of space was made possible by the material qualities of sound: vibrations on the floors, walls, seats and table, resonance in the body, physical sensations and tone inflections all enabled the emergence of a different order that supplants the structure of the White governance of Segue (see Ella's quotation).

For Saldanha (2007, p. 10), racial difference is the result of processes that unfold "at different levels of organisation", which suggests that the way in which certain factors (space, bodies, location) constellate, shapes power and resistance. Just like with sound, attending to these factors invite us to look beyond discourse and representations (without undermining their influence on shaping lived realities). Similarly, emergence is processual and constellates in ways that are unpredictable through, in this case, a series of transgressive practices of social and spatial norms at different levels. That is to say, there is no single form of resistance, and resistance is, as in Cindi Katz's typology (Katz, 2001), only one form of political response that can drive change, but should not be romanticised.

In this case, emergent resistance manifests itself through a series of non-predetermined, transgressive practices that eventually break with the status quo. In Segue, these practices operated spatially and sonically against the backdrop of a culturally normative understanding of migrants' socialising behaviours. As a result, by encouraging the exploration of a new neighbourhood and the highly coded space of the pub, migrants challenged the widely held belief that for cultural reasons they should not be found in pubs, and reclaimed a space from which they are structurally excluded. In terms of sonic transgression, it was the improvisation of a riff and collaborative songwriting that served as a tacit invitation to reshape power dynamics by giving migrants a platform.

SOCIO-SPATIAL TRANSGRESSIVE PRACTICES

Even if so-called 'parallel lives' and 'self-segregation' could not be demonstrated in the North East of England, Nayak's (2012, p. 458) study showed that the absence of people of colour in everyday social spaces (for example, the pub) should not be dismissed as solely a matter of cultural difference. Rather, these absences reflect structural obstacles. That is because these processes of racialisation are fundamentally about the material conditions of people who are in the asylum system. Their im/mobilisation is infused with silencing; since they are cast away spatially and cannot afford regular public transport, their absence is also sonic. As their material conditions do not enable them to take part in and shape the urban sound/landscapes on their own terms, their political response may not be outwardly one of contestation. In the pub, their very presence operates a shift in the routines of regulars, as in their own, a 'rupture in the given' (Isin and Nielsen, 2008). The presence of 'strangers' or 'otherness', as Mark expresses in the quotation below, evokes the process of 'cultural destabilisation' defined by Amin as a moment where people are "encouraged to step out of their routine environment, into other everyday spaces" (Amin, 2002, p. 969):

> Mark: ... they might have been a little bit like, 'oh!' because it's just out of their norm, this is their one little thing of a week that they do, it's just like they know who

goes and it's all quite a part of a comfortable routine. So, there might have been some reactions someone perhaps acting a little awkward. I would say that that's probably more to do with just anyone being in the space and time that they are used to, in their routine place. Obviously, the element of otherness about it will have an effect as well, but the kind of people who go [there] would not intellectually be put off (Interview with Mark, 11 June 2020)

If they are finally seen in that space as Black and Brown, people in the asylum system are also heard, through their voices, their bodies, their music and rhythmic taps. These are "imprinted with, and can intervene in, the circuits and flows of power in these public spaces. These dynamics of domination and cooperation modulate and influence ... modes of expression, that is to say the voice is deployed in geographies of complicity, sympathy, antagonism, defiance, and so on" (Lazzarato, 2009, p. 2 in Kanngieser, 2012, p. 345). "This is how spaces manifest sound", adds Kanngieser (2012, p. 345). As such, sonic transgressions occur on the backdrop of a normalised/normative model (for example, sonic/material, social, spatial) that excludes the presence of racialised bodies and sounds in the urban space, and particularly that of the pub, and momentarily transform the space. The transgression of these norms must occur in an account of emergent resistance, but it is not predetermined as explicit opposition, because the material and structural norms upon which the events occur are not always known or conscious, hence emergence can only be identified *a posteriori*. In sum, we can identify three moments of socio-spatial transgressions in this vignette: the rupture between tutors/students and the White governmentality of the charity system, the disrupted routines of the regulars and migrants, and finally, the fact of occupying the pub as a racialised space.

IDENTIFYING EMERGENCE

Through this reading of the event, I align with Hughes's (2020) and Griffin's (2023) call to consider resistance beyond intention and identify resistance on a spectrum/trajectory. By that, I do not wish to undermine the value of 'macropolitics' and overt political activism, nor do I "romanticise molecular movements as inherently transgressive or liberatory actions" (Merriman, 2018, p. 8). Instead, I would like to draw attention to emergent resistance as an organic, unpredictable, improvised process that involves multiple space-times, that can emerge in multiple directions, and that is composed of relational, material and infrastructural arrangements, as the three moments of transgression above express. In the quotation below, the organic nature of resistance in emergence emerges as the result of barely noticeable relational and spatial transgressions, and encourages us to look beyond the lyrics of the song that was written:

> [W]hat happened last night, was just really organic. We did some work with the Boomwhackers, we did some of the choir songs with the Boomwhackers and then said, *oh well* we will have a jam, and then there was this new kind of riff going on and I didn't know what it was, and Mark was like singing and stuff, and then they, I think they had been discussing some words on peace and they had written some lyrics, and then there was this vamping kind of riff, and then I just thought oh well, and then Mark said that they were writing a new song, so I just wrote a little violin part and the violins joined in, and it was a song just like that. (Ella, meeting recording 14 January 2020)

Ella's vocal inflection reflected her surrender to a collective creative energy ('oh well') and a slight destabilisation. However, this allowed her to improvise the writing of a violin part for the emerging song. The power geometry, in which she is normally visible as the leader, had to shift in tandem with the usual structure of the music session. Critically, destabilisation and surrender represented opportunities for Segue's reorganisation. This, however, was not known at the time. Talking about outcomes is an impossible exercise when emerging possibilities of becoming are unfolding.

According to Hughes, the trajectory of resistance in emergence is what makes it an important object of study. It is for all those whose resistance does not or cannot be expressed outwardly and explicitly, as well as for all those acts that we undertake when affect and emotion, rather than intentional or deliberate thought, drive our actions. As a result of their interconnectedness, these cumulative acts allow for a reshaping of the terms for im/mobilised bodies and their relationships with civil society. Although the policies are not necessarily changing as a result, these forms of seemingly non-political mobilities (for example, leaving one's neighbourhood, entering a space from which one is excluded) do constitute resisting precarious conditions set up in the hostile environment (for example, dispersal scheme, asylum hotels). In the trajectory of Segue, this event not only offered a rupture with the constraints of the dispersal scheme, but also opened possibilities for future music sessions to be more open-ended. It opened a space for critical questioning, which is itself a political response that can lay foundations for resistance in-becoming.

At the time of writing, Segue is rethinking its charity status in light of the bureaucratic barriers that the formal status implies, and is considering trading off financial 'security' in order to reclaim its ethical commitment to non-hierarchical forms of governance. In terms of the musical project itself, writing this in 2021, the coming months will see the launching of weekly 'open sessions', with no preassigned agenda, which will take place on a different day than the music lessons.

CONCLUSIONS

In summary, this chapter has demonstrated how understanding resistance in emergence can provide an opportunity for radical political refashioning. The bodies of migrants in the UK are im/mobilised, racialised, and particularly vulnerable to violent sanctions, and to pain. This prevents many of them from participating in society, let alone engaging in outward forms of active resistance. This, however, does not imply that they are passively enduring the conditions imposed on them by a hostile asylum regime. In addition, charities are often forced to adhere to a state-sanctioned model of racialised governance, precluding the expression of a political stance. Within those organisations, however, members of staff also engage in critical questioning of these structures and their position within it. In this chapter, I have argued that paying attention to (un)intended transgressions of normative expectations is an intriguing point of focus for identifying resistance in emergence. Paying attention to commonly held beliefs about where migrants should or should not be found, how to 'deliver' them a 'service', and the discourse on charity in that context, exposes subtler resistance.

This chapter also provides a short methodological contribution by demonstrating how an engaged form of ethnography can support the process of radical refashioning for charitable organisations that work with migrants, and is ideally suited to capture the unfolding of emergent resistance. To illustrate this, I recounted an event which I co-organised with Segue, a charity that provides free music lessons to migrants, that struggles to evolve into the grassroots organisation it aspires to be. A comparison of the qualities of Segue's ordinary music sessions with those of an exceptional session held at a local pub demonstrates the importance of focusing on subtle, socio-spatial transgressive practices to openly address how racial difference underpins the experience of Black and Brown bodies in much of the charity sector. Indeed, this event metaphorically enabled the group to let out some of the pain endured through the system and 'fill the space with joy'.

NOTES

1. The term 'migrant' is used in this chapter in accordance with Scheel and Tazzioli's (2022) definition drawn from the autonomy of migration literature, which defines it as 'a person who, in order to move to or stay in a desired place, has to struggle against bordering practices and processes of boundary-making that are implicated by the national order of things' (Scheel and Tazzioli, 2022, p. 3).
2. The venue appeals to young crowds for their weekly club nights and artistic events, but does not seem to draw in people who are in the asylum system.
3. Sessions are free to attend, and travel costs are covered.

4. In terms of its location and structure.
5. Also see Sharma (2020) for more on the histories of failing empires and the birth of nations.
6. Destitution is a phenomenon that can affect anyone seeking asylum in the United Kingdom. When someone is destitute, it means that they have lost access to the National Asylum Support Service (NASS), welfare provision (accommodation, financial assistance), which often leads to people becoming unhoused. This agency was established specifically to manage the influx of immigrants into the country, and it is well known for its disbelief culture, lengthy wait times, and for subcontracting essential services such as housing.
7. Black and minority ethnic.
8. All names have been changed.
9. The name of the pub has been changed.
10. Boomwhackers are plastic tubes coming in different sizes and colours that are tuned to a particular pitch (thanks to their length). They are used as percussion instruments.
11. 'What a Moonlit Night' in English.

REFERENCES

Adams, T.E., Jones, S.H., Ellis, C., 2014. *Autoethnography*. Oxford University Press, Oxford.

Ainsworth, D., 2018. David Ainsworth: Why is the Charity Sector so White? WWW Document. https://www.civilsociety.co.uk/voices/david-ainsworth-why-is-the-charity-sector-so-white.html (accessed 6 December 2022).

Amin, A., 2002. Ethnicity and the Multicultural City: Living with Diversity. *Environment and Planning C* 34, 959–980.

Billo, E., Mountz, A., 2016. For Institutional Ethnography: Geographical Approaches to Institutions and the Everyday. *Progress in Human Geography* 40, 199–220.

Bonnett, A., 1990. Anti-Racism as a Radical Educational Ideology in London and Tyneside. *Oxford Review of Education* 16, 255–267.

Brown, M., Knopp, L., 2008. Queering the Map: The Productive Tensions of Colliding Epistemologies. *Annals of American Geographers* 98, 40–58.

Brown-Vincent, L.D., 2019. Seeing It for Wearing It: Autoethnography as Black Feminist Methodology. *Taboo: The Journal of Culture and Education* 18. https://doi.org/10.31390/taboo.18.1.08.

Cahill, C., 2007. The Personal is Political: Developing New Subjectivities through Participatory Action Research. *Gender Place and Culture* 14, 267–292.

Charity So White, 2019. Charity So White. WWW Document. Charity White. https://charitysowhite.org (accessed 6 December 2022).

Chowdhury, E.H., Pulido, L., Heynen, N., Rini, L., Wainwright, J., Inayatullah, N., Nagar, R., 2016. Muddying the Waters: Coauthoring Feminisms across Scholarship and Activism. *Gender Place and Culture* 23, 1800–1812.

Clayton, J., Vickers, T., 2019. Temporal Tensions: European Union Citizen Migrants, Asylum Seekers and Refugees Navigating Dominant Temporalities of Work in England. *Time and Society* 28, 1464–1488.

Darling, J., 2014. Asylum and the Post-Political: Domopolitics, Depoliticisation and Acts of Citizenship: Asylum and the post-political. *Antipode* 46, 72–91.

Darling, J., 2016. Privatising Asylum: Neoliberalisation, Depoliticisation and the Governance of Forced Migration. *Transactions of the Institute of British Geographers* 41, 230–243.

Ellul-Knight, B., 2019. Listening Otherwise: Attuning to the Caring-Chaos of a Refugee and Asylum Drop-In Service. *Cultural Geography* 26, 505–517.

Freire, P., 2017. *Pedagogy of the Oppressed.* Penguin Classics, New York.

Griffin, P. (2023). *Resistance.* In International Encyclopaedia of Geography (eds D. Richardson, N. Castree, M.F. Goodchild, A. Kobayashi, W. Liu and R.A. Marston). https://doi.org/10.1002/9781118786352.wbieg2120 Accessed 31st May 2023.

Haraway, D., 1988. Situated Knowledges: The Science Question in Feminism and the Privilege of Partial Perspective. *Feminist Studies* 14, 575–599.

Hesse, B., 1996. White Governmentality. In: Westwood, S., Williams, J. (eds), *Imagining Cities.* Routledge, London, pp. 86–103.

Hoy, D.C., 2004. *Critical Resistance: From Poststructuralism to Post-Critique.* MIT Press, Cambridge, MA.

Hughes, S.M., 2016. Beyond Intentionality: Exploring Creativity and Resistance within a UK Immigration Removal Centre. *Citizenship Studies* 20, 427–443.

Hughes, S.M., 2018. Rethinking Resistance: Creativity and Potentiality within the UK Asylum System. PhD thesis. Durham University, Durham.

Hughes, S.M., 2020. On Resistance in Human Geography. *Progress in Human Geography* 44, 1141–1160.

Isin, E.F., Nielsen, G.M., 2008. *Acts of Citizenship.* Zed Books, London.

Kanngieser, A., 2012. A Sonic Geography of Voice: Towards an Affective Politics. *Progress in Human Geography* 36, 336–353.

Katz, C., 2001. On the Grounds of Globalization: A Topography for Feminist Political Engagement. *Signs* 26, 1213–1234.

Kindon, S., Pain, R., Kesby, M. (eds), 2007. *Participatory Action Research Approaches and Methods: Connecting People, Participation and Place.* Routledge, Milton Park.

Kneale, J., 2021. Good, Homely, Troublesome or Improving? Historical Geographies of Drinking Places, c. 1850–1950. *Geography Compass* 15(3), 1–14.

Mayblin, L., James, P., 2019. Asylum and Refugee Support in the UK: Civil Society Filling the Gaps? *Journal of Ethnic and Migration Studies* 45(3), 375–394.

Mayblin, L., Wake, M., Kazemi, M., 2020. Necropolitics and the Slow Violence of the Everyday: Asylum Seeker Welfare in the Postcolonial Present. *Sociology* 54(1), 107–123.

McKittrick, K., 2020. *Dear Science and Other Stories.* Durham, NC: Duke University Press.

Merriman, P., 2018. Molar and Molecular Mobilities: The Politics of Perceptible and Imperceptible Movements. *Environment and Planning C* 37, 65–82.

Mullings, B., 1999. Insider or Outsider, Both or Neither: Some Dilemmas of Interviewing in a Cross-Cultural Setting. *Geoforum* 30, 337–350.

Nagar, R., Shirazi, R., 2019. Radical Vulnerability. In: Antipode Editorial Collective, Jazeel, T., Kent, A., McKittrick, K., Theodore, N., Chari, S., Chatterton, P., Gidwani, V., Heynen, N., Larner, W., Peck, J., Pickerill, J., Werner, M., Wright, M.W. (eds), *Keywords in Radical Geography: Antipode at 50.* John Wiley & Sons, Hoboken, NJ, pp. 236–242.

Nayak, A., 2012. Race, Religion and British Multiculturalism: The Political Responses of Black and Minority Ethnic Voluntary Organisations to Multicultural Cohesion. *Political Geography* 31, 454–463.

Phillips, D., 2006. Moving Towards Integration: The Housing of Asylum Seekers and Refugees in Britain. *Housing Studies* 21, 539–553.

Rose, N., Miller, P., 1992. Political Power beyond the State: Problematics of Government. *British Journal of Sociology* 43, 173–205.

Saldanha, A., 2007. *Psychedelic White: Goa Trance and the Viscosity of Race*. University of Minnesota Press, Minneapolis, MN.

Scheel, S., Tazzioli, M., 2022. Who is a Migrant? Abandoning the Nation-State Point of View in the Study of Migration. *Migration Politics*. https://doi.org/10.21468/MigPol.1.1.002.

Scott, J.C., 1985. *Weapons of the Weak: Everyday Forms of Peasant Resistance*. Yale University Press, London.

Sharma, N., 2020. *Home Rule: National Sovereignty and the Separation of Natives and Migrants*. Duke University Press, Durham, NC.

Tolia-Kelly, D.P., 2006. Affect – An Ethnocentric Encounter? Exploring the 'Universalist' Imperative of Emotional/Affectual Geographies. *Area* 38, 213–217.

Tolia-Kelly D.P., 2016. Feeling and Being at the (Postcolonial) Museum: Presencing the Affective Politics of 'Race' and Culture. *Sociology* 50, 896–912.

Tyler, I., Gill, N., Conlon, D., Oeppen, C., 2014. The Business of Child Detention: Charitable Co-option, Migrant Advocacy and Activist Outrage. *Race and Class* 56, 3–21.

Wood, N., Duffy, M., Smith, S.J., 2007. The Art of Doing (Geographies of) Music. *Environ Plan D* 25(5), 867–889.

14. Around, despite, and without reference to domination: crafting oppositional human geographies in migrant detention

Leah Montange

INTRODUCTION

As one spends time around the Northwest Detention Center (NWDC) in Tacoma, Washington, handmade crafts spill out of the facility and into one's field of vision. Colorful trinkets made of folded soup and food wrappers sit in the offices and homes of all kinds of people who interact with the detention center: inside the trailer that receives people as they are released, sitting next to a bowl of granola bars, is a little dog made of folded wrappers, just 5–6 cm tall; on the desk of an immigration attorney, a picture frame made of folded wrappers; inside the home of someone released from detention, another picture frame holding the school portraits of his children.

The NWDC is a 1575 bed facility owned and operated by private prison company the GEO Group (GEO), on behalf of United States Immigration and Customs Enforcement (ICE). The NWDC is one of two adult long-term detention facilities in the Seattle ICE Field Office area at the time of my research, and one of the more than 200 facilities that make up the US Immigration and Customs Enforcement's migrant detention system. All but five of these are owned and operated by private companies, local law enforcement agencies, or other third-party providers.

The research that informs this chapter was part of a study of the spatial and temporal ordering of carceral immigration enforcement in the US Pacific Northwest, centering on the NWDC. Geographers and social scientists who study immigration detention often must do so from the side, "periscoping" in (Hiemstra, 2017), or reading between redacted lines (Hiemstra and Conlon, 2021), as data about and access to these sites is highly restricted (Maillet et al., 2017). For my study, I interviewed 65 people with direct experience or expertise regarding immigration enforcement, such as people who ICE has arrested and detained, immigration attorneys, social service providers, and others. I received consent from all who I interviewed. I attended public events where detention was addressed, and volunteered with a social service organization that works with people as they leave detention. I also maintained long-term (1–3 year) pen pal and visitation relationships with several people inside the detention center, three of whom agreed to inform my research once they were out of confinement. Crafting was not the object of my study, but in this chapter I trace my encounters with crafts and crafting in my fieldwork. I do so in order to consider what crafting reveals for our understanding of resistance, opposition, and space in migrant detention.

In this chapter, I discuss resistance to spatial and temporal domination, the ordering of space and time in places such as migrant detention centers and camps, where non-citizens' agency, visibility, and mobility are restricted in ways that exclude them not only from political subjecthood within the national space, but also from the category of deserving human. Geographers studying migrant detention have identified spatial and temporal orderings such as confinement, punishment, forced mobility, isolation, distancing, and criminalization that characterize detention sites and contribute to harmful conditions (Martin, 2015; Mountz et al., 2013; Mountz, 2020; Hiemstra, 2013; Mountz and Loyd, 2014; Campos-Delgado, 2021). These spatio-temporal orderings shape detention centers into spaces marked by the production of not only relations of migrant exclusion, but also dehumanization, exposure to premature death (Gilmore, 2007), and the production of human hierarchy.

While dissent and resistance are difficult, risky endeavors in a detention center, people invent ways of confronting or challenging domination anyway (Montange, 2017). Not all the ways that people use or make oppositional space are legible as politics. I argue that crafting in the NWDC is an oppositional use of space, a resistant practice of producing a human geography despite, around, and without reference to spatial and temporal domination in the detention center. I engage with frameworks from two Black feminist thinkers, Saidiya Hartman and Katherine McKittrick, in order to frame this argument and explore the multiple valences of craft-making in the oppositional production of space and time in detention. Hartman and McKittrick, who both interrogated everyday opposition in the context of plantation life and chattel slavery, offer important concepts for apprehending what opposition can look like in other contexts of spatial domination and human hierarchy, such as migrant detention.

I begin in the following section with a discussion of approaches to understanding resistance and politics in bordering zones or spaces such as migrant detention centers. I emphasize how Saidiya Hartman's (1997) conceptualization of "everyday practice" and Katherine McKittrick's (2006) production of space and alternative, human geographies provide a fruitful framework for understanding resistance in a context of spatial and temporal domination such as a detention center. Next, after a brief section that outlines the logics of spatial and temporal domination at the NWDC (isolation, austerity, extraction, and wasting), I examine the activity of making and circulating crafts in detention in terms of everyday spatial and temporal practices. In doing so, I make an intervention in the debates on political subjectivity, space, and resistance in abject spaces such as detention centers. That is, I draw attention to a way that people in detention resist domination not through making political claims or exerting rights, but by making space and place around, despite, or without reference to spatio-temporal domination. I demonstrate how such forms of spatial practice are ambiguous, do not fall neatly under the category of politics and resistance, but nevertheless re-shape space and time in detention. This analysis offers a dimension to the conception of resistance beyond the question of political subjectivity.

RESISTANCE, AGENCY, SPACE, PRACTICE

Debates on migrant agency, resistance and politics have hinged upon the question of how to conceptualize the politics of those non-citizens and "abject" others to whom the state ascribes a very constrained set of rights (Isin and Neilson, 2008; Nyers, 2010; Jones, 2012; McNevin, 2013; Squire, 2015; Maestri and Hughes, 2017). Within liberal democracies, the possibilities for politics and resistance are formally proscribed by political belonging and citizenship: who has the right to speech, voice and protest? And yet, non-citizens and immigrants take part in politics by protesting, occupying space, and claiming or even "taking" rights not formally ascribed to them (Nyers, 2010).

Within the literature on resistance in detention, and other spaces of border-making, the predominant scholarly discourse emphasizes the political activity or subjectivity of non-citizens in relation to state sovereign control over borders and citizenship. Many scholars have focused on rupturous acts such as hunger strikes or outward protest, theorizing these through the rubrics of political subjectivization (Montange, 2017), contentious politics (Ataç et al., 2016), counter-conduct (Conlon, 2013), subversion of sovereign power and abjectification (Edkins and Pin-Fat, 2005), or as tactics for seizing political opportunity and connecting across struggles (McGregor, 2011). What all of these analyses have in common is the notion that non-citizens can and do contest state sovereign control over their bodies and mobilities, even where their political claims are ambivalent, or reinscribe exclusionary discourses, institutions and practices (McNevin, 2013). In this chapter I shift the gaze to forms of opposition in spaces of domination that do not look like protest and direct contestation of state-sovereignty, but instead are subtler forms of using and making space around, despite, or without reference to various forms of spatio-temporal domination.

Space is not only the setting where non-citizens make political claims or enact resistance to state sovereignty, bordering, or domination. Space is at once produced through these processes, and shapes the possibilities of struggle and agency (Maestri and Hughes, 2017; Isin and Rygiel, 2007; Jones, 2012; Erensu, 2016; Martin et al., 2020). Isin and Rygiel (2007) conceptualized sites such as camps, border zones, and detention centers as "abject spaces" where the personhood of migrating people are made invisible, and that thus attempt to render migrants and displaced persons inhabiting them as "inexistent beings" (p. 184). But, as Isin and Rygiel (2007) point out, spaces of citizenship are nestled within abject spaces. In other words, the spatio-temporal orderings that produce invisibility of personhood do not actually erase the agency, resistance, or activity of people who make claims to the rights, space, and voice that they do not have. This line of thinking is also echoed by other scholars who have theorized "spaces of refusal" in which "sovereign state practices interact with alternative ways of seeing, knowing, and being" (Jones, 2012, p. 687). That is, non-citizens contest the relation between sovereign state and migrant through mobilities that evade state control, or through a "simple dismissal of the state's claim to define subjects and activities in those spaces," even without necessarily making outwardly contentious or political claims (Jones, 2012, p. 687).

The social and spatial relations of detention sites are not wholly defined through (non-)citizenship and state sovereignty: there remains a need to theorize human geographies and uses of space beyond this specific relation (Squire, 2015). Here, I build on a turn in migration and border studies from understanding bordering and detention practices as bent on migrant exclusion and the performance of state sovereignty, to understanding these practices as marked by physical, social, and political death (Mountz, 2020), racial violence (Ordaz, 2021), and forms of dehumanization (Montange, 2017; Mainwaring, 2019). I suggest that to meet this context, we need to expand our concepts for understanding forms of resistance, opposition, and life-making in detention. In this chapter, I address agentic, oppositional space-making beyond the state–abject non-citizen relation. The frameworks of Black feminist theorists and geographers (Hartman, 1997; McKittrick, 2006) who look at the question of oppositional spatial practices in the context of chattel slavery gives us a pathway to conceptualize how this might work in migrant detention.

In the book *Scenes of Subjection*, Saidiya Hartman (1997) focused on ambiguous forms of resistance to chattel slavery that she calls "everyday practice." Hartman's conceptualization of everyday practice, an extension of de Certeau's (1984) term "practice," emerged through her theorization of enslaved peoples' pleasure and cultural production. Hartman analyzed the ways that enslaved people in North America made life and acted with agency despite domination, which she describes as the "brutal exercise of power upon the captive body," the subjugation and terror facilitated by "preying upon the flesh, heart, and the soul" of enslaved people (Hartman, 1997, p. 5). Geographers and other spatial thinkers have drawn on de Certeau to analyze the agentic ways in which oppressed social groups tactically maneuver or narrate space to express themselves agentically and politically (Secor, 2004; Elwood and Mitchell, 2012; Garmany, 2017). These works prompt a consideration of how political subjectivity or "citizenship is continuously being reconfigured from the bottom up" (Secor, 2004, p. 365). Hartman's conceptualization of everyday practice is distinct, because she is analyzing a context characterized by a denial of personhood and an impossibility of political subjectivity. Instead of conceptualizing how political subjectivity, rights, or a kind of citizenship is claimed or constituted, Hartman addresses how non-citizenship also expresses itself through spatial practices and tactics that are agentic; that are not merely capitulating to spatialized and temporalized dominance.

For her, everyday practices include ways that people maneuver within a context of domination by "exploiting the limits of the permissible, creating transient zones of freedom, and reelaborating innocent amusements" in ways that "undermine, transform, and redress the condition of enslavement" (Hartman, 1997, p. 50). Hartman examines tactics such as enslaved people sneaking out to visit one another, attending a prayer meeting, or singing an encoded critique of slavery. These practices sought pleasure and unauthorized personal connections, or imitated but also surpassed what was allowed. These practices are inherently ambiguous: they do not demonstrate the resistant political subjects claiming rights and attempting to undermine the order of slaveholder hegemony, nor harmony and consent to such an order. Such ambiguous practices are "excluded from the locus of the 'political proper'" (p. 61) and yet are evidence of a "subterranean politics" (p. 50). Hartman's concept of everyday practice offers a way to identify and theorize activity and expressions of agency that do not necessarily assert political subjectivity, but nevertheless sidestep or exceed the limits of spatio-temporal domination. They operate "in and against the demands of the system" (p. 51).

In her book *Demonic Grounds*, geographer Katherine McKittrick (2006) connects everyday practices to the production of space, drawing attention to intertwining, overlapping spaces of domination and opposition. McKittrick (2006) analyzes what she calls the spatial practices of Black women on plantations to look for "alternative patterns that work alongside traditional geographies" of domination (p. xiv). In particular, she emphasizes the ways in which spaces structured around the denial of personhood and dehumanization sit alongside or are overlaid with agentic, human geographies produced through spatial practices that demonstrate the persistence of human subjectivity and life beyond domination. Through their spatial practice, various Black women re-spatialize the geographies of dehumanization and human hierarchy, for instance by re-signifying their own bodies on the auction block, or signifying a space of confinement, a garret. What is important in McKittrick's contribution on the production of space is her insistence that what she calls "traditional geographies"—dominant modes of producing and representing space—organize social difference through racial and sexual hierarchies, which "place" people of various social groups in particular geographical arrangements, which are then deemed "natural" or transparent and unremarkable. For McKittrick, racism and sexism are spatial relations necessary to the "overarching traditional geographic projects" which require that Black women "be placed and displaced" (p. 12). But for McKittrick, space is also produced through ruptures, contestations, and alternative place-making.

McKittrick excavates spatial practices through which enslaved Black women inhabit space and make place in ways that are an alternative to, but overlap with, spatial domination; in this way, these spatial practices are an important vector in the production of space and in the re-working of human hierarchies (Gilmore, 2002). Without necessarily asserting a political personhood, these are spatial practices which use and produce oppositional space that are "new, or unacknowledged, strategies of social struggle" (McKittrick, 2006, p. xvi). They do not express a kind of citizenship, and they do not necessarily address a contest with state sovereignty, but they nevertheless express a human geography that exceeds domination and contests the way that spaces have configured and then naturalized human hierarchy.

Hartman and McKittrick developed their conceptualizations of everyday practice, spatial practice, and alternative, human geographies through studies of Black women's opposition to chattel slavery. This form of domination was enshrined in law but took on economic, cultural, and social forms, including denial of personhood, that Hartman argues are a specific, violent, and persistent characteristic of anti-Black racism. Without drawing a parallel between detention and the distinct racial-spatial formations that are the legacy of chattel slavery in North America, I offer that ICE detention centers in the US are also spaces of domination, in their own historically and geographically specific ways. In these spaces, space and time are ordered not just to exclude migrants from the US population, but also to subordinate them (Montange, 2021). Everyday practice and alternative, human geographies provide us with a framework for analyzing spatial practices in detention that often go unacknowledged as resistance, without collapsing these practices into an assertion of citizenship, and while also acknowledging that the forms of domination found in detention amount to a production of not only state sovereignty, but also racial violence and hierarchy. I offer that Hartman's and McKittrick's concepts of practice and the production of space provide us with a pathway to think about resistance and space in detention differently, as they "open up a conceptual arena through which more humanly workable geographies can be and are imagined" (McKittrick, 2006, p. xii).

In this chapter I offer a reading of the activity of crafting in the detention center in these terms, as an agentic practice that does not demonstrate political subjectivization, or acquiescence with spatio-temporal domination, but rather demonstrates an alternative, human geography. Those who exist within spaces of domination such as immigration detention centers use and make space and place around, despite, or without reference to the logics of spatio-temporal domination.

SPATIO-TEMPORAL DOMINATION IN THE NWDC

ICE and the GEO Group order space and time in the NWDC through logics of isolation and segregation, austerity and deprivation, financial extraction and wasting (see also Montange, 2021). Altogether, these logics amount to a form of spatio-temporal domination, in which people's everyday lives, mobilities, uses of space, and daily rhythms are highly structured and controlled, in ways that are difficult for detained people to tolerate.

The NWDC is an isolating, austere, and extractive space. It is organized through segregation and isolation: the facility is divided into men's and women's units, which are further sub-divided by security levels ranging from low to high, mostly based on criminal record. The use of the buildings is regulated through schedules and movements that prevent mixing and interaction between security levels and gender categories. Isolation and segregation are even more pronounced in solitary confinement. Spatial practices associated with isolation contribute to the invisibility of people in detention and make possible the unfreedoms and harms that can happen there (Hiemstra, 2013; Mountz and Loyd, 2014).

Within the space of segregation and isolation, people must survive with austere provisioning. The metal furnishings, thin mattresses, and lack of privacy in the open dorms are often described as "cold" and "hard." The GEO Group provides people with a basic uniform, undershirt, underwear (used, sometimes stained), and socks (used, sometimes holey); three meals calculated to contain enough calories for sustenance; and stocks the restrooms monthly with hygiene supplies such as soaps and shampoos. However, the food served is unappetizing and sometimes comes spoiled; the uniforms that are provided are thin, while the air is cool; and the toiletries provided by the detention facility are not adequate and often run out.

Spatial isolation and austerity at the NWDC imbricates people in micro-economies of extraction, as many find supplemental food, garments, and toiletries a necessity. A commissary provided by Keefe Group sells snack items, microwavable soups, coffees, toiletries, sweatsuits that people can layer with their uniforms for warmth, and other items that people might want such as playing cards and stationery. The coupling of deprivation with supplemental services and goods for a fee imbricates detained people in the extraction of value (Hiemstra and Conlon, 2017). While some people can afford to make these purchases through outside support, many others have only one option to do so, which is by participating in the Volunteer Work Program, through which ICE and the GEO Group pay people $1/day to clean, prepare and distribute food, sort and fold laundry, clean their units, and more.

Meanwhile, temporalities of detention at the NWDC are best understood as both arbitrary and wasting: people do not have a sense of when or how their confinement will end, and meanwhile their time, resources, relationships, and health are all put under strain, depleting and wasting away (Montange, 2021; see also Khosravi, 2010, pp. 100–102). The length of time a person will remain in detention is ordered through the rhythms of the immigration court and ICE deportations regulate time. In the US detention system, arbitrariness of both transfers and the time frames of deportation cases combine to create a chaotic, non-transparent system that cloaks any alternatives to deportation that may exist for people (Hiemstra, 2019). People wait for their cases to be processed, without concrete and specific information about how long this will take and whether they have a chance. Meanwhile, daily rhythms at the NWDC are structured through population counts and meal calls, with very few activities available to occupy time in between other than sleeping, watching TV, reading, playing games, and exercising. Time spent in detention is not cumulative or progressive; it is monotonous. The only organized activities are weekly religious services and legal orientations. People in detention must waste their time, sitting and waiting, while also undergoing a process of wasting as their physical and mental health deplete.

The craft-making of those detained migrants work in relation to these logics of isolation, austerity, extraction, and wasting that pervade the NWDC. In the next section, I analyze crafting in the NWDC as a spatial practice that neither directly contests nor rehearses these spatio-temporal logics of domination, but that instead makes and uses space differently. Crafting produces, to adapt Katherine McKittrick's phrase, geographies "predicated on human life" (McKittrick, 2013, p. 3).

CRAFTING IN THE NORTHWEST DETENTION CENTER

Unlike migrant detention facilities in the United Kingdom, which have art rooms and some (restricted) cultural offerings (see Bosworth and von Zinnenburg Carroll, 2017; Hughes and Forman, 2017), the NWDC provides no creative activities or materials. People detained there turn to craftwork anyway. They make knick-knacks, toys, home decorations, and functional items—animals, picture frames, pillow covers, purses, wallets—at a range of sizes. They craft under the constraint of regulations around the kinds of materials that can circulate in the detention center. Any item for personal consumption or use that has not been cleared first through the Warden or purchased in the commissary is considered contraband. Thus, many crafts incorporate food wrappers gleaned from the waste stream of one's pod. People create adhesives for their crafts out of toothpaste, and string or fibers out of twisted plastic bags. People also purchase yarn and colored paper at the commissary, or a friend or family member outside can send them these materials (after pre-arrangement and approval).

The act of crafting and the circulation of crafts do not amount to an assertion of political subjectivity or a direct challenge to state sovereignty. Nevertheless, crafting as oppositional spatio-temporal practice signals the simultaneity of creative human activity and space or place-making with domination (McKittrick, 2006). In my encounters with crafts from the NWDC, I observed this activity's multiple valences in the navigation of spatio-temporal domination in the detention center: a way to express friendship and connection despite the isolation of detention (gifting); a way to make place within the austere detention space (place-making); a way to earn income outside the extractive work relations of the detention center (livelihood); and a way to survive the monotonous, wasting temporality of the detention center (spending time). Below I outline each of these four valences by which detained people make or use crafts in ways that are shaped by but also exceed the spatialities and temporalities of domination in NWDC. That is, through crafting, people in detention navigate and survive spatio-temporal domination without acquiescing to it, but also without claiming crafting as a political practice.

Gifting

One of the ways in which people circulate crafts in and around detention is through gifts. Through making and giving hand-crafted gifts to one another and to people outside the facility, detained people form spaces of interaction that express connection, care, and mutual obligation. They do so despite the isolation, segregation, and deprivation that organize the facility, as described above. During my fieldwork and interviews, I heard people describe crafts which they or others had made as gifts: toys and decorations to give to their children outside, or as personal accessories or decorations for one another's bunks inside. For example, one of my participants, Patricia, explained to me that while a friend of hers was in solitary confinement for two weeks, a form of heightened segregation and isolation within the already isolating detention space, she crocheted her a hat. When this same friend's court date to decide on her deportation was approaching, she and others in the pod made her another gift (I did not find out what it was), in case she left.

Gift-giving is constrained by the austere conditions inside detention—lack of income, and lack of access to a wide array of materials—but hand-made crafts, whether made by the giver or acquired through trade, are possible. Through giving crafts, people co-create a social space that is centered on care, appreciation, or social bonds that the isolation and segregation of detention interrupt. In this way, gift-giving of hand-made crafts is an everyday practice that produces an alterative to the space of domination, even as the constraints of spatio-temporal domination shape this practice.

Place-Making

Shortly before she was deported, Patricia asked me to come to the center to pick up a craft she had made: it was a vase full of flowers. The vase was constructed out of individual pieces of brightly colored folded paper slotted together, striped in rainbow order. The flowers, also made of paper, have green stems and bright petals, also in an assortment of rainbow colors (see Figure 14.1). Patricia told me that she had had it sitting beside her bunk, as a decoration. I asked her about other decorations that she had, and she told me that she had a little rainbow pillow (for lesbian, gay, bisexual, and transgender, LGBT, pride) which she had crocheted. She described making a similar pillow for her girlfriend's bunk, also in the pod. When she was deported, Patricia had been living in the detention center for over two years, and in this time she had adopted a perspective that she summarized like this: "They [the guards] work here, but I live here." She had found multiple strategies for inhabiting the space and expressing herself within it, including through markers of domesticity (a vase and flowers), sexual orientation (the rainbow), and relationship (matching pillows).

In the austere conditions of detention, property is highly regulated. According to The GEO Group's Detainee Handbook, rules enforced by routine and unannounced bunk checks regulate how much "property" people are allowed to keep at their bunks (GEO Group, 2016). The personal space and belongings of people in detention are both tightly controlled and kept austere. Meanwhile, crafted items that people make inside the center out of wrappers or other materials from the commissary become an area of negotiation, a possibility for making one's personal space in the detention center one's own, and for expressing one's individuality in the austere, highly regulated space. I read the place-making associated with crafting as a practice that remakes the detention space despite spatial austerity, deprivation, and control.

Figure 14.1   Vase of flowers made by Patricia at the Northwest Detention Center, USA

Livelihood

Inside the home of Ronaldo, a formerly detained man who I was interviewing, I encountered a set of small picture frames made of folded red and silver instant soup wrappers. During a pause in our interview, I looked around the room, noticing the frames. I recognized these immediately as a bit of the detention center decorating his home. I asked him about them when he sat back down with me. Inside each frame was a school photo of each of his children, who went with his partner to Mexico when ICE deported her earlier in the year. I asked him if he had made them in the NWDC. Ronaldo said no, he had not. He had commissioned them from someone in his unit at the detention center.

He remarked that he himself had had financial support from an immigrant solidarity network in his community, supplying him with money for phone calls and commissary items, but most people in the detention center did not. He had used his money to buy commissary items desired by someone in his pod who crafted, in exchange for the photo frame. In addition to these kinds of exchanges among people in the same pod, some people try to set up ways to sell their crafts to people outside the detention center, such as by sending them to family members or friends who can sell them.

This is one way to work around the coercive, extractive micro-economies of detention (Hiemstra and Conlon, 2017), and to invent alternative economies inside the detention center that sidestep extraction. Rather than amounting to a politicized and collective withdrawal from these economies, as a strike would, Ronaldo's pod mate had used his time in an unsanctioned way to work out alterative economies, beyond the extractive spatio-temporal ordering that he lived in.

Spending Time

As I explore elsewhere (Bisaillon et al., 2019), crafting is also a practice to negotiate temporal domination. Despite the arbitrary, wasting temporalities of detention, people express their creativity and metabolize the wastes—food wrappers, time—that are remnants of the extractive process which they find themselves in. The act of crafting—producing objects—becomes a method for reclaiming temporality by re-working wasted time and resources into creation. One of my participants, Michael, submitted his craftwork to a mixed-media art show entitled 'Immigration: Hopes Realized, Dreams Derailed' at Spaceworks Gallery in Tacoma, WA in the summer of 2017. His artist statement commented: "It is sad that there is not much we can do here. When i was in prison i made metal art, wood art, leatherwork, Native American beadwork and so much more. In NWDC it feels like my hands are tight [*sic*]." Michael told me that one of his intentions in participating in the show, in addition to being productive with his time and creative energy, was to add to his portfolio, which he assembled to demonstrates his positive attributes. It was a form of self-promotion in his attempt to fashion himself into an entrepreneurial, deserving subject. Although this is not a particularly resistant subject position in a capitalist society, in the face of the denial of personhood and human warehousing it marks the fashioning of an alternative spatio-temporal practice, an attempt to make the time in detention cumulative, despite the wasting monotony.

Each of these four valences offers a way to counter logics of spatio-temporal domination that exists within detention: isolation, austerity, extraction, and wasting. Rather than expressing a set of rights, claims, or even critiques of the detention center, through the activity of crafting people produce new or alternative spatio-temporal relations around, despite, or without reference to domination. Despite their isolation, they create ways to connect with one another and to express their connections with people outside of detention through making and giving gifts. They produce decorations for their bunks and a distinct set of crafts that signal the detention center as a place, in a practice that both expresses and subverts the austerity of the detention center. They work around the conditions of deprivation and extraction that they are imbricated in by creating their own micro-economies of production and trade. They reclaim time and waste through their crafting. In each of these four valences, I read crafting as an everyday spatial and temporal practice (Hartman, 1997), through which people in detention make oppositional spaces and times (McKittrick, 2006) around, despite, or without reference to spatio-temporal domination in the detention center.

Ambiguities

The activity of crafting has its ambiguities or ambivalences as an oppositional practice. Strictly speaking, the possession of crafts and the repurposing of commissary items is against the rules outlined in the NWDC Detainee Handbook. According to the Handbook, items that are altered from their original condition are defined as contraband (GEO Group, 2016, p. 19); the possession of contraband leads to disciplinary action. The crafts themselves are fashioned through altering the original condition of materials such as wrappers. Some of the crafts, particularly those made of yarn, involve using tools that are technically not allowed: one of my interview participants informed me that knitting and crochet needles cannot be supplied or purchased, and must therefore be fashioned out of materials on hand such as an old toothbrush. Although this breaks a rule in the Detainee Handbook, officers overlook this practice, and accommodate crafting. From my field notebook:

> At NWDC to visit and pick up a gift from my pen pal today. I was sort of juggling looking up the A number and writing it and chatting with the guard—she knows R___ and brightened up to see her name. I told her I was getting a swan, and so she wanted to chat enthusiastically about the industriousness of detainees and all the different things they make—the swans, the cars made of soap, the purses made of wrapper. The glues made of toothpaste and flour that holds the stuff together. The string made of saran wrap—she said they get on the top bunk and hang the wrap down to spin the wrap into string. While she talked to me, the officer from property came out and gave me a box with two swans in it, each a foot [30 cm] tall. She said they had been sitting there for a long time and she was glad to get them cleared out. I took them out and the other guard admired them. She spotted playing cards among the folded paper. She told me about how GEO got permission from ICE to let the detainees do all this crafting, how it started getting really big in about 2014, but then

they had had to figure out how to store all the things—property office got full, but you also couldn't have detainees with those things at their bunks because of fire hazards she said, but also because they would trade them, bet on them, sell them, and then you start getting into favors and manipulations and debts, which she said is not good. (Field notes, October 2017)

This interaction reveals some of the ambiguity of crafting in the detention center. That crafting helps people to tolerate the detention center with its austerity and its arbitrary, wasting timelines has meant that it has been accommodated into ICE and GEO Group's management of the center. Although this management does not involve structured activities to keep detained people occupied (and docile), GEO Group accommodated crafting insofar as it is a kind of self-organized, self-occupation. In its accommodation, GEO Group limited how many crafts people can store at their bunk and stored other crafts in the detention center's property office in the name of preventing illicit economies and fire safety. GEO Group has thus incorporated crafting into the spatio-temporal ordering of detention.

One reading of the situation is that the crafting activity that people in detention engage in is something that is easily incorporated into spatio-temporal domination, and that it is therefore not resistance to power. But a more productive reading, one prompted by my reading of Hartman and McKittrick, is that the ambiguity of crafting in relation to power is a hallmark of everyday spatial and temporal practice. The ambiguities of resistance and politics among non-citizens has been explored by theorists who have noted that when non-citizens enact citizenship, they are inherently reinforcing a social order that excludes (McNevin, 2013; Squire, 2015; Erensu, 2016). In this chapter, I locate ambiguity within Hartman's (1997) concept of everyday practice and McKittrick's (2006) geography of intertwined spaces of domination and opposition. For Hartman (1997), practice refers to activities that at once "are determined by, exploit and exceed the constraints of domination" (p. 54). Such practices overlap and coexist with relations of spatial (and temporal) domination.

The accommodation of crafting is not a signal of GEO Group's benevolence and humanitarianism, nor of an attempt to actively undermine the smooth functioning of the NWDC's spatio-temporal order. It is, however, a signal that crafting is an improvisation of activities that exist despite domination, a manifestation of the human geography of detention, and a process of producing space and time that exceeds the spatio-temporal domination, and that GEO Group must therefore accommodate. The material practice of crafting re-shapes the detention space-time, asserting a human geography beyond the austere, isolating, extractive, and wasting spatio-temporalities of the detention center. At the same time, the oppositional and human spatial practices are very much shaped by the spatio-temporal domination with which they intertwine.

CONCLUDING DISCUSSION

Crafting happens in the NWDC despite, around, and without reference to spatio-temporal domination in detention. While these spatial and temporal practices do not offer a direct or explicit critique of detention's logics of spatial and temporal domination, they speak to the ways that such geographies of domination overlap and intertwine with alternative, human geographies of opposition. In making this argument, I have drawn on Black feminist thinkers Saidiya Hartman and Katherine McKittrick, whose theorization of everyday forms of opposition and perseverance of life in contexts of racial violence offer concepts and tools for apprehending opposition in carceral spaces of non-citizenship, such as migrant detention. Hartman's everyday practice and McKittrick's conceptualization of the production of space and alternative geographies offer a framework for understanding agentic actions that are shaped by spaces of racial violence, hierarchy, and subjugation, but are not fully reducible to these conditions.

The lens of everyday practice (Hartman, 1997) offers us a way to understand the multiple valences of crating as processes of creating oppositional, alternative human geographies and temporalities in a context of domination. Crafting involves productions of space and time that re-work or exceed domination. Spatio-temporal orderings such as isolation, deprivation, austerity, and wasting shape the everyday geographies and temporalities of detention without completely defining them; through the spatio-temporal practice of crafting, people in detention produce an alternative geography (McKittrick, 2006). These alternative geographies and temporalities do not (or do not necessarily) invoke political subjectivity or directly contest detention. Nevertheless, they exceed the forms of spatio-temporal domination that shape the possibilities for using and creating space and time in detention.

What this points to is the limitations of a rubric for engaging opposition and resistance in detention as an activity that often is understood in relation to a struggle over state sovereignty and control over borders. Space and time are constituted through the simultaneity of multiple relations: in detention, these include struggle over state control of borders and the abjection of non-citizens, but also social relations that figure those in detention into a subordinate position on the human hierarchy, naturalizing their emplacement in conditions of exposure to death and racial violence. Space and time are also constituted through the production of human geographies and relations of opposition to abjection or subordination. The production of these human geographies signals a refusal of domination, the active agency and presence of people in detention who will not be dominated.

REFERENCES

Ataç, I., Rygiel, K., and Stierl, M. (2016). Introduction: The Contentious Politics of Refugee and Migrant Protest and Solidarity Movements: Remaking Citizenship from the Margins. *Citizenship Studies*, *20*(5), 527–544.

Bisaillon, L., Montange, L., Zambenedetti, A., Frascà, P., El-Shamy, L., and Arviv, T. (2019). Everyday Geographies, Geographies Everyday: Mundane of Mobilities Made Tangible. *Acme: An International E-Journal for Critical Geographies*, *18*(4), 1025.

Bosworth, M., and von Zinnenburg Carroll, K. (2017). Art and Criminology of the Border: The Making of the Immigration Detention Archive. *OAR: The Oxford Artistic and Practice Based Research Platform*, *1*. http://www.oarplatform.com/art-criminology-border-making-immigration-detention-archive/.

Campos-Delgado, A. (2021). Abnormal Bordering: Control, Punishment and Deterrence in Mexico's Migrant Detention Centres. *British Journal of Criminology*, *61*(2), 476–496.

Conlon, D. (2013). Hungering for Freedom: Asylum Seekers' Hunger Strikes—Rethinking Resistance as Counter-Conduct. In D. Moran, N. Gill, and D. Conlon (eds), *Carceral Spaces: Mobility and Agency in Imprisonment and Migrant Detention* (pp. 133–148). Ashgate Publishing.

de Certeau, M. (1984). *The Practice of the Everyday Life*. University of California Press.

Edkins, J., and Pin-Fat, V. (2005). Through the Wire: Relations of Power and Relations of Violence. *Millennium - Journal of International Studies*, *34*(1), 1–24.

Elwood, S., and Mitchell, K. (2012). Mapping Children's Politics: Spatial Stories, Dialogic Relations and Political Formation. *Geografiska Annaler. Series B, Human Geography*, *94*(1), 1–15.

Erensu, A.I. (2016). Notes from a Refugee Protest: Ambivalences of Resisting and Desiring Citizenship. *Citizenship Studies*, *20*(5), 664–677.

Garmany, J. (2017). Strategies of Conditional Cash Transfers and the Tactics of Resistance. *Environment and Planning A*, *49*(2): 372–388.

GEO Group (2016). *Northwest Detention Center Detainee Handbook*.

Gilmore, R.W. (2002). Fatal Couplings of Power and Difference: Notes on Racism and Geography. *Professional Geographer*, *54*(1), 15–24.

Gilmore, R.W. (2007). *Golden Gulag: Prisons, Surplus, Crisis, and Opposition in Globalizing California*. University of California Press.

Hartman, S.V. (1997). *Scenes of Subjection: Terror, Slavery, and Self-Making in Nineteenth-Century America*. Oxford University Press.

Hiemstra, N. (2013). "You Don't Even Know Where You Are": Chaotic Geographies of US Migration Detention and Deportation. In D. Moran, N. Gill, and D. Conlon (eds), *Carceral Spaces: Mobility and Agency in Imprisonment and Migrant Detention* (pp. 57–76). Ashgate Publishing.

Hiemstra, N. (2017). Periscoping as a Feminist Methodological Approach for Researching the Seemingly Hidden. *Professional Geographer*, *69*(2), 329–336.

Hiemstra, N. (2019). *Detain and Deport: The Chaotic U.S. Immigration Enforcement Regime*. University of Georgia Press.

Hiemstra, N., and Conlon, D. (2017). Captive Consumers and Coerced Labourers: Intimate Economies and the Expanding US Detention Regime. In D. Conlon and N. Hiemstra (eds), *Intimate Economies of Immigration Detention: Critical Perspectives* (pp. 123–139). Routledge.

Hiemstra, N., and Conlon, D. (2021). Reading Between the (Redacted) Lines. *ACME: An International Journal for Critical Geographies*, *20*(6), 666–686.

Hughes, S.M., and Forman, P. (2017). A Material Politics of Citizenship: The Potential of Circulating Materials from UK Immigration Removal Centres. *Citizenship Studies*, *21*(6): 675–692.

Isin, E.F., and Nielsen, G.M. (eds) (2008). *Acts of Citizenship*. Palgrave Macmillan.

Isin, E.F., and Rygiel, K. (2007). Abject Spaces: Frontiers, Zones, and Camps. In E. Dauphinee and C. Masters (eds), *The Logics of Biopower and the War on Terror* (pp. 181–203). Palgrave Macmillan.

Jones, R. (2012). Spaces of Refusal: Rethinking Sovereign Power and Resistance at the Border. *Annals of the Association of American Geographers*, *102*(3), 685–699.

Khosravi, S. (2010). *"Illegal" traveller: An Auto-Ethnography of Borders*. Palgrave Macmillan.

Maestri, G., and Hughes, S.M. (2017). Contested Spaces of Citizenship: Camps, Borders and Urban Encounters. *Citizenship Studies*, *21*(6), 625–639.

Maillet, P., Mountz, A., and Williams, K. (2017). Researching Migration and Enforcement in Obscured Places: Practical, Ethical and Methodological Challenges to Fieldwork. *Social and Cultural Geography*, *18*(7), 927–950.

Mainwaring, Ċ. (2019). *At Europe's edge: Migration and Crisis in the Mediterranean* (1st edition). Oxford University Press.

Martin, D., Minca, C., and Katz, I. (2020). Rethinking the Camp: On Spatial Technologies of Power and Resistance. *Progress in Human Geography*, *44*(4), 743–768.

Martin, L. (2015). Noncitizen Detention: Spatial Strategies of Migrant Precarity in US Immigration and Border Control. *Annales de Géographie*, *702–703*, 231–247.

McGregor, J. (2011). Contestations and Consequences of Deportability: Hunger Strikes and the Political Agency of Non-Citizens. *Citizenship Studies*, *15*(5), 597–611.

McKittrick, K. (2006). *Demonic Grounds*. University of Minnesota Press.

McKittrick, K. (2013). Plantation Futures. *Small Axe*, *17*(3), 1–15.

McNevin, A. (2013). Ambivalence and Citizenship: Theorising the Political Claims of Irregular Migrants. *Millennium*, *41*(2), 182–200.

Montange, L. (2017). Hunger Strikes, Detainee Protest, and the Relationality of Political Subjectivization. *Citizenship Studies*, *21*(5), 509–526.

Montange, L. (2021). The Spatio-Temporal Ordering of Migrant Detention: Exclusion, Hierarchy, and Human Disposal. *Population Space and Place*, *27*(5): e2478

Mountz, A. (2020). *The Death of Asylum: Hidden Geographies of the Enforcement Archipelago*. Minneapolis, MN: University of Minnesota Press.

Mountz, A., Coddington, K., Catania, R.T., and Loyd, J.M. (2013). Conceptualizing Detention: Mobility, Containment, Bordering and Exclusion. *Progress in Human Geography*, *37*(4), 522–541.

Mountz, A., and Loyd, J.M. (2014). Transnational Productions of Remoteness: Building Onshore and Offshore Carceral Regimes across Borders. *Geographica Helvetica*, *69*, 389–398.

Nyers, P. (2010). Abject Cosmopolitanism. In N. De Genova and N. Puetz (eds), *The Deportation Regime: Sovereignty, Space, and the Freedom of Movement* (pp. 413–441). Duke University Press.

Ordaz, J. (2021). *The Shadow of El Centro: A History of Migrant Incarceration and Solidarity*. University of North Carolina Press.

Secor, A. (2004). "There Is an Istanbul That Belongs to Me": Citizenship, Space, and Identity in the City. *Annals of the Association of American Geographers, 94*(2), 352–368.

Squire, V. (2015). Acts of Desertion: Abandonment and Renouncement at the Sonoran Borderzone: Acts of Desertion. *Antipode, 47*(2), 500–516.

Index

Abrahams, N. 134
act of bearing witness 195
act of crafting 225, 228
act of resistance 18, 139, 182–3
activism and resistance 92–4
    activist dispositions 103–4
    hierarchies of action
        direct action 95–7
        everyday activism 97–100
        quiet, implicit and slow
            activism 100–102
activist dispositions 93, 102–4
activist organisation 208
activist sensibility 72
actor network theory 9, 109
acts of activism 94, 97, 103
acts of defiance 128
acts of resistance 13, 14, 35, 86, 88, 94, 108, 132, 134, 139, 147, 170, 199
Agamben, G. 187
Ahmed, Sara 66
Alldred, P. 110
amalgamated knowledge 174
ambiguity of crafting 230
Amin, A. 210
Amoore, L. 12
anarchist/anti-capitalist movement 69
Anderson, Jon 95
animal activism 42, 54
animal campaigns 48
animal resistance 16, 41, 53, 54
animal scholarship 43
anthropocentric framework 16, 54, 80
anthropocentric framings 88
anthropocentric tendency 45
anthropocentrism 77, 84, 88
anthropomorphism 53, 79
anti-austerity campaign groups 128
anti-Black racism 222
anti-Brexit campaign 145
anti-Brexit neologisms 148
anti-Brexit protest group 146

anti-colonial feminist theory 205
anti-discrimination legislation 125
anti-fascist principles 69
anti-gentrification activism 109
anti-road protest movement 95, 104
anti-trans campaigns 67
Arab Spring 174, 175
Armiero, M. 85
Articles 19, 27 and 28 of the UN
    Convention on the Right of
    Persons with Disabilities 126
Ash, J. 85
Askins, K. 100, 101, 104, 195
asylum policy 185–7
asylum system 2, 7, 185, 200, 201–4, 208, 210, 211, 213
austerity regime 168
auto-ethnographic account of pub visit
    with racialised migrants 206–10
'autonomous spaces' 97
Awcock, Hannah 17

Bagelman, J. 13
'BAME communities' 202
'banal activist disposition' 100
Bassel, L. 130–132
Bates, E. 64
Bayat, A. 101, 102, 104
bedroom tax 18, 168–70, 179
    discretionary housing payment and
        legal loopholes 176–7
    legal geographies, intimate life and
        emergent resistance 170–172
    legally challenging government
        172–3
    virtual legal spaces 174–6
befriending scheme 104
bell hooks 42
Bennett, J. 10, 93, 104
Bentham, Jeremy 192
Benwell, M.C. 146

Beraldo, D. 146
Bhabha, H.K. 9
Biehl, João 156
Blomley, Nicholas 170
Board of Trustees 202, 203
The Body Multiple (Mol) 112
'Bollocks to Brexit' 138, 146
    chronology of Brexit through stickers 140–145
    designing and producing protest stickers 145–8
    interacting with protest stickers 148–9
border management practices 195
border management processes 189
Boyer, Kate 29
Braverman, I. 188, 190
Brice, Sage 16
Brickell, K. 170, 171, 173
British socialisation spaces 206
British welfare system 168
Brown, G. 93
Browne, Kath 67
Butler, J. 65, 117, 124, 190
Butler-Rees, Angharad 17

Cameron, David 168, 169
Camilo, Juan 157, 160, 162
Campbell, J. 125
Canadian labour market 117
capitalist society 127, 228
capitalist violence 54
carceral immigration enforcement 217
Carmichael, Jacqueline 172
Caroll, Kimberley 49
Cartesian concept of the thinking 66
case law approach 173
case studies 111–18
Caygill, H. 3
charitable organisations 213
Charity So White campaign 202
Chatterton, P. 9, 12, 13, 34, 93, 96–8, 130, 149
    'Give up activism' 96
Chilean mobilisation 85
chronic health conditions 131
classic 'fishbowl' exercise 70
climate activism 94
climate crisis 94
'climate disobedience' 96

Cloke, P. 4
cognitive intentionality 64
collective identities of resistance 147
collective ownership approach 202
Colling, S. 44
Collins, Patricia Hill 132
Colombian Constitution 164
community-based activism 175
'compulsory able-bodiedness' 132, 133
'compulsory able-bodiness' 132
Conservative–Liberal Democrat Coalition government 168
Conservative Party 144
conservative taxation 170
contemporary feminist scholarship 26
'contentious branding' 146
conventional conceptualisation of resistance 92, 188
conventional research methods 107
'conventional' research practices 110
Corbyn, Jeremy 151
Cott, Nancy F. 34
crafting in Northwest Detention Center 224
    ambiguities 229–31
    gifting 225–6
    livelihood 227–8
    place-making 226
    spending time 228–9
Cresswell, T. 4, 12, 15, 64, 96
criminal and political violence 159
critical animal geographies 43
Critical Geographies of Resistance 3, 15–18
'cultural destabilisation' 210
Cuomo, D. 170, 171, 173
Curran, Amelia 17
Currans, E. 183
'cyber-material alliances' 86

Dandelion Collective 61, 67, 68, 72
Davies, Barbara 41
de Certeau, M. 5, 220, 221
decision-making mechanisms 203
de la Cadena, M. 79
DeLanda, M. 10
Delaney, D. 170, 178
Deleuze, G. 10, 65, 199
DeLyser, Dydia 33
Demonic Grounds (McKittrick) 221

Department of Social Prosperity (DPS) 154
depoliticise asylum 203
Derrida 13
Desmond, M. 113
deterrent effect 71
DeVerteuil, G. 130
differential mobility 64
disability activism 17, 129, 131
disability campaign group 135
disability campaigning 132
Disability Discrimination Act 1995 125
disability geographies 171
disabled people
 citizenship 125
 existence 133
Disabled People's Direct Action Network 125
'discrete modes of activism' 100
Discretionary Housing Payment (DHP) 176, 177
discretionary housing payment and legal loopholes 176–7
'disposition of things' 93
distinctive colour scheme 146
'doing feminism' 37
do-it-yourself (DIY) 45
domestic violence 173
dominant classification systems 33
dualistic oppositional form 71
Duque, Iván 163

'ecologising politics' 77
Eichorn, Kate 38
Einwohner, R.L. 14, 183
emblematic activism 96
embodied bordering 115–18
Emejulu, A. 130–132
emergence, identifying 211–12
emergent resistance 114, 118, 154, 170–172, 205, 208–11, 213
empathetic resistance 41
empathetic stakeholders 178
Employment Support Allowance (ESA) 127, 168, 176, 177
empowerment 33
'engaged ethnography' 205
Enlightenment thinking 81
entanglements of law 171

Entanglements of Power: Geographies of Domination/Resistance 2–3
entrepreneurial activities 162
environmental campaigns 82
environmental direct action (EDA) 96
Equalities Act 2010 68
Equality and Human Rights Consortium (EHRC) 126
Ethics Committee 72n4
ethnography 111, 213
EU Flag Mafia 138, 142, 144, 146
European Union (EU) referendum 17, 138
European Women's Thesaurus 33
exploitative hierarchy 53

Fannin, Maria 16
farmed animals' resistance 41
far-right political extremism 175
Fava, A. 85
Featherstone, D. 86
Feigenbaum, A. 149
Feinberg, Leslie 66
 Stone Butch Blues 65
feminine qualities 101
feminism 26–7
 archives and resistant practice 34–6
 Feminist Archive South 28–34
feminist activism 26, 36
Feminist Archive North 32
Feminist Archive South 27–36, 38
feminist campaigns 37
'feminist geolegality' 170–171
feminist geopolitics 171
feminist liberatory epistemologies 69
feminist methodological approaches 111
feminist political engagement 26
'Fight Climate Change with Diet Change' 45
First-Tier Tribunals 172, 179
fiscal austerity measures 126
fiscal retrenchment 126
Fisher, D.X.O 186
Flusty, S. 4
formal institutional privilege 35
Foucauldian-inspired theorizations 108
Foucauldian system of governmentality 201
Foucault, M. 7, 8, 10–12, 53, 154, 155, 160, 164, 192, 208

Fox, N.J. 110
Free Housing Programme projects 153–4, 156, 158–61, 163–4
Freer, Jean 30, 32
'Friends Not Food' campaign 44–6, 48, 54
friendship-as-resistance 42

Galis, V. 86
gender-diverse facilitators 70
Gender, Place and Culture 34
Gender Recognition Act 2004 (GRA) 68, 73n7
generative friction 64–7
Gentry, C.E. 171
geographical scholarship 6, 16
Geographies of Resistance 2
Gill, N. 7, 189
Giraud, E. 54
Gitlin, T. 128
'Give up activism' (Chatterton) 96
global capitalism 63
global financial crash 168
global political activism 174
'Go Veg' bus ad campaign 45
Goldberg, Jess 65
Golubchikov, O. 130
GoVeganWorld 45
grassroots community 130
grassroots resistance movements 175
Griffin, P. 211
Guattari, F. 10, 65, 199

Hall, E. 64
Haraway, D. 43
'hardworking *femme*' project 73n12
Hargreaves, Jane 32
Harrison, Brian 206
Hartman, Saidiya 18, 130, 218, 221, 222, 230, 231
  Scenes of Subjection 220
Hasselberg, I. 185, 186
Hawkins, G. 82
Hedva, J. 128
hegemonic bureaucratic system 191
Herzog, H. 45
Hesse, B. 201, 202
Heynen, N. 96
Hobson, K. 82

Hocknell, S. 46
Hollander, J.A. 14, 183
home office reporting 184–5
homogenisation 54
Horton, J. 93–5, 97, 99–101, 103, 104, 127, 149
hostile environment 184–5
housing and welfare charities 176
housing associations 176
  and charities 177
Housing Benefit and Council Tax Benefit (Consequential Provisions) Regulations 2006 177
housing project functions 156
Hovorka, A. 84
Hoy, D.C. 13
Hribal, J.C. 44
Hughes, S. 33, 43, 46, 59, 61, 76, 80, 86, 92, 108, 109, 149, 171, 189, 208, 212
Hughes, S.M. 211
human–animal border 43
human disposition 93
human entities 110
human geography 15, 76, 218, 222, 230
  of detention 230
  resistance in 79
Human Rights Act 173
humanitarian assistance 154

immigrant solidarity network 228
Immigration Acts 2014 and 2016 184
im/mobilisation 200–201
'implicit activism' 100
Independent Living Fund (ILF) 126, 135
indigenous politics 79
initial impact assessment 169
institutionalised decision-making processes 84
'insurgent posthumanism' 76
interlinked dualisms 78
'interspecies alliances' 86
'interspecies democracy' 44
'interspecies resistance' 87
Isaacs, J.R. 43
Isin, E.F. 220
Iverson, Karen Schouw 17

Jindal, Priyanka 62

Johnson, Boris 148
Johnston, L. 6
Jones, Pattrice 49, 50
Jones, R. 11, 13
Joronen, M. 13
Jullien, F. 93

Kanngieser, A. 208, 211
Karanth, K.K. 83
Katz, C. 4, 5, 27, 103, 108, 189, 194, 210
Koopman, S. 190
Kraftl, P. 93–5, 97, 99–101, 103, 104, 149
Kurasawa, F. 187, 189

labour market 155, 157–60, 200
labour migration 108, 115–18
Labour Party 169
Lalić-Krstin, G., 148
language assessments 115, 117
La Plaza De La Hoja in Colombia 153–5
 new opportunities for resistance 161–3
 technology of invisibility 156–60
large-scale public protests 168
learning disabilities 64
Lee, Charlotte 17
legal geographies 171
Legg, S. 10
lesbian, gay, bisexual and trans (LGBT) equality 67
leveraging privilege 189–91
Liberal Democrats 138
liberal-progressive narrative 69
liberatory movements 59
liberatory politics 63
Linder, C. 133
Lo, Samantha 138
Lorde, A. 124, 130
Lorimer, J. 78
Luger, J. 149

Machsom Watch (MW) 188
MacLeavy, Julie 16
'macropolitics' 211
Maiguashca, B. 188
Margulies, J.D. 83
Martin, D.G. 14, 92, 99, 101
Marxist framework 6

Marxist oppositional accounts of resistance 6
'masculine gendered performances' 100
Massey, D. 8, 155, 160
Massey, D.B. 164
Masuda, J.R. 10, 109
May, Theresa 184, 196
McDonagh, Briony 34, 35
McFarlane, C. 80
McGranahan, C. 187
McGuirk, P.M. 10
McKittrick, Katherine 18, 218, 222, 224, 230, 231
 Demonic Grounds 221
McRuer, R. 132, 133
Meehan, K.M. 83
Meijer, E. 44
mental health condition 193
Meziant, Kahina 18
migrant detention facilities 224
mobilities scholarship 175
Moffatt, S. 170
Mol, A. 48, 112
 The Body Multiple 112
Molfese, Carlotta 16
Montange, Leah 18
more-than-human assemblages 78
'more-than-human collectives' 86
more-than-human friendship 54
'more-than-human' geographies 42–4, 54, 55, 78
more-than-human political theory 81–4
'more-than-human' resistance 54
more-than-human theory of resistance 76
 end of nature and its politics 77–9
 more-than-human political theory 81–4
 non-anthropocentric conceptualisation of resistance 84–7
 resistance in more-than-human worlds 79–80
more-than-human thought 43
Mullings, B. 205
Murrey, A. 4, 101

Naseemullah, A. 4
Nash, Catherine 67
National Asylum Support Service (NASS) 214

National Health Sevice (NHS) 184
Nature–Culture binaries 79
Nature–Society dichotomy 78
Nature–Society dualism 78
Nayak, A. 201, 202, 210
Naylor, L. 7
Nealon, J.T. 13
neo-Marxist 4
No One is Too Small to Make a Difference (Thunberg) 99
non-anthropocentric conceptualisation of resistance 76, 84–8
non-anthropocentric framework 16, 76, 85, 86, 88
non-anthropocentric framework of resistance 86, 88
non-hierarchical forms of governance 212
non-hierarchical multiplicity 10
non-human animals 42, 77, 86
non-human entities 110
non-human material entities 118
non-human resistance 42
non-political mobilities 212
non-profit organisations 29
non-representational geographies 61
non-transparent system 224
North East for Europe 145
Northwest Detention Center (NWDC) 217, 219, 224
    crafting in 224
        ambiguities 229–31
        gifting 225–6
        livelihood 227–8
        place-making 226
        spending time 228–9
    spatio-temporal domination in 223–4
Nowicki, Mel 18
nuance binary approaches 18
NWDC Detainee Handbook 229

Occupy movement 4, 98, 174
Olarte, C.O. 161
Oliver, Catherine 16
Oliver, M. 125
ontological binary 78
ontological dualism 78
oppositional dualism 71
oppositional spatio-temporal practice 225

oppositional stance 71
Ortega-Alcázar, I. 129

People's Global Action (PGA) 80
People's Vote campaign 144
Philo, C. 79
Pickerill, J. 9, 12, 13, 34, 93, 95–8, 130, 149
Pickering, S. 183
Pierce, J. 6, 14, 92
Pile, S. 12, 15
'pluralities of resistance' 3
'political amnesia' 178
political entanglements 48
political geography 7, 9, 76, 81, 82, 109
political subjectivity 81–3
political subjectivization 18
political theory 77
'politicising ecology' 77
'politics of discomfort' 186
politics of 'resourcefulness' 32
'poll tax' 170
post-colonial contributions 3
post-colonial scholarship 9
'post-heroic' forms of activism 189
posthumanist thinking 76
post-political approach 6
post-political scholarship 6
'post-qualitative inquiry' 120
post-structuralist conceptualisations 7
Pottinger, L. 101
praxis as liberation 204–6
pre-screening process 116
Presidential Decree 1077 of 2015 157
protest stickers
    designing and producing 145–8
    interacting with 148–9
punitive welfare reforms 129
punitive welfare system 130, 131

queer culture 62
'quiet activism' 101
'quiet encroachment' 101
quiet politics 100–101
'quiet resistance' 124

racial violence 231
racism 62
Radcliffe, S. 9

radical democracy 14
radical relationality 109
'ready-made' methods 111
referendum campaign 140, 142
refugee befriending scheme 100
refugee 'crisis' 1
relational assemblages 110
'relational effect' 83
relational ethics of accountability 114
relational ethnographic approach 119
relational ethnographic orientation 107
relational ethnography 112, 113, 117
relational ontologies 77–9
Research Excellence Framework (REF) 38
residual anthropocentrism 88
resistance 60, 124, 200–201
    activism and (see activism and resistance)
    as always-already entangled with power 7–10
    conceptual vocabulary for 1
    conceptualisation of 1, 2
    'everywhere' dilutes purchase of term 10–13
    and feminism (see feminism)
    as friction 67
    in more-than-human worlds 79–80
    more-than-human theory of (see more-than-human theory of resistance)
    movements 18, 146, 172
    as oppositional 4–7
    pluralities of 3
    requires intention 14–15
    in rescue 49–53
resistance-orientated activism literature 97–8
Rezvani, L. 87
'ricochet' effects of asylum policy 186
'ritualised movement' 186
'romance of resistance' 189
Rose, M. 4, 11
Rose, N. 127
Rosenberg, Rae 62
Routledge, P. 80, 96, 98
Ruddick, S. 93, 94
Rule 35 of the Detention Centre Rules 193
Rupp, Leila J. 34

Ryan, Frances 178
Ryder, Richard D. 49
Rygiel, K. 220

Said, Edwards 9
Saldanha, A. 201, 209
Santos, Juan Manuel 153, 160, 163
Scenes of Subjection (Hartman) 220
Scheel, S. 213
Schmid-Scott, Amanda 18
Scott, J.C. 14, 15
Scotton, G. 51
Sepúlveda-Luque, C. 85, 86
Serano, Julia 61
shark rehabilitation programme 44
Sharma, N. 214
Sharp, J.P. 7, 8, 11, 155
Silaški, N. 148
Simpson, P. 85
'single-sex spaces' 68
Sjoberg, L. 171
Slicer, D. 46
'slow resistance' 129
social disenfranchisement 158
social housing tenants 169, 178
social identity approach 147
social media in legally challenging, role of 174–6
social movements 5, 7, 44, 79, 86, 99
    complexities of 11
    feminist 31
    ontological multiplicity of 146
    theory 132
social service organization 218
social tenants 174, 175, 178
socio-economic barriers 163
socio-economic geographical barriers 175
socio-economic marginalisation 155, 156, 163, 164
socio-economic rights 157
sociomaterial assemblages 110
socio-political barriers 175
socio-spatial transgressions 211
socio-spatial transgressive practices 210–211, 213
Sokolowski, R. 42
sonic transgressions 210, 211
"spaces of refusal" 220
Sparke, M. 5, 9, 26

spatial injustice 178
spatial isolation and austerity 223
spatio-temporal domination 221, 223–5, 230, 231
spatio-temporal orderings 220, 230, 231
'speech act' 187
Stanley, Eric 59
Stoddard, E.A. 84
Stone Butch Blues (Feinberg) 65
'Stop Brexit' 139
Stroud, S. 42
'structural reform' 126
"subterranean politics" 221
subtler prefixes 102
Summerton, J. 86
'symbolic spaces' 112

Taş, H. 139
'Tamworth Two' 41
Taylor, Verta 34
Tazzioli, M. 213
'technology of invisibility' 156, 159, 163
Thatcher, Margaret 169
Thrift, N. 8, 92
Thunberg, G.
   No One is Too Small to Make a Difference 99
Tolia-Kelly, D.P. 201
'traditional' case studies 111
traditional conceptualisations of resistance 88
"traditional geographies" 222
traditional political ecology accounts 79
traditional qualitative methodologies 110
'transgression' 79, 96
'trans-individual' politics 65
Trump, Donald 175
Tsing, Anna Lowenhaupt 63, 64

UK
   asylum system 2, 7, 185, 200, 201–4, 208, 210, 211, 213
   austerity programme 125
   climate activism 95
   immigration policy 195
   legal system 172
UK Equalities Act 2010 7
Union Flag 146, 147

United Nations Committee on the Rights of Persons with Disabilities (UNCRPD) 126
United States Immigration and Customs Enforcement (ICE) 217
Upper Tribunals 172, 179
urban geography 10
US detention system 224
US Immigration and Customs Enforcement 217

Vancouver Humane Society (VHS) 45
Vegetarian Society 55n2
vegetarianism 55n1
'vibrant materiality' 10
Vigsø, O. 145
virtual legal spaces 174–6
voluntary and community sector (VCS) 199, 202, 203
Volunteer Work Program 224
vulnerability 124
'vulnerable' population group 124

Wadiwel, Dinesh 53
Wall, I.R. 161
Weaver, H. 65, 66
Welfare Act 170
Welfare Reform Act 168
Welsh Independent Living Grant (WILG) 127
Whatmore, S. 42, 43
Whatmore, S.J. 82
'What's Wrong with McDonald's?' campaign 46
White governmentality 201–4, 206
whiteness 200–201
Wideman, T.J. 10, 109
Wiebe, S.M. 13
Wilbert, C. 15
Wilkinson, E. 129
Williams, O.R. 6
witness as resistance 187–9
Women's Liberation Movement 27, 31
Work Capability Assessments (WCAs) 168, 178

Yeo, C. 196

Zell, Sarah 17

Žižek, S. 6